D1557034

**Peter Lavrov and the
Russian Revolutionary Movement**

Peter Lavrov and the Russian Revolutionary Movement

Philip Pomper

The University of Chicago Press
Chicago and London

The University of Chicago Press, Chicago 60637
The University of Chicago Press, Ltd., London
© 1972 by The University of Chicago
All rights reserved. Published 1972
Printed in the United States of America
International Standard Book Number: 0–226–67520–3
Library of Congress Catalog Card Number: 72-84407

To Alice

Contents

Preface

Nine years ago when I conceived this study, Peter Lavrov seemed to be an all but forgotten figure. Since that time, largely as a consequence of revived interest in Russian revolutionary populism, two dissertations besides my own, and a number of publications—most notably James P. Scanlan's excellent translation of Lavrov's *Historical Letters,* and a large number of documents relating to Lavrov's career edited by Boris Sapir—have appeared. Aside from these one could list a number of articles, monographs on the revolutionary movement, and heretofore unpublished Lavrov manuscripts issued by Soviet scholars.

It has been my good fortune to be able to correct and amplify my earlier work on Lavrov through additional archival research and through access to the new materials made available by the International Institute for Social History and by Soviet historians. During the academic year 1962–63, under the auspices of the cultural exchange and the Inter-University Committee on Travel Grants, I had the opportunity to work in the Soviet Union, where members of the history and philosophy faculties of Moscow State University provided me with sound guidance and access to archival sources. In 1963–64, thanks to a Ford Foundation Foreign Area Fellowship and Professor Jan Meijer's invaluable aid, I was able to take advantage of the incomparable resources of the International Institute for Social History. Anna Mikhailovna Bourgina of the Hoover Institution Archives made it possible for me to find my way through the wealth of materials in the Nicolaevsky collection, and Lev Magerovsky of the Columbia University Russian Archives introduced me to the important correspondence between Lavrov and Alexandra Weber.

The advice and criticisms of several scholars helped me to improve this biography of Lavrov, and if it remains deficient, the blame is mine. Professor Leopold Haimson saw it through as a dissertation. Professors Michael Confino, Richard Wortman, and James Billington provided valuable comments about the manuscript at various stages. I acknowledge a special debt to the late Boris Nicolaevsky and to Boris Sapir, without whose painstaking efforts and expansive knowledge Lavrov's and V. N. Smirnov's papers might have remained in considerable disorder for years to come.

I am grateful to my colleagues in the Department of History at Wesleyan University for their spiritual and material support of this endeavor, and to Wesleyan's administration and trustees for the summer research grants which permitted me to travel to the sources when necessary. Mrs. Dorothy Hay and Rhonda Kissinger helped to prepare the manuscript for publication.

My final and deepest gratitude goes to the person whose knowledge of Russian, critical skill, and careful assistance made her a genuine collaborator in this project at every stage. The book is dedicated to her.

Introduction

Occasionally, the lucky traveler to the Soviet Union will discover one of those circles of men and women who keep alive the best traditions of the Russian intelligentsia—the intellectual and spiritual intensity and complex humanism that are still best exhibited in the literature of the nineteenth and early twentieth centuries. During a gathering of one such circle, the moment arrived for the singing of revolutionary songs. Several were sung loudly and with feeling. The traveler remembered having read that one of Peter Lavrov's poems had been set to music and had been sung as a kind of anthem by the revolutionary masses in 1917. He asked whether anyone knew the song that began

> We renounce the old world!
> We shake its dust from our feet!

Without hesitation the company took up the song, delivering the refrain with redoubled vigor:

> Rise up, lift yourself up, working people!
> Rise up against your enemies, starving brother!
> Let the cry of popular vengeance resound!
> Forward!

They did not know that the poem had been written in 1875 by Peter Lavrov, but why should they? It was part of their revolutionary heritage, safely transmitted by tradition rather than pedantry. An obelisk in the Aleksandrov garden outside the Kremlin walls is another part of that heritage. Among the names of the great utopian and revolutionary thinkers inscribed there is Lavrov's and the monument itself testifies to the historical awareness and relative fair-mindedness of the men who were trying to create a new social order in the years immediately following the revolution of 1917. The revolutionary tradition also lives in the names of streets, boulevards, and squares and in the numerous commemorative plaques that one finds everywhere in Leningrad and Moscow. The street in Leningrad where Lavrov lived before his arrest and exile is now named for him. And so the revolutionary cause that he served for more than thirty years until his death in 1900 did not forget him, even though it was taken over by men who opposed the particular revolutionary tradition to which Lavrov belonged.

Nonetheless, Lavrov has remained a relatively obscure figure. To be sure, any educated Soviet citizen could identify him as a major theoretican of the *narodnik* movement of the 1870s. Those educated since the mid 1950s, since de-Stalinization in the historiography of the revolutionary movement, might know what was "progressive" about the *narodnik* movement and what role Lavrov played in its history. The gradual resurrection of the *narodniki* during the past fifteen years, after more than twenty years of entombment in the formulas of the Stalin era, has rescued Lavrov from total obscurity, without making him a vivid historical figure. An important moment in his rehabilitation came with the republication in 1965 of some of Lavrov's most important philosophical and sociological essays, along with several previously unpublished manuscripts, in a two-volume anthology. This was the first collection of Lavrov's writings to be published in the Soviet Union since 1935, and the introductory essay is coauthored by I. S. Knizhnik-Vetrov, Lavrov's biographer in the 1930s. It contains Lavrov's brief, impersonal autobiography, first published in 1910 and republished in the 1934–35 collection. Despite the fact that much of Lavrov's correspondence has been preserved, and despite the rich memoir literature about him, no recent Soviet historian has yet produced a full biography of him. There is only a short biography written for school children, in which Lavrov is presented in storybook fashion as a revolutionary hero. Thus, although Lavrov's name has long been associated with a theoretical tendency and a strategy of Russian revolutionary populism, he himself has never been presented fully as a thinker and actor in the movement. In this respect, he is possibly the most neglected of all the major figures in the history of the Russian revolutionary movement.

One cannot attribute this neglect to the injustices of Soviet historiography alone. The corpus of Lavrov's writings is vast. His lengthy and complex essays and treatises were forbidding even during the second half of the nineteenth century, when German scholars were producing even weightier tomes. Lavrov was regarded by his contemporaries as a Germanic writer, and they were fully justified in that judgment. Furthermore, he was a polymath, one of the most fully educated men of his times. In order to follow him through his intellectual journeys, one must be prepared to confront almost the entire range of Victorian theoretical knowledge, from epistemology to neurology. There are numerous essays about Lavrov's work by experts in several areas—philosophy, sociology, anthropology, literary criticism, and the history of thought, including the history of science—and one gains the total impression that he possessed an extraordinary mind. One also gains the impression that he attempted too much and therefore did not make an enduring contribution in any given area of scholarship. It is not the purpose of the present study to reassess Lavrov's contribution in the several areas of scholarship mentioned above. Probably, only a team of scholars could do that adequately. It is hoped, however, that the more limited scope of this study will permit narrower focus upon the character of Lavrov's thought and its relationship to his revolutionary career.

Lavrov's unusual career defies easy classification. Had he never become a revolutionary, he still would have earned a place for himself in Russian intellectual history. He might have been remembered best as the man whose philosophical essays of the late 1850s and early 1860s served as points of departure for some of the most important statements of Nicholas Chernyshevskii and Dmitrii Pisarev, the leading radical publicists of the 1860s. Or he might have been remembered primarily as the founder of the Russian school of "subjective sociology." Still another possibility—he might eventually have produced a bulky and unreadable history of human thought, written from a vaguely socialist point of view, and incorporating the findings of several disciplines. Despite his involvement in the revolutionary movement, Lavrov did manage to produce lengthy articles and even book-length portions of his projected magnum opus. All of these have gone the dusty way of forgotten Victorian scholarship. His reputation and his place in Russian history rest largely upon

his contribution to Russian revolutionary populism. More specifically, his *Historical Letters,* published serially in Russia in 1868–
69 and then in several single-volume editions, the first appearing in
1870, strongly influenced more than one generation of Russian
revolutionaries. In the period 1873–76, Lavrov edited and guided
the policy of the revolutionary socialist periodical *Vpered!* (Forward!), which circulated more widely than any other Russian émigré
journal of that time. He and his colleagues on the journal were also
responsible for the publication of some of the most important propaganda pamphlets written for the peasants—pamphlets which were
still being used more than thirty years later by Socialist-Revolutionary propagandists and agitators. Again, in 1883–86 he was coeditor of *Vestnik Narodnoi Voli* (Messenger of The People's Will),
the overseas organ of the most important party to emerge from the
revolutionary populist movement of the 1870s—the party that assassinated Alexander II in 1881. Though he remained an ally of
Narodnaia Volia ("The People's Will") until his death in 1900,
Lavrov is still best remembered for his influence during the 1870s.

Under close scrutiny, a life history can become a case. Furthermore, revolutionary careers are unusual, almost by definition. Yet
some cases are more puzzling than others, and some revolutionary
careers are more unusual than others. I. S. Turgenev, who was
friendly with Lavrov and contributed small amounts of money to
Lavrov's journal, wrote in a letter that Lavrov was a dove trying
to pass himself off as a hawk. An early Soviet student of Lavrov's
career, P. Vitiazev, carefully examined the personal events in
Lavrov's life which narrowed his choices and forced him into a revolutionary career. Although Turgenev's insight and Vitiazev's thesis
are valuable, they should not be used to "explain" Lavrov's career.
An approach of this sort could be used, for example, to "explain"
Lenin, who almost certainly entered the revolutionary movement because of the execution of his brother, Alexander. On the other hand,
it is true that the character of a revolutionary's long-term involvement can be related to the nature of his original commitment, which
is largely shaped by his preceding personal history. Of course, the
term "preceding personal history" means not only the accidents of

personal history, but also an individual's cultural and generational inheritance. Some of the peculiarities of Lavrov's career can be traced to the fact that he was almost the only representative of his generation to play an important direct role in the revolutionary movement of the 1870s. More specifically, Lavrov was in most respects closer to the generation of radicals who achieved their mature philosophies in the 1840s than to the generation which he influenced.

The decade of the 1840s was the great theoretical period in the history of modern revolutionary thought—the years when the "algebra of revolution" was derived from Hegel, later to be systematized in Marxist and anarchist doctrines. Russian gentry radicals of that period who took the path of left-wing Hegelianism and became attracted to Pierre Proudhon's anarchism were the real theoretical innovators in the early history of the Russian revolutionary movement, later to be followed by able and effective popularizers who were responsible for both the elaboration and theoretical vulgarization of the ideas of the 1840s. The young émigrés of the 1840s, Alexander Herzen, Michael Bakunin, and a lesser light, Nicholas Ogarev, founded Russian socialism. As middle-aged men, they became associated with the radical movement that developed in Russia during the early 1860s. The revolutionary émigrés of the generation of the 1840s were the first to experience the problems created by distance from the movement in Russia, and by the "new men" who came abroad, often with the intention of exploiting the reputations and resources of the older émigrés.

After the revolutionary movement of the 1860s had run its hopeless course, little remained but wrecked reputations. Herzen died in 1870, when the Nechaev scandal was effectively terminating the movement and when Lavrov was fleeing Russia with the intention of joining Herzen abroad. Ogarev was neurotic, dissipated, and no longer fit for serious work. One is tempted to say the same of Bakunin, but the latter, a man of enormous energy, was still capable of inspiring followers, writing important anarchist tracts, formulating grandiose schemes, and undermining Marx's designs for the First International.

Lavrov, too, belonged to the generation of the 1840s. He was born about a decade later than most of the leading figures of that period, but he shared their culture, and, belatedly, their fate. Lavrov did not enter the literary scene until the late 1850s, largely because he had devoted himself to a teaching career in mathematics. During the late 1850s his writings show traces of the "reconciliation with reality" characteristic of the men of the 1840s before their full radicalization. However, Lavrov was temporarily reconciling himself to a different kind of "reality"—to the dramatic interval full of hope and foreboding that followed the death of Nicholas I in 1855 and Russia's failure in the Crimean War. As the era of the Great Reforms unfolded during the reign of Alexander II, Lavrov completed his evolution towards radicalism. After each important crisis of the 1860s, Lavrov moved closer to the general outlook of the radicals, even though he shared neither their culture, style, nor basic philosophical position. His tenuous ties with the radical subculture of the 1860s led to his arrest and internal exile after Dmitrii Karakazov's attempt on the life of Alexander II in 1866. Lavrov's flight to Europe in 1870, his experience of the Paris Commune in 1871, his exposure to the ideas of the First International, and the unexpected severing of important personal ties all altered the nature of his commitment to the revolutionary movement. Once again one is reminded of the careers of the men of the 1840s, especially Herzen's. Indeed, when Lavrov founded his revolutionary journal less than three years after Herzen's death, he unquestionably had in mind a historically updated version of Herzen's *Kolokol* (The Bell). Thus, in terms of the commonly used genealogy of the Russian revolutionary movement, Lavrov belonged to the fathers' generation culturally, entered the movement as a moral ally of the sons, and became an intellectual leader—a *vlastitel' dum*—to the grandsons of the 1870s. Lavrov tried to join forces with Bakunin, the last of the great Russian radicals of the 1840s, but the latter was nearing the end of his career, and his banner was being taken up by younger men hostile to Lavrov. Given Lavrov's and Bakunin's personalities and theoretical positions, there is no reason to believe that the two would ever have gone very far in any kind of collaborative venture.

In a sense, Lavrov was left stranded by the disappearance of the Russian revolutionaries belonging to his cultural generation. There is a revealing photograph of the group that edited and published *Vpered!*. Lavrov, a bearded, patriarchal figure in a suit stands out alongside the younger men dressed in workers' costume. There is also something ironic about Lavrov's posing beside the printing apparatus. Lavrov's extreme myopia and almost total helplessness in manual matters were well-known traits. His gingerliness about the little spirit-lamp in his apartment amused at least one memoirist. Ultimately, he was a lonely figure, whose theoretical and moral stature in the movement could never quite compensate for the generational and personal differences between him and the young men and women with whom he worked.

For the reasons sketched above, it is not difficult to understand why Lavrov never really entered the field of "practical" activity—unless one includes his attempts to intercede on the behalf of Russian political "criminals" abroad, or the famous closet in his Paris apartment, which harbored numerous political fugitives over the years. His lack of "practical" experience made him unique among the major figures in the émigré community after the 1860s. Bakunin, Tkachev, Plekhanov, Aksel'rod, Deutsch, Zasulich, Tikhomirov, Kravchinskii, Kropotkin—all had been involved in student movements, propaganda activities in the cities and countryside, underground organizations, abortive insurrections, demonstrations, assassinations, prison escapes, and other revolutionary adventures. Men closer to Lavrov's generation and culture, like Turgenev, could immediately see that Lavrov did not belong among these "hawks," and Lavrov himself knew that he was not so much a comrade as a colleague in the cause. Yet he remained firmly committed to the movement for almost thirty years, and at the time of his death he stood for a more radical tendency in the movement than did any of those in the above group who were still alive.

The series of very important choices that Lavrov made between 1870 and his death in 1900 reveals remarkable consistency, in that he continually chose to associate himself with the party that he judged to be the revolutionary vanguard of the moment. If we examine his career before he was forced to emigrate in 1870, we discover the same consistency. After 1870 he moved toward a role for which he was ill-adapted by personality and life-long habit, a role which he accepted reluctantly and diffidently after two years abroad. During those two years, a series of extraordinary events, both personal and historical, determined the nature of his commitment to the "party of progress" without fundamentally altering his long-established modes of adaptation. He was forty-nine years old when he worked out a rather strange but functional compromise in which he reluctantly served the historical agencies of revolutionary socialism in the capacity of publicist. However deficient the historically concrete "party of progress" proved to be, Lavrov believed that it had to be served. Thus, although he can be criticized retrospectively for his choice of historical vanguards, he cannot fairly be accused of capriciousness or inconsistency.

A problem arises, however, when one attempts to find consistency in Lavrov's doctrinal positions. At the intellectual level, he achieved a complex neo-Kantian orientation in which there was a perpetual tension between relativism and absolutism, subjectivity and objectivity, and free will and determinism. The first terms in these antinomies suggest a detached perspective, a degree of individualism, and flexibility, each of which would presumably discourage rigid, sectarian loyalty. But Lavrov, like most members of the intelligentsia, needed to commit himself *absolutely* as a moral actor to the noblest causes of his time. He thus chose to act as if a given doctrine were absolutely true, bowing to the "scientific" authority of the critically thinking vanguard. In this way he resolved one of the most painful dilemmas of a historically-minded, secular intelligentsia. However, it is one thing to yield to the authority of a doctrine, and quite another to accept the demands made by a party engaged in a life or death struggle with existing authority. Lavrov ended by supporting doctrines and parties because they were useful instruments or weapons in the struggle, even though they seemingly contradicted his own theoretical and strategic positions. He believed that he was yielding only "secondary" or "nonessential" points.

Thus the courtly, gentle, comically myopic teacher of mathematics, the scholar who had loved to declaim verses to the ladies at St. Petersburg soirees, became an ally of a party of young men and women who attacked the Russian authorities with daggers, pistols, dynamite, and pyroxylin. This was the final outcome of Lavrov's successive stages of self-subordination to the historical vanguards of revolutionary socialism. The process of doctrinal narrowing to socialism in general and to revolutionary populism in particular, and Lavrov's evolution in *partiinost'* ("party spirit") from a vague commitment to the socialist party to his affiliation with Narodnaia Volia are traced in the ensuing chapters.

1.
The Early Years

Peter Lavrov's childhood and adolescence must be reconstructed from very scanty material. The little information about his early years that has survived comes to us mainly through Nicholas Rusanov, one of Lavrov's colleagues and friends in the Russian socialist émigré community. Especially during the 1890s, the aging socialist patriarch used to confide memories of events that had occurred sixty years and more ago to men whom he must have known might soon be his biographers. In the late 1880s Lavrov wrote a brief and studiedly impersonal autobiography, in which he referred to himself in the third person. It contains even less information about his early years than Rusanov's later efforts.

The picture of the young Lavrov that Rusanov conveys to us is that of a sensitive and precociously studious little *barchuk*. Rusanov suggests that the absence of close siblings (his only brother was six years older than he, his sister eleven years older) and play companions, and, more generally, the impoverished character of Peter's play life tended to produce the seriousness and bookishness that remained with Lavrov throughout his life.[1] Peter's companions were adults and books, even in infancy and childhood. Rusanov's theory seems plausible enough. As a grown man, Lavrov's primary modes of sociability were the exposure and exchange of "developed" ideas and feelings, and he never seems to have learned to play, in the ordinary sense of that word.

One can infer from Rusanov's and other accounts that Lavrov liked to contrast his life as a young aristocrat with his later career rather than to describe himself as a young rebel. There is no story

---

1. N. S. Rusanov, *Biografiia Petra Lavrovicha Lavrova* (St. Petersburg, 1899), p. 5. Another short biography of Lavrov by Rusanov appeared as an essay: "P. L. Lavrov," *Byloe,* 1907, no. 2, pp. 243–86. Also see N. S. Rusanov, *Sotsialisty zapada i Rossii* (St. Petersburg, 1908), pp. 200–266; and "Lavrov, chelovek i myslitel'," *Russkoe bogatstvo,* 1910, no. 2, pp. 220–56.

of a youthful awakening to the brutality of the serf system or to the injustice and irrationality of Russian life. Lavrov chose rather to describe a childhood full of protections and restrictions, which encouraged the development of a thoughtful, sensitive, and physically dependent person. In presenting this retrospective view, Lavrov, always the teacher, probably wanted to do more than merely provide an amusingly inappropriate prologue to his later career as a revolutionary socialist. One of the central themes in Lavrov's writings is that idleness and one-sidedness are bred into a leisure class in a society based upon exploitation. In his imaginative descriptions of the socialist society of the future he always stressed the diverse kinds of physical and intellectual work in which each individual would engage. Thus, on a conscious ideological level he both resented and apologized for a childhood which had so clearly belonged to the old order, and which had developed only one side of him. This was especially true in later years, when Lavrov sometimes felt acute embarrassment about the relative safety of his position as an émigré publicist and about his continuing dependency upon the initiative of young activists.

There may also be deeper symbolic meanings contained in some of the anecdotes which Lavrov told his friends about his aristocratic childhood, especially in those describing his nurse's protectiveness. For example, he sometimes told about the bathing expeditions to the river near his home.[2] Little Peter's nurse would take him there to bathe, but she also carried a tub with her. Instead of bathing her charge directly in the river, she dipped water into the tub for his bath. In another anecdote, he described an illustrated German chronicle, one of his favorite childhood books. His nurse would turn the pages while he sat on her lap and looked at the pictures. He was particularly fond of a print of Horatius fighting the Curiatii, and was moved to tears by one of Charlemagne smashing a hideous Saxon idol. In order to spare her barchuk a few tears, Peter's nurse tried to skip the latter illustration, but the boy always demanded that she show it to him, refusing to be denied the stimulus for a strong emotion or its expression.[3] In this respect at least, Lavrov depicted himself as a rebel. But it was a curious kind of rebellion,

2. Rusanov, "P. L. Lavrov," p. 247.
3. Rusanov, *Biografiia,* p. 9.

for it issued from contact with an image of violence and ugliness
rather than from a real immersion in a truly dangerous situation.
The boy was still in the tub, not the river, and to some extent this
symbolized his entire career. Even after many years as an exile,
Lavrov seemed to feel that his contacts with reality were in some
way mediated, and he never overcame a sense of distance, of being
on the periphery of things, or of nonbelonging.

Although much of Lavrov's sense of distance in his later career
is attributable to his position as an émigré and to ideological, cultural, and generational differences between him and a varied assort-
ment of revolutionary colleagues, one can speculate that an even
more basic psychological distancing was involved. What was true
of Lavrov in emigration was true, to a greater or lesser extent, in
every step of his career. Lavrov's tendency to see everything in historical perspective—indeed to do so in midstream—is another
manifestation of this fundamental psychological trait in him. Yet he
was more firmly dedicated to the cause of revolutionary socialism
than many of his coworkers who condemned him for lack of revolutionary passion, but who frequently abandoned the cause after a
few months or years of passionate involvement, or else ended by
taking a much more moderate position. Ultimately, Lavrov's unusual critical detachment, and the almost courtly decorousness that
was bound up with it, did not prevent him from remaining stably involved while others fell by the wayside.

The origins of the fundamental values and life style that Lavrov
exhibited in some fashion or other throughout his long career are
discernible in other glimpses of his childhood. Lavrov's family was
one of substance, though by no means wealthy. One of Lavrov's
biographers, writing under the constraint of "proletarian" ideology,
tried to minimize the importance of the family holdings in Pskov
province, but they were not insubstantial.[4] The family's most important land holding was the village of Melekhova. On the basis of
information gathered during the period of the serf reform, we can

    4. I. S. Knizhnik-Vetrov, "P. L. Lavrov ot pervykh publitsisticheskikh
vystuplenii do izdaniia 'Vpered!' (1857–mart 1872)," in P. L. Lavrov,
Izbrannye sochineniia na sotsial'no-politicheskie temy, ed. I. A. Teodorovich,
4 vols. (Moscow: Izdatel'stvo vsesoiuznogo obshchestva politkatorzhan i
ssyl'no-poselentsev, 1934–35), 1:17–18. (Hereafter cited as *Izbrannye sochineniia.*)

ascertain that Lavrov inherited an estate which included 297 field serfs and 16 house serfs. The total area of the estate was 2,120 *desiatin* (approximately 5,274 acres), almost two-thirds of which was manorial land.[5]

Peter grew up in a cultural environment full of the contradictions that had troubled the Russian *dvorianstvo* ("gentry") for more than a century. His father, Lavr Stepanovich, had retired from a military career with the rank of colonel in the artillery and had spent the remainder of his life indulging a taste for horticulture and art, without, however, relinquishing the military qualities instilled in him by the exacting standards of the First Cadet Corps.[6] Lavr Stepanovich's love of order extended to matters ordinarily removed from estate management. One story has it that he dosed his serfs with a patent medicine in order to guarantee their proper intestinal functioning.[7] He was also interested in more theoretical problems of estate management and, evidently unaware of its content, asked young Peter to read Fourier's *Treatise on Domestic-Agricultural Association.*[8]

The picture of Lavr Stepanovich that one can piece together from fragmentary information is that of a loyal subject and strict father, who raised his children in the tradition of the military-administrative elite to which he and his father before him had belonged. However, Lavr Stepanovich was also a product of the period of the legal "liberation" and cultural westernization of the Russian gentry. After being wounded in 1807 in the war of the Third Coalition against Napoleon, he could retire to his library and garden.[9] His estate was located in the northwestern part of the vast empire, within the cultural sphere of the westernized capital. It was evidently placed conveniently for visitors from St. Petersburg who were traveling south to the Black Sea vacation areas. Alexander I himself stopped at the estate in 1825 on his way to the royal residence at Livadia

5. Ibid., p. 17.

6. Lavrov's great-grandfather had been the general adjutant of Count Apraksin, chief admiral during the reign of Peter I. His grandfather had sired twenty-two children, among them Lavr Stepanovich (Rusanov, *Biografiia,* p. 5).

7. Rusanov, "Lavrov, chelovek i myslitel'," p. 221.

8. Rusanov, "P. L. Lavrov," p. 248.

9. Rusanov, *Biografiia,* p. 5.

in the Crimea, where he died shortly thereafter.[10] Both geographically and culturally, the Lavrov estate belonged to the Western ambience in Russia. Lavr Stepanovich belonged to the stratum of Westernized gentry who had escaped the demands of the barracks and avoided the routine of the bureaus, and for whom old Russian culture has increasingly become a set of empty forms and rituals. Although he obeyed religious forms, to the point of inviting priests to dinner on appropriate occasions, he was not a religious man. He vigorously opposed the systems of thought which were associated with radicalism during the reigns of Catherine II and Alexander I—the Masonic movement, for example—yet collected the works of the Encyclopedists in his library. The latter possession, like his busts and oil paintings, probably signified devotion to the new cultural forms rather than to their substance. Lavr Stepanovich did what was fitting for a man of his position, including hiring a Swiss tutor for his son.[11]

In a peculiar way, Peter's career was an extension of his father's, in that the military function was further attenuated, though not entirely abolished, the old religious forms vigorously repudiated, and the process of cultural Westernization elaborated and deepened. Interestingly, both father and son married women who were not Russian. Lavr Stepanovich's wife, Elizaveta Karlovna Handwig, was the daughter of a Russified Swede who managed a Siberian metal factory.[12] Peter married a woman of German origin.[13] (There was also German ancestry on Lavrov's mother's side.)[14] While Lavr Stepanovich's wife was Orthodox (and much more interested in re-

10. Ibid., p. 6.
11. Lavr Stepanovich evidently belonged to the dvorianstvo type described by Marc Raeff: "The nobleman frequently tried to run his estate the way he had been accustomed to run a regiment or administrative office. He issued rules regulating the daily activities of his peasants and domestics that at times reached ridiculous extremes of pedantry and pettiness." See Marc Raeff, *Origins of the Russian Intelligentsia* (New York: Harcourt, Brace and World, Harbinger Books, 1966), pp. 78–79.
12. Rusanov, *Biografiia,* p. 5.
13. "Iz materialov o P. L. Lavrove," *Krasnyi arkhiv* 3 (1923): 220.
14. I have not seen this fact established elsewhere. Lavrov himself provided the information in a document in his own hand: "Réponse sur l'enquête sur l'état psychique des artistes et des scientistes par A. Hamond" (MS in International Institute for Social History, Amsterdam, Netherlands; hereafter referred to as IISH).

ligion than was her husband), Peter's wife, Antonina Khristianovna, remained Lutheran.[15] Another curious fact, both father and son achieved the rank of colonel in the artillery despite otherwise dissimilar careers.

However, Lavr Stepanovich's friendship with Count Arakcheev, who was responsible for the most hated internal reforms of Alexander I's reign, suggests the huge distance that ultimately separated the son from the father. Stern patriarch that he was by all accounts, Lavr Stepanovich could control his son's formal career up to a point, but he failed in the end to shape his loyalties. The aristocratic values of honor, duty, and service which were inculcated in young Peter by his father were later enlisted in causes quite unthinkable to Lavr Stepanovich.

It is more difficult to measure the extent of Elizaveta Karlovna's influence on her youngest child. We do know that some of her friends were, in Lavrov's retrospective assessment, religious zealots; that she was gentle and educated; and that she helped her son to learn German.[16] Her closeness to him was later revealed when she joined him in exile in northern Russia, despite her advanced age and infirmities. Elizaveta Karlovna expressed tender concern for her grown son in several letters written to him during his exile.[17] She also played a role in his escape from internal exile. One feels that the absence of any extended discussion of her in his memoirs is attributable to Lavrov's extremely developed sense of propriety rather than to any lack of regard for her. Indeed, all of the later evidence points to his being something of a mamma's boy, extremely dependent upon feminine care, and as a grown man always quite needful of a woman's attention. The fact that he was somewhat weak, sickly, and physically underdeveloped as a child may help to explain this aspect of his character.

There are some aspects of young Peter's development and his intellectual orientation that cannot be explained easily by environmental influences alone. The picture that he presented to a French

15. "Iz materialov o P. L. Lavrove," p. 220.

16. Rusanov, *Biografiia,* p. 11.

17. Several of these letters are preserved in the Nicolaevsky Collection at the Hoover Institution on War, Revolution, and Peace, Stanford, California.

psychologist, A. Hamond, many years later was that of a very special kind of intellectualism. Lavrov described himself as having a good memory for words, facts, and the products of his own imagination. General concepts also stayed with him well. (Associates described his memory as extraordinary.) On the other hand, he could not remember melodies or colors, and did not perceive vividly the concrete objects in his environment—this in spite of the fact that his home in Pskov province had been filled with objets d'art and surrounded by gardens.[18] He never showed much interest in music or the plastic arts. At an early age he became absorbed in mathematics, filling copybook after copybook with arithmetical problems.[19] There is little question that he began to show a propensity and an unusual capacity for abstract thought early in childhood, although the influences in his environment, if anything, tended to work in another direction.

His nurse, his parents, and his tutor, Berget, transported their charge into an enchanted, vivid world of antique heroes. He read mainly history, drama, and poetry. From the German chronicle of his early childhood, he progressed to the histories of Charles Rollin and Jean Baptiste Louis Crevier. At the age of five or six he had mastered French sufficiently to read Jean-Pierre Claris de Florian's *Numa Pompilius*.[20] Whether in the context of an epic antiquity or a legendary medieval Christian world such as that created by Friedrich Heinrich Karl Lamotte-Fouqué in *Der Zauberring,* young Peter was steeped in the most romanticized aristocratic values.[21] Heroes were brave, strong, virtuous, and wise. Honor was always endangered and defended, wrongs were righted, dilemmas resolved. The good cause never lacked for champions. Heroines were severely tried. At the age of ten the boy wept over the plight of the heroine in Beaumarchais's *Eugénie*. His tutor had him commit to memory a speech from Voltaire's *Zaïre*.[22] One message clearly conveyed in all this

18. The gardens were evidently quite impressive, and in Maria Negreskul's letters to her father there are wistful references to them. See Rusanov, *Biografiia,* p. 8.
19. Ibid., p. 15.
20. Ibid., p. 10.
21. Ibid., p. 11.
22. Ibid., pp. 13, 15.

literature was that it is better to die for a good cause than to live falsely, and that truth and virtue always win out somehow. An extremely sensitive and teachable child, Peter internalized the values and models of behavior placed before him, and began to build an identity around them. Twenty-five years later, Elena Shtakenschneider, whose salon provided a framework for Lavrov's coming out in the St. Petersburg literary world, was able to detect in the myopic professor of mathematics (with hands "white and plump, like a Bishop's") the romantic, knightly spirit that remained with him from childhood.[23]

Berget also exposed his pupil to the splendid and awesome images of more contemporary struggles. Peter learned passages from Hugo's "Lui" and Schiller's "Das Lied des Glockes."[24] The same historical climate which produced the Hegelian synthesis inspired in poets a fascination for the vast processes of creation and destruction surrounding the French Revolution and the Napoleonic era. Through poetry the boy learned about the promise and tragedy of the revolutionary period.

To a serious, sensitive child with a vivid imagination, neo-classical and romantic literature conveyed models for a life of heroic struggle, a life in which actions arose spontaneously from passionate convictions. As boy and man, however, Lavrov exhibited traits almost antithetical to those of the romantic hero. As noted above, he was a sickly, bookish, and housebound child. The adult Lavrov was extremely myopic and sedentary, a "cabinet scholar" almost inevitably attracted to the most theoretical and abstract areas of the disciplines which engaged his interest.

This apparent contradiction between the child and the adult can be understood by recognizing the peculiar illusions created by a special response to acculturation. During the process of acculturation, when children are exposed to ideals and models of behavior, they often do not have a clear sense of the distinction between responding to and internalizing ideals and models, and acting them out or externalizing them. Since cultures reward children for master-

    23. E. A. Shtakenschneider, *Dnevnik i zapiski* (Moscow: Academia, 1934), p. 148. (Hereafter cited as *Dnevnik i zapiski*.)
    24. Rusanov, *Biografiia*, p. 15.

ing and internalizing symbols, ideals, and models, a child's sense of goodness and moral achievement can grow out of his successes during the process of internalization itself, even if his subsequent development fails to prepare him for the heroic exploits whose images helped to form his identity. Most individuals realize at a certain point in their development that ideal or heroic action is not possible for them, but some do not. The latter must usually find some way to reconcile their capacities with their ideals. Lavrov did this mainly by shifting the emphasis from heroic action to the activities of critically examining and forming convictions, and teaching others to do the same. But at crucial moments in his career he reaffirmed his commitment to action—to the struggle for the externalization and concretization of ideals—a commitment which contemporaries like Elena Shtakenschneider perceived beneath his restrained, academic exterior. Lavrov experienced considerable frustration during the last thirty years of his life because he was totally adapted to the sedentary, well-regulated life of a scholar and pedagogue. Eventually he was forced to work out a compromise by creating for himself the career of a revolutionary socialist theoretician, propagandist, and scholar.

Throughout his childhood young Peter evidently suffered few shocks or threats to his self-esteem. He was an obedient child and an apt pupil who advanced so quickly that his Russian teacher, Slobodchikov, soon discovered that his services were superfluous. By late childhood, Peter knew French and German and had begun to study English.[25] He never lost his passion for foreign literature, and the corpus of his writings gives the impression that, by comparison, he read very little in Russian.

During early adolescence, poetry was Peter's true passion, something not entirely surprising in view of the mystique which poets enjoyed at that time in Russia as well as in Europe. But, like many a sensitive young dvorianin, Peter was uprooted from his family environment and thrust into the quasi-military world of a cadet academy. In 1838, at the age of fourteen, he entered the elite Mikhailovskii Artillery School.[26] The new environment did not stifle

25. Ibid., pp. 10, 15.
26. "Iz materialov o P. L. Lavrove," p. 220.

Peter's literary aspiration, but reinforced his propensity for mathematics and, more generally, confirmed his bookishness. He found it difficult to adjust to the rough and tumble competitiveness of most of his peers. A typical young intellectual, he found a small circle of boys with literary interests who did not haze him for his poetic expressiveness and romantic dreaminess. Quite to the contrary, they shared their literary adventures and found ways to acquire the forbidden books in the school library.[27]

In early adolescence, while acquiring conventional technical skills demanded by the conservative regime of Nicholas I, Lavrov wrestled with traditional antinomies in European thought—determinism and free will, God and the laws of nature. He decided that the laws of nature had been created by God, but that God could not intervene in their operation.[28] Lavrov's youthful deism was, of course, a common variety of eighteenth- and nineteenth-century rationalistic thought, but he chose it for a romantic reason—not because it was the most *rational* description of the working of the universe, but because it was the most *poetic* one.[29] Lavrov exaggerated the role of poetry in life and thought. He felt that it could explain things which science could not, that it was a mediating intelligence which somehow bridged the misunderstandings separating faith from science.[30] The necessary alliance of poetry and science, one of the central conceptions of Lavrov's adolescent philosophy, still appeared

27. N. N. Firsov, "Vospominaniia o P. L. Lavrove," *Istoricheskii vestnik* 1907, no. 1 (January), pp. 101–2. According to Rusanov's account, Lavrov matured early intellectually and morally, but late physically. By the time that he reached the age of sixteen, however, he was one of the tallest boys in his class.

28. Rusanov, "P. L. Lavrov," p. 249; and *Izbrannye sochineniia,* 1:89.

29. *Izbrannye Sochineniia,* 1:89.

30. Ibid. Johan Gottfried von Herder's explanation of the first part of the Book of Genesis provided Lavrov with the inspiration for this idea and also for a poem, "Pervaia glava knigi bytiia" (The first chapter of the Book of Genesis), which, like most of his early philosophical religious poetry, was not published. One of these poems, "Predopredelenie" (Predestination), written in 1857, appeared in a collection of revolutionary poems and essays published in Leipzig in 1875. See *Izbrannye sochineniia,* 1:471 n 123; also, S. A. Reiser, ed., *Vol'naia russkaia poeziia vtoroi poloviny XIX veka* (Leningrad: Sovetskii pisatel', 1959), pp. 221–22. "Predestination" somewhat melodramatically sums up Lavrov's early deterministic philosophy, which I believe reflected a fundamental trait in his personality. Lavrov's sense of mission is expressed in the idea that he had to pursue "an unknown aim . . . along a slippery path." He

in his poetry and essays of the 1850s. Another element of the mystique of poetry was perhaps even more important for Lavrov's later thought. The preeminence of poetry lay in the poet's presumed closeness to cosmic forces—to nature and her secrets. The poet expressed his insights in harmonious and whole images, transmitting beauty and truth. Harmoniousness and wholeness, however, were not merely aesthetic principles. They were independent values applicable to all human activity. Lavrov displayed devotion to these values throughout his life. They appeared in his later thought in many guises.[31]

Lavrov tried his hand at both verse and drama, but only one product of his adolescent literary labors was published, a romantic poem entitled "Beduin."[32] It is a historical poem, full of exotic proper nouns and imbued with high pathos derived from the young poet's sense of the tragic degradation of Arab civilization. It recalls the past splendor of the Arab world and contrasts it with an inglorious present. In one of the dramas that he wrote, the hero rebels against society, but neither the drama nor a summary of its contents has been preserved.[33] At best one can say that his early literary efforts reflected the emotionalism (which he often referred to as "pathos" in his later writings on aesthetics) and the love of flamboyant and heroic actions and gestures appearing in so much of the romantic literature of the period.

Peter's literary career and his adolescent romanticism in no way interfered with his steady progress through the ranks. He began

---

also expressed another deep conviction that he was the instrumentality of a merciless "deity" in these words: "My hand trembles, but I hear a voice: 'Be firm! I realize my thoughts through you, I speak by means of you.' While I repeat: surely, God is merciless." The inner voice that guided Lavrov was the collection of deeply internalized ideals that formed his moral personality—his "merciless" and demanding conscience. Lavrov's precocious conscience and his later career fit quite well into Erik Erikson's picture of the development of a distinct type of personality—that of the *homo religiosus*. However, as shall be seen, merciless logic, an idea of progress, and belief in a scientific ethic became Lavrov's inner voice, his "deity."

31. I think that one can find them in his concepts of unity (*edinstvo*) and solidarity (*solidarnost'*), for example. They appear in his idea of progress as the integral development of the individual in "physical, intellectual, and moral aspects."

32. P. L. Lavrov, "Beduin," *Biblioteka dlia chteniia* 46, no. 1 (1841):5–7.

33. Rusanov, *Biografiia*, p. 15.

service in February 1838 as a *Feuerwerker* ("cannoneer"), within two years achieving the rank of *Junker* ("cadet"), and a year later that of a *Portupei-Junker* ("distinguished cadet"). In August 1842, when he was nineteen years old, Lavrov became an ensign in the artillery, but instead of entering military service he remained in the Mikhailovskii Artillery School as a science tutor. In September 1843 he was promoted to the rank of second-lieutenant for his distinguished scholarship, and in June 1844 started his rise in the academic hierarchy as a *Repetitor* ("coach") in mathematics.[34] Throughout this period, and indeed until 1848, when he received his first modest compensation, Lavrov was wholly dependent upon his father for financial support.

One can only speculate why Lavrov decided to continue in the Mikhailovskii Artillery School after his class had graduated. The simplest answer is that he was encouraged to continue by his teachers, and that a secure career in the capital lay ahead of him. He was unsuited to military service, and a literary career, even in the capital, was not a well-defined or secure kind of employment in the 1840s. During the reign of Nicholas I, when the military functions of the gentry were emphasized and the cadets were encouraged to reject inappropriately intellectual habits, a cadet school could not have been a very congenial environment for a hyper-intellectual young man. But Lavrov evidently saw no real alternatives, and he chose to advance along a path that he knew.

Lavrov complicated his life in 1847 by marrying Antonina Khristianovna Loveiko, the beautiful widow of a titular counselor, thereby provoking his father's wrath and putting himself in a difficult economic position. Without a paternal dole, Lavrov was forced to supplement his token salary (145 rubles semiannually in 1848) by giving private lessons in boarding schools for the gentry.[35] To complicate things further, he soon had two children to support as well: Mikhail, born in November 1848, and Elizaveta, born in November 1849.

Lavrov's wife, Antonina Khristianovna, was older than he and

34. Firsov, "Vospominaniia," p. 97.
35. "Iz materialov o P. L. Lavrove," p. 220. Lavrov's salary is listed here. The factual information given in Firsov's account is sometimes erroneous, but most of it checks out with Lavrov's own information.

quite beautiful. According to Elena Shtakenschneider, who first saw her in 1857, when Antonina Khristianovna was still a young girl, the artist K. P. Briullov had encountered her on a street in St. Petersburg and had been so impressed by her beauty that he had wanted to paint her as the Madonna.[36] Shtakenschneider described her as stately and beautiful in the late 1850s, at a time when she was the mother of four children. Their third child, Maria, was born in November 1851, and their youngest, Sergei, in May 1855.

Lavrov must have been under some strain during the late 1840s and early 1850s, even though the extreme reaction following the revolutions of 1848 did not affect him directly. He was not connected with any of the groups of intelligentsia, such as the Petrashevskii circle and its satellites, that had formed in St. Petersburg. Completely absorbed in his teaching, his reading, and his family, Lavrov evidently stood apart from the centers of criticism among the intelligentsia in the capital, but his sensibilities and idealism were of a kind with theirs, and he must have suffered during these years, as did the entire educated class. Furthermore, the cadets at the Mikhailovskii Artillery School had a rather low opinion of him. They thought that he was superficial and a money-grubber because, instead of concentrating on his specialty, mathematics, he gave lessons in French, German, and history in private boarding schools.[37]

Lavrov was nicknamed the "red dog" by the cadets. He was a very tall man, with a somewhat gaunt face, carelessly brushed, light red hair, and unkempt mustache. He had a prominent nose, neither aquiline nor quite the Russian "potato nose." A myopic squint and protuberant grey eyes gave him an intense appearance. In his earliest photographs he posed without spectacles, although he undoubtedly needed them. In later photographs, small, metal-rimmed spectacles rest firmly upon his nose. Even as a young man he was extremely near-sighted and had to put his face so near whatever he was reading that his mustache scraped the page.[38]

In society, however, Lavrov was a man of considerable presence.

36. *Dnevnik i zapiski,* p. 148.
37. Firsov, "Vospominaniia," p. 103; also see *Izbrannye sochineniia,* 1:17.
38. Firsov, "Vospominaniia," p. 96. Firsov described one of Lavrov's poetry readings—something at which he excelled—at a St. Petersburg soiree, during which he reached for what he thought was a chocolate, but instead plucked a cigar butt from an ashtray (ibid., p. 109).

He spoke fluently, with a slightly exaggerated uvular *r* that had been the source of some hazing from fellow cadets during adolescence, but that now gave his speech a pleasant luxuriance in polite company. Though it is difficult to picture him on the dance floor, he sometimes stepped out with Antonina Khristianovna, who was frequently the belle of the ball. It is probably wrong to say that Lavrov was a part of St. Petersburg society during the late 1840s and early 1850s. He did not really "come out" until the mid-1850s.

When his father died in 1852, and his older brother in 1853, Lavrov became the head of an extended family, for his mother and sister moved into a house adjoining his own in St. Petersburg.[39] It was at this time also that, through his inheritance, he achieved financial independence. These new circumstances signified a kind of liberation. Lavrov's only overt rebellion against his father during the latter's life had been his marriage to Antonina Khristianovna, but bitter resentment of paternal tyranny is quite evident in several of the articles that he wrote in the late 1850s, and in the stories about his father that he apparently told to close friends, such as the poet V. G. Benediktov.[40] Benediktov described Lavrov as a model husband, father, son, and brother, but there are no detailed descriptions of his conduct as a paterfamilias or of his domestic environment. One can only assume that he attempted to establish a domestic life quite unlike his father's regime. It is likely, however, that despite his desire to replace arbitrary authority by just and rational guidance, Lavrov's own penchant for formalism and regularity strongly affected the rest of the household. He had close ties only to his daughter Maria and had distant or strained relationships with his two sons, Mikhail and Sergei, if their behavior after his arrest and exile is any indication of their earlier association.

Although it is not possible to find a clear and distinct dividing line between Lavrov's early career as an accomplished but relatively anonymous pedagogue and his coming out in the world of the St. Petersburg intelligentsia, the year 1855 does serve as a kind of

39. *Izbrannye sochineniia,* 1:17; and *Dnevnik i zapiski,* p. 147.
40. Benediktov described Lavrov's father as an "extremely cruel" man, and this description was no doubt based upon Lavrov's own account. See *Dnevnik i zapiski,* p. 147.

boundary. It was an important historical boundary in that Nicholas I's long and repressive reign ended with his death in that year, and the empire seethed with resentment, anger, and bitterness over the fall of Sevastopol in the Crimean War. The capture of Sevastopol by an English and French expeditionary force signified the end of Russian military predominance in Europe, while the failure of Russian arms called into question the entire social, economic, and political system upon which Russian military might presumably rested. It posed the kind of threat which aggravated existing tensions and, rather than creating patriotic unity, produced a wide front of both open and clandestine criticism, the likes of which had not been seen in Russia during Nicholas's reign. Criticism assumed several forms. Some of it was directed against the European powers who had formed a coalition against Russia, but much of it came in the shape of new demands for political and social reforms—above all for the granting of a constitution and the abolition of serfdom.

During this period of defeat, crisis, and, later, controversy over Sevastopol, Lavrov served his only active military duty as an assistant to the commander of the Narva garrison—far from the Crimea. He probably played only a clerical role, and in later years he looked back on the episode with a wry smile. However, although the experience of war itself did not affect Lavrov in any significant way, the debates and discussions among the intelligentsia in 1855–56 heightened his political and social consciousness. Despite a seeming immersion in technical subjects, Lavrov had been reading omnivorously and possessed a vast store of knowledge from all of the humanistic disciplines and social sciences, such as they were, except economics. His earliest published articles (1852–56) were, according to his own account, quite unrelated to his major interests. They appeared in *Voennyi entsiklopedicheskii leksikon (The military encyclopedic dictionary)* and *Artilleriiskii zhurnal (The artillery journal).*[41] But Lavrov continued to write poetry and to express his philosophical, social, and political views in verse. He was still struggling with the problem of reconciling faith and science and was trying to combine

41. For a bibliography and brief description of the content of these articles see the annotated bibliography compiled by I. S. Knizhnik-Vetrov in *Izbrannye sochineniia,* 1:493–503.

patriotism and progressive social and political views in a harmonious civic philosophy.

Between 1852 and 1856 the *points fixes* of his civic philosophy were the most elevated slogans of the French revolution—liberty, equality, and fraternity. His poems, by his own definition highly perishable "political lyrics," are filled with disappointment and anger over European politics—especially France's failure to consolidate and advance the revolutionary movement—and Russia's role as suppressor of liberation movements. He used Napoleon III and Nicholas I as symbols of despotism, deceit, and illegality. But he predicted that the day of reckoning would come, and that the masses would liberate themselves if the rulers did not recognize basic civil liberties. Lavrov addressed his poems to the French and Russian masses and to the Russian tsars, first to Nicholas and then to Alexander II after the latter's coronation in 1856. Although fundamentally westernizer in substance, they contained several characteristically slavophile ideas about Europe's corruption and decadence, Russia's suppressed vitality, the possibility of a benign relationship between tsar and people, and the traditional Russian idea that a new tsar might play the role of liberator if he could only free himself from the corrupt influences surrounding him— the pomp and ceremonialism of the court, and the predators and parasites that flocked to the throne. However naïve these ideas may seem in retrospect, they were common currency among the intelligentsia of that period.[42]

Lavrov's pamphlets in verse evidently struck a sympathetic chord in the reading public of the mid 1850s, for several of his poems were widely circulated and declaimed. Two of the poems were mistakenly attributed to the prominent slavophile A. S. Khomiakov, whose underground verse did indeed resemble Lavrov's in its righteous vehemence and in its manner of address.[43] In a climate of frustrated

42. Lavrov's political poems are gathered together in A. M. Bikhter, ed., *Poety-demokraty 1870–1880-kh godov* (Moscow: Sovetskii pisatel', 1962), pp. 59–91, and in Reiser, *Vol'naia russkaia poeziia.*

43. *Dnevnik i zapiski,* p. 146. The poems "K russkomu tsariu" or "Novomu tsariu" (To the Russian tsar, or To the new tsar) and "Russkomu narodu" (To the Russian people)—written respectively in December 1854 and August 1856, the former during the siege of Sevastopol and the latter on the corona-

patriotism, resemblances between men of all shades of thought were not uncommon, and ordinarily bitterly opposed westernizers and slavophiles joined in the demand for full publicity of ideas about social and political reforms.

Like many other members of educated society, Lavrov wanted to avoid the bloodshed of revolution and called for timely reforms from above. However, he did not believe that Russia was ready for the radical social and economic reforms which Herzen propagated in *Poliarnaia zvezda* (The polar star). Lavrov entered the ranks of the opposition as a conciliator. He did not exhibit a systematic political philosophy, but rather a style of thought whose major feature was the idea of conciliation *(primirenie)*. In a letter to Herzen written in 1856 as an accompaniment to several poems, three of which Herzen published with the letter in *Golosa iz Rossii* (Voices from Russia), a supplement to *Poliarnaia zvezda,* Lavrov used the idea of primirenie in a seemingly conservative vein. The influence of the Hegelian vision of progress is apparent in this letter, but unlike Herzen, Lavrov emphasized the conciliation of Russia's past with her future, rather than a decisive negation of the past. Nonetheless, he also admitted the necessity of "shocks" and "sacrifices" similar to those experienced in other historical revolutions.[44]

While naming some ideological groups and showing awareness of the wide range of social and political thought within the St. Petersburg intelligentsia, Lavrov did not dismiss any of them as harmful or irrelevant, but, in keeping with his basic idea of conciliation, tried to show that they all agreed about the need for freedom of thought. This approach is quite characteristic for Lavrov, and he used it repeatedly in the more radical context of the revolutionary movement. At this earlier point in his career, he was much more interested in the importance of convictions, and in the process of forming critical convictions.

---

tion of Alexander II—were almost responsible for Khomiakov's arrest. Lavrov was prepared to confess authorship of the poems in order to save Khomiakov. The epigraph of "Russkomu narodu" is taken from Khomiakov's poem "Noch' " (Night), also written in 1854. See Bikhter, *Poety-demokraty,* p. 537.

44. *Izbrannye sochineniia,* 1:111–12. Lavrov's "Pis'mo k izdateliu" (Letter to the editor) is printed in full in *Izbrannye sochineniia*. It first appeared in *Golosa iz Rossii,* Knizhka ("booklet") 4, in 1857.

Much of his letter to Herzen is a statement of Lavrov's own credo—his ideas about historical progress and his more specific notions about Russia's present and future. Lavrov expressed historical optimism alongside pessimism about the Russian government's ability to carry out a rational program of reforms.

The problem of the abolition of serfdom was, of course, the central concern of that period. There is a curious contradiction—or what seems to be a contradiction—between the image of the ominously stirring masses in his poetry and his description of the Russian peasants in the letter to Herzen. The former was not simply a matter of rhetoric or poetic diction. The grand and awesome poetic image of the masses fashioned by Lavrov belonged to his wider historical vision. History told him that this was the age of the liberation of the masses and that popular revolutions were inevitable. When discussing Russia's immediate problems, however, he abandoned any idealization of the Russian peasants. Quite to the contrary, patriotic considerations were at least as important for him as social justice, and he opposed a land settlement which would place too much land in peasant hands, jeopardizing Russia's position in the grain trade and endangering the national economy. Thus, in 1856, he could write: "The logical injustice of slavery is apparent, but history has its rights, and logic must solve historical problems without disclaiming them."[45] In 1856 Lavrov was not a spokesman for the peasants or laboring classes. He presented a tentative program for national advancement in which the petty gentry (*melkoe dvorianstvo*) were to play the role of Russia's *tiers état* because they were the group most likely to lead the nation in agricultural entrepreneurship.[46]

Acceptance of revolution in the abstract, fear of a bloody upheaval, belief in the idea of historical progress, patriotism, and pessimism about Russia's immediate future could not easily be combined in a consistent program. Lavrov found himself in the strange position of reproaching Herzen for the latter's critique of the idea of progress in *S togo berega* (*From the Other Shore*), while at the same time cautioning him about the possibilities of radical reform in Russia. Ironically, twenty years later Lavrov would find himself

45. *Izbrannye sochineniia,* p. 112.
46. Ibid.

in much the same position as Herzen, advocating revolutionary strategies for Russia from abroad and exposing himself to the criticism of firsthand observers of Russian conditions.

Lavrov's program for the period immediately following 1855 bears some resemblance to his first revolutionary program (1873), in that it advocated preparation for major historical changes rather than an immediate historical upheaval. There is an element of academic thoroughness and cautiousness in his proposals. For example, he proposed intensive study of local conditions over a period of two or three years under conditions of full publicity before any attempt to convene deputies in St. Petersburg or Moscow for the purpose of drawing up a plan for the liberation of the serfs.[47] This kind of approach inspired his later critics to apply to him and his followers the sobriquet "preparationists" in the mid-1870s. Although Lavrov belonged to a much more radical portion of the spectrum of social thought in the 1870s, his inexpugnable academic streak showed through nonetheless. Thus, both a propensity for conciliation and a "preparationist" bias are already clearly visible in the only published document which reveals Lavrov's positions during the debates about the serf reform after 1855.

The substantive philosophical, historical, social, and economic ideas in the letter to Herzen do not yield much in the way of clues to Lavrov's later development. Some ideas expressed in the letter adumbrate Lavrov's mature philosophy of anthropologism. But, on the whole, the ideas are much more deterministic and gradualistic than his later revolutionary socialist thought. His social thought, expressed in fragmentary form, suggests that the French Revolution and the revolutions of 1848 were quite important historical models for him. His characteristically superficial opinions on economic questions were, as is indicated in the letter itself, echoes of arguments and discussions stimulated by rumors about the liberation. Having spent most of his life in the rarefied atmosphere of poetry, mathematics, and philosophy, Lavrov was rather dependent upon the knowledge and advice of others when he descended into the terrestrial murk of political, economic, and social questions. He exhibited the fear, typical for educated Russians, of the time when Russia, like Western

47. Ibid., p. 113.

Europe, would develop an impoverished industrial proletariat as one of the social consequences of a hasty liberation. The absence of a large-scale industrial proletariat in Russia was one of the factors determining the course of Russian social thought for several decades, and schemes to avoid the proletarianization of the serfs appeared in both conservative and radical doctrines. It was not so much a belief in the promise of native Russian social institutions as the anticipation of new and possibly greater social problems that made Lavrov an advocate of agricultural entrepreneurship led by the gentry, and of a period of something akin to wardship for the serfs.

The substantive social, political, and economic ideas in the letter to Herzen written in 1856 reveal less about Lavrov than does the ideological temperament which informs them. However conservative his proposals seem, they did not issue from a conservative ideological temperament. Lavrov belonged to that species of humane, forward-looking thinkers who wanted to pay the cheapest price for progress, to minimize the bloodletting and social dislocation entailed by it. When his views became more radical, Lavrov chose a revolutionary ideology which promised to cut short the period of social misery in Russia by preventing the development of industrial capitalism there. In 1856 he showed the influence of his peers, mostly members of the gentry like himself, men outside the government who considered themselves to be a rational, oppositional force, whose duty it was to save Russia from ruin. Within a few years Lavrov moved toward a more extreme ambience of radical publicists and student activists without, however, severing all his ties with the salon opposition which had nurtured him during the period of his coming out.

Buoyed up by the success of his political verse, launched by Herzen as a publicist, Lavrov nonetheless remained fully committed to a pedagogical career. Affirming his commitment to a life of study and moral purity, he prescribed something similar for all patriotic Russians. Indeed, this was his preparationist program for the late 1850s: "To prepare oneself and fulfill one's duty. . . . To prepare oneself through study and purification."[48] Himself a man of disciplined intellect and encyclopedic knowledge, Lavrov resented the

48. Ibid., p. 115.

petty squabbling of intellectual factions. The superficiality of St. Petersburg salon intellectualism irritated him. In addition, he decried the lack of moral fiber in his contemporaries—their unwillingness to advertise their convictions. Lavrov demanded intellectual wholeness and moral purity through work and the discipline of science. He believed that, having formed critical convictions, one was dutybound to enlighten and morally cleanse one's fellows, so that when the disease within the body politic reached its "crisis," there would be a corps of mature thinkers who could help ease Russia into the new era.[49] Lavrov lapsed into vague, metaphorical language in the only portion of his letter to Herzen where he might have provided a clear picture of his conception of the change from the old to the new order. In the last analysis, the letter is more a form of self-advertisement or self-affirmation than a social or political program, for Lavrov was simply demanding of others what he himself had been practicing. He evidently wanted to reshape Russian educated society in his own image.

Lavrov's concern with the general corruption in Russian society and his critique of the intellectual and moral capacities of his contemporaries no doubt issued from literary as well as from direct encounters. The plays, novels, and stories of the naturalistic and realistic schools exhibited in excruciatingly vivid detail all of the ugly and degrading features of Russian life. Even typical "cabinet scholars" like Lavrov could, through the mediation of literature, encounter the suffering spirit and flesh that populated both the cities and the countryside. But Lavrov tended toward the abstract, and he preferred writers like Herzen who could discuss the human condition with literary skill and compassion yet still examine it "scientifically." Furthermore, Herzen had suffered persecution, imprisonment, and exile for his convictions. An embattled knight of secular causes, he was an attractive figure to Lavrov, in whose memory were etched images of antique and medieval virtue.

Not fully prepared to break a lance in a fruitless cause, Lavrov set himself the more modest task of helping to raise the intellectual and moral level of his countrymen. All of this was undertaken in an elevated civic and patriotic spirit, but it was, after all, a program of

49. Ibid., p. 116.

"small deeds." His first articles and letters on contemporary questions published in Russia (several of them signed "One of Many") were fully consistent with the program suggested in his letter to Herzen.

There are several recurring ideas and approaches in Lavrov's essays of the late 1850's. He was engrossed with what one might call aesthetic-synthetic principles: unity, wholeness, harmoniousness, and perfection. As noted earlier, these principles had achieved the status of values in Lavrov's early world view. They became the guiding principles of his program of education and enlightenment for Russia. Beside the satires and radical critiques of Russian society that Gogol and Belinsky had, by their genius, established as major modes of expression within the Russian intelligentsia, Lavrov's ideas and critical manner were hopelessly academic and old-fashioned. To be sure, censorship was a problem, even in a period of relative relaxation, but the earnest, righteous, and elevated character of Lavrov's critique is not attributable to fear of censorship alone. He was constitutionally incapable of expressing biting scorn, of pinioning the object of his criticism with a peremptory phrase. Even the first of his anonymous "Letters on Various Contemporary Problems," in which he consciously attempted to satirize every Russian species of drawing-room babbler, mandarin, and semi-educated professional, never achieved satire.[50] In this and two other letters Lavrov balanced "satire" and criticism with an abstract discussion of a harmonious unity of knowledge, feeling, and action. The truly educated man, he wrote, applied himself to questions of truth (*istina*), justice, and civics (*grazhdanstvennost'*).[51] Lavrov was one of those thinkers who typically group their major principles into triads. One can see, without much difficulty, that his various

50. [Lavrov], "Pis'ma o raznikh sovremennykh voprosakh: Pis'mo k redaktoru," *Obshchezanimatel'nyi vestnik,* 1857, no. 1, pp. 45–49.

51. Ibid., p. 49. Although Lavrov wrote three such letters for *Obshchezanimatel'nyi vestnik* in 1857, the censor passed only the first and third. The second letter appeared under the title "Vrednye nachala" (Pernicious principles) in *Illiustratsiia,* 1858, no. 39, pp. 222–23. The open attack upon authority in "Pernicious Principles" is the probable reason for its being censored. See P. Vitiazev, "P.L. Lavrov v epokhu 60–kh godov i ego stat'ia 'Postepenno'," *Kniga i revoliutsiia,* 1922, no. 6, p. 11. The third letter appeared in the sixteenth issue of *Obshchezanimatel'nyi vestnik,* 1857.

triads contain homologous ideas or principles. For example, in his article "Pernicious Principles" he related three principles—authority, individuality, and sociality (*obshchestvennost'*)—to three areas of life: faith, science, and practical affairs.[52] in another article written in 1857 he named religion, poetry, and science as the three major aspects of human spiritual activity. The idea of creativity (*tvorchestvo*) was his major unifying principle.[53]

Most of Lavrov's articles published during 1857–58 were attempts to translate his educational philosophy into a program that would produce a truly educated man and enlightened citizen. "Pernicious Principles," however, contained an attack upon the principle of authority. Although the attack seems to be directed more against cultural than political authority, it nonetheless troubled the censors. Lavrov's affirmation of active criticism and struggle against authority was the dynamic factor in his aesthetic-synthetic system. "Where there is struggle, there is still both life and the possibility of development."[54] This was the maxim behind Lavrov's critical attitude in the late 1850s. He followed his own prescription by criticizing Herzen, probably the only contemporary Russian thinker whom he esteemed as an authority.

The most important moral teaching in Lavrov's essays of this period centered around the concepts of respect (*uvazhenie*), duty, and self-sacrifice. In Lavrov's usage, uvazhenie did not connote deference to authority, but rather perception and understanding of the dignity of one's fellow man. Another major moral principle, one which recurs in his later social thought with somewhat different implications, is the idea of duty (*dolg*). In Russian, the word dolg also connotes debt, and deep in the psychology of every Russian dvorianin who had internalized the values of his forebears, there was a sense of something owed to the state. The Russian intelligentsia, drawn largely from the gentry, reviewed and elaborated the idea of dolg in the course of historical changes in their relationship to the throne, and according to their shifting allegiances. Later in his career, Lavrov provided the revolutionary intelligentsia with

52. Lavrov, "Vrednye nachala," p. 222.
53. Ibid.
54. Ibid.

a developed rationale for repaying its "debt" to the Russian masses, but in the late 1850s he used dolg in a most general moral sense as duty or responsibility to oneself, to other individuals, to one's society, and to the abstract ideas which lie at the basis of every society.[55] Closely connected with Lavrov's conception of duty was a belief in self-sacrifice—another persistent motif in his thought.

In 1857–58 Lavrov hadn't yet systematically worked out a doctrine in which he could reconcile his intellectual commitment to individuality and egoism with the promptings of his conscience. Instead, he employed an aesthetic device, not unlike his aesthetic-synthetic principles, a version of the *juste milieu.* Since the major evils of Russian society were egoism and pride, the good pedagogue had to counteract them by instilling in his students a capacity for self-sacrifice and respect for other human beings; and since Russian society was overwhelmingly petty and practical, the student should be taught to strive for ideals and broad solutions to social problems.[56] In this way a healthy balance would be struck. Lavrov

55. P. L. Lavrov, "Po povodu voprosa o vospitanii," *Otechestvennye zapiski,* 1857, no. 9, p. 132. One might add to the concepts dolg and uvazhenie those of *tselost'* ("wholeness") and *edinstvo* ("unity"). In several articles on education, Lavrov gave full expression to his deeply internalized values of wholeness and unity.

56. Ibid., pp. 131–32. Aside from the article on education cited in the preceding footnote, Lavrov wrote several other articles on education in a broad sense and pedagogy in a narrower sense. These were "Neskol'ko slov o perevodakh istoricheskikh sochinenii," *Syn otechestva,* 1857, no. 51; "Neskol'ko slov o sisteme nauk," *Obshchezanimatel'nyi vestnik,* 1857, no. 11; "Ekzameny," *Zhurnal dlia vospitaniia,* 1858, no. 10; "O sisteme vospitaniia molodykh liudei," *Biblioteka dlia chteniia,* 1858, no. 2.

Lavrov's theory of education contained several fundamental assumptions. He believed that three major formative influences shaped the individual's development in society: the material circumstances of life, the influence of people, and the individual's own process of reflection. Education, for Lavrov, belonged to the second category of influences upon the individual. It was preceded by a period of "accidental" formative influences, and followed by the individual's assumption of control over his own development. According to Lavrov's theory, the first stage of "accidental" influences ended at the age of twelve, and the third stage, that of self-governing development, began at the age of twenty-four. His theory of education seems to be patterned roughly on his own intellectual development: rearing at home under the influences of his parents and tutors until the age of fourteen, followed by formal education in a cadet school, and finally, self-emancipation in the form of marriage against his father's wishes at the age of twenty-four, and criticism of con-

protested against utter selflessness before society, yet all of his programs, early or late, educational or revolutionary, contain in some form an idea of self-sacrifice or self-subordination.

It is not difficult to understand why Lavrov's articles on education and pedagogy and his "Letters on Various Contemporary Problems" evoked little interest and added little to his reputation. Some of them were written for relatively obscure periodicals; some of them were anonymous; and not one of them dealt with major philosophical or social issues in a direct way. They are mainly of biographical interest, revealing that in this transitional period in the development of his public identity, Lavrov displayed remarkable continuity of temperament, style, and morality with both his earlier and later careers. He carried to every subject a need to reconcile seemingly clashing elements and to synthesize them in one harmonious system, a tendency to historicize, and a very strong civic morality. He aimed his most censorious remarks at dogmatism, authority, hypocrisy, superficiality, and one-sidedness, opposing to them his program of individual development and social progress. It was mainly a program of social progress through cultural enlightenment.

---

victions instilled by both his family and his formal education. Lavrov's rebellion occurred considerably later in life than that of many members of the intelligentsia.

2.
Radicalization

Between 1858 and 1861 Lavrov acquired a new public identity, but not as a poet, educator, or social critic. He made his reputation as a philosopher at a time when philosophy was a forbidden subject in Russian universities. His articles and lectures on philosophy, however, did not interfere with his teaching career. In April 1858 he achieved the rank of colonel in the artillery and was awarded the Order of Anna, third degree.[1] Evidently he was a much more popular teacher in these years, at least partly because of the change in atmosphere in even cadet institutions after the end of Nicholas' reign.[2] He also began to cut more of a figure in society as a member of Elena Shtakenschneider's salon. Finally, during the late 1850s and early 1860s Lavrov resolved for himself some of the philosophical, historical, and sociological problems that he had been struggling with, and emerged with his doctrine of anthropologism. All of these activities widened his ties in the literary world of St. Petersburg, involving him in the burning philosophical and ideological issues of the day and with the radical proponents of views that did not always coincide with his own but that had the same ideological tendency.

Lavrov was at first something of a puzzle to Elena Shtakenschneider, the daughter of a wealthy St. Petersburg court architect whose luxurious home on *Millionnaia* ("million") Street, near the Hermitage, served as a meeting place for poets, novelists, philosophers, and other eminent cultural figures in the late 1850s and 1860s. Among those who frequented the Shtakenschneider salon were the novelists Ivan Turgenev, Ivan Goncharov, and Fedor Dostoevsky, the poets Apollon Maikov, Nikolai Shcherbin, Vladimir Benediktov, and Iakov Polonskii, and the agronomist Alexander Engel'gardt, who became a leading populist writer in the 1870s.

1. "Iz materialov o P. L. Lavrove," p. 220.
2. One can find a brief description of Lavrov's evolution as a teacher in Firsov's memoirs ("Vospominaniia," pp. 102–7).

Benediktov recommended Lavrov to Shtakenschneider in January 1857, at a time when his reputation still rested largely on his clandestine verse of the Crimean War period.[3] To Benediktov, Lavrov was like a figure out of Plutarch, possessing a rare combination of virtues and skills. Elena Shtakenschneider, who recorded in her diary the high moments of her mother's salon, commentaries on its habitués, and notes about personal and historical events, was an intense young woman in her early twenties when she first met Lavrov. At that time she was seeking an *homme supérieur,* someone who could answer the burning questions that troubled her.[4] What puzzled her about Lavrov was his simultaneous projection of external discipline and inner longing for some heroic, idealistic exploit. By April 1858 she had concluded that of all the members of the salon, Lavrov was the only man with a truly revolutionary spirit, despite his self-imposed restraint and his tendency to moderate the effusions of the outspoken but harmless parlor revolutionaries surrounding him. To her, Lavrov was the only man who meant what he said.[5] At moments, while listening to his compelling discourse, Elena Shtakenschneider felt that she was experiencing the spiritual birth of a new era, for the world of the salon was a strange mixture of frivolousness and religious intensity.

At times, on the ground floor of our luxurious home on Millionnaia, Lavrov spoke while we all listened attentively, usually in the winter garden or in the room with the arches alongside the garden, from which drifted the aroma of tropical plants and, quite audibly, the sound of drops falling from the glass dome onto the wide banana leaves or the flagstone floor; and I imagined the Roman catacombs and the first Christians, the new people sheltering themselves, perfecting their new form of worship, serving an apostle.[6]

History finally resolved the ambiguous situation of the oppositional groups in Russian society—although the Shtakenschneider

3. *Dnevnik i zapiski,* p. 147.
4. Ibid., p. 170.
5. On 10 April 1859 she wrote in her diary, "I somehow feel that Lavrov has an ideal, perhaps dread and merciless, but real; the others, including Turgenev, haven't any at all." (Ibid., p. 199.)
6. Shtakenschneider, quoted in "Iz vospominanii E. A. Shtakenschneider o P. L. Lavrove," *Golos minuvshego,* 1915, no. 7–8, p. 302. These are memoirs supplementary to her diary.

salon was not an oppositional circle in any true sense. Parlor liberalism was a hothouse plant that failed to survive the first con-
frontations between the government and genuine radicals during
the era of the Great Reforms. Indeed, Lavrov was one of the few
persons of that era who remained firm and outspoken in the face
of government repression. Ironically, Million Street is now Khalturin
Street, named for Stepan Khalturin, a worker who joined Narodnaia
Volia, the revolutionary organization which assassinated Alexander II in 1881. Lavrov spent the last years of his life as an ally of
Narodnaia Volia, true to the real radical possibilities which Shtakenschneider had early recognized in his personality—a peculiar combination of academic open-mindedness, "merciless" revolutionary
idealism, and personal compassion.

Shtakenschneider believed that Lavrov was basically a very sen-
timental man, a "dreamer-idealist" who somehow had arrived at
the conviction that "for the sake of humanity one had to be a revolutionary and cruelly to negate everything." Some of the members
of the salon regarded him as "mercilessly" logical.[7] Thus Lavrov
accepted many of the ideas of Fourier and St. Simon and spoke
matter-of-factly about the probable disappearance of the family and
social classes. Yet when he asked Shtakenschneider one day what
she thought about Fourier's phalansteries and she petulantly replied
that any imaginable disorder would be preferable to that kind of
arrangement, he reacted like a man whose own deeper feelings had
been surprised, and laughingly assented.[8] What Lavrov accepted in
the abstract did not prevent him from expressing his regard for the
convictions of real people.

Toward 1860 Lavrov's growing reputation as a philosopher surprised Shtakenschneider, for whom he had become the central figure in the salon but who had not followed his philosophical writings in *Biblioteka dlia chteniia* (Reader's library), *Otechestvennye
zapiski* (Notes of the fatherland) and *Russkoe slovo* (The Russian
word). Neither of the latter two journals belonged to the radical
camp at this time, and Lavrov's articles were lengthy discussions
of German thought, based largely upon the historical and critical

7. *Dnevnik i zapiski,* pp. 174, 207.
8. Ibid., p. 240.

writings of German scholars.[9] However, Lavrov's articles on Hegel, Hegelianism, the mechanistic world view, and German theism contain his own characteristic critiques. Lavrov was as much concerned with the character of thought as with its substance. For example, Lavrov recognized the extraordinary importance that Hegel's phenomenology of the spirit bore for nineteenth-century thought, but he condemned Hegelianism for its dogmatism and its obsequiousness before authority—in short, for its violation of the spirit of science.[10] Lavrov's meticulousness about the distinction between dogma and hypothesis, between religious blindness to other points

9. Lavrov was something of a cultural Germanophile, and his hopeful projection of Russian cultural development was based upon the German model. His own prose had a rather Teutonic character, acquired after years of reading German philosophical, historical, and psychological literature. Lavrov's major articles of this period (1858–60) were "Gegelizm" [Hegelism], *Biblioteka dlia chteniia,* 1858, nos, 5 and 9; "Prakticheskaia filosofiia Gegelia" [Practical philosophy of Hegel], *Biblioteka dlia chteniia,* 1859, nos. 4 and 5; "Mekhanicheskaia teoriia mira" [Mechanistic theory of the universe], *Otechestvennye zapiski,* 1859, no. 4; "Sovremennye germanskie teisty" [Contemporary German theists], *Russkoe slovo,* 1859, no. 7; "Ocherk teorii lichnosti" [Sketch of a theory of personality], *Otechestvennye zapiski,* 1859, nos. 11 and 12; "Laokoon, ili o granitsakh zhivopisi i poezii" [Laocoön, or on the boundaries of painting and poetry], *Biblioteka dlia chteniia,* 1860, no. 3; "Sovremennoe sostoianie psikhologii" [Contemporary state of psychology], *Otechestvennye zapiski,* 1869, no. 4; and "Chto takoe antropologiia?" [What is anthropology?], *Russkoe slovo,* 1960, no. 10.

10. Lavrov, "Gegelizm," *Biblioteka dlia chteniia,* 1858, no. 5. Lavrov had begun to elaborate and modify the position that he had taken in his letter to Herzen in 1856, where he had written: "In the flight of a feather, circling in the air, alongside all of its visible aimlessness, there exists a law, and this law leads to the measurement of a small number of accelerations, defining the motion. Does such a law exist in the history of mankind? Perhaps no, perhaps yes—science cannot decisively speak up for one or the other, but by failing to arrive at a solution, it permits man to create, by means of his own imagination, a solution which does not contradict the data. The analogy with the physical world permits, it seems, with considerable certainty, the necessity of all moral-historical phenomena rather than their fortuity. Indeed, it seems to me that one can assert in place of Hegel's "all that is real—is rational" another dogma: "all that is real is necessary." But the desire for a better life, for greater justice, for the fullest development of life is one of man's spiritual phenomena. As a real, necessary, constant force this desire must produce results. Perfection in some areas, in some definite periods of time is a historical fact. Given this, nothing contradicts the dogma of my religion—the gradual and necessary perfection of mankind." *(Izbrannye sochineniia,* 1:111.)

of view and the open-ended kind of approach that was both critical (Kantian) and historical, eventually embroiled him in controversies with several camps. Everywhere in Lavrov's writings of this period one finds a tension between his desire for positive knowledge and his sense of the historically conditioned character of thought. When he spoke of positive knowledge, he did so with Kant's epistemological strictures clearly in mind and with his understanding that men were shaped by traditions. From this tension there emerged another triadic formulation, which permitted Lavrov to criticize other systems of thought for their one-sidedness. He believed that all past philosophies had tended to emphasize one of three principles—the external world (Nature), individual consciousness, or tradition—at the expense of the other two.[11] Once again he demanded a harmonious, balanced approach in which man would be examined in his three-fold relationship to his consciousness, the external world, and tradition.[12] Lavrov himself believed that consciousness had to be the starting point for any philosophy.[13]

Another kind of critical approach to the philosophical systems that he reviewed in his articles of the period 1858–59 also reveals Lavrov's moral and civic focus: he did not criticize other philosophical systems on the basis of their violation of the spirit of science, their epistemological failings, or their one-sidedness alone. He never failed to add the moral dimension, the sphere of practical action for a chosen end, to his discussion. Thus his final assessment of a philosophical school or tendency included considerations of moral purpose and civic action. Having repudiated the idea of a search for answers to metaphysical questions which were, according to the Kantian critique, insoluble, Lavrov felt free to concentrate upon problems of practical philosophy. It was in this spirit that he approached contemporary materialism in his essay "Mekhanicheskaia teoriia mira" (The mechanistic theory of the universe).

11. Lavrov, "Gegelizm," *Biblioteka dlia chteniia,* 1858, no. 9, p. 28.
12. Lavrov, "Mekhanicheskaia teoriia mira," *Otechestvennye zapiski,* 1859, no. 4, p. 491.
13. Ibid. For a good brief discussion of Lavrov's philosophical position see James P. Scanlan, "Peter Lavrov: An Intellectual Biography," in Peter Lavrov, *Historical Letters,* ed. James P. Scanlan (Berkeley: University of California Press, 1967), pp. 11–30 (hereafter cited as *Historical Letters*).

Although he felt constrained to review the phenomenalistic critique of materialism, Lavrov was much more concerned with the moral implications of a materialistic and deterministic world view. Deterministic materialism dwarfed the significance of human action by reducing humanity to an insignificant aspect of matter in a vast universe and by rendering all human actions and doctrines equally valid because inevitable. In a word, Lavrov believed that deterministic materialism was fundamentally pessimistic and that it could never be more than the "religion of a minority."[14] He already viewed all concepts and systems of thought as instrumentalities whose usefulness he measured by their consequences for human development and human morality. He did this in spite of his own profound psychological fatalism, for which he had found doctrinal support in his adolescence and which had attracted him to Hegel in the mid 1850s.

Lavrov was searching for a doctrine which would make the struggle for justice and truth an ethical imperative and not merely an involuntary gesture. Kantianism was the key to the solution, because it opened the way toward an instrumental view of human consciousness while simultaneously upholding the idea of duty that was so central to Lavrov's world view. Through Kantianism he was able to explain the inevitability of some of the phenomena of human consciousness. Lavrov learned that one could accept the limitations of human consciousness, yet still arrive at a voluntaristic and optimistic conclusion. The neo-Kantian perspective encouraged Lavrov to engage in conscious self-manipulation and to act as if he were a free actor, freely choosing his goals. He never quite overcame his own psychological fatalism, however, and ended by seeing not only his consciousness but also *himself* as an instrumentality. He was not always consistently able to maintain the balance between voluntarism and determinism, the former as a consciously held critical doctrine and the latter as a personal psychological trait. This doctrinal-psychological contradiction led, on one hand, to Lavrov's anthropologism and, on the other, to a drifting toward the left without any hard commitment on his part.

As a result of these philosophical probings, Lavrov found himself in the peculiar position of having attained a level of critical

14. Lavrov, "Mekhanicheskaia teoriia mira," p. 490.

sophistication that was beyond the reach of the youthful radicals around him, although his fundamental sympathies lay with them. The unusual complexity of Lavrov's philosophy linked him to Herzen's generation, and, not unlike Herzen, Lavrov had to communicate with younger intellectuals whose philosophies, as well as temperament and style, were alien to him. However, Lavrov's pedagogical orientation, his historical vision, and his stern moralism overrode any intellectual or personal misgivings that he felt about the new generation of radicals, who, while fleeing from the metaphysical systems of the idealists and spiritualists, had mistakenly embraced the equally metaphysical materialism of Büchner, Vogt, and Moleschott. Lavrov was sufficiently astute to understand that this was a typical kind of extreme reaction against a prevailing orthodoxy. Furthermore, epistemological meticulousness was not the major aim of his articles. He felt real kinship with men whose philosophies were epistemologically unsound but whose moral and civic goals were similar to his own, and he discovered among the radical materialists men who placed human will and morality at the center of their doctrine in spite of the fact that they had chosen a rather inappropriate epistemological foundation for it.[15]

Lavrov's own scholarly career and his career as a publicist were very much influenced by his philosophical conclusions. In order to be true to his own system he could not accept the materialists' belief that the proper study of mankind was physiology. He concluded that one had to study the variegated historical products of human consciousness.[16] Consequently Lavrov committed himself to the

15. For example, although Lavrov did not agree with the materialism of Helvétius, Holbach, and Diderot, he held them in higher esteem than he did Büchner, Vogt, and Moleschott. The civic virtue of the Encyclopedists, their intense concern with morality and politics, more than compensated for their epistemological errors. On the other hand, the contemporary vulgar materialists were little concerned with morality and politics. Büchner's *Kraft und Stoff*, very popular among Russian intellectuals in the late 1850s and early 1860s, narrowly focused upon metaphysical questions and, worse still, was implicitly amoral. Although one could not disprove mechanical determinism, it could not serve as the basis for the kind of philosophy which Lavrov demanded. Human consciousness, human will, and human morality were rendered insignificant by mechanical determinism.

16. Lavrov, "Mekhanicheskaia teoriia mira," p. 491.

phenomenology of the spirit at a time when vulgar materialism and physiology were all the rage and when young intellectuals, with self-conscious asperity, were examining and discussing the hard facts of economic, social, and political reality. Lavrov undertook his new role as a critic of contemporary philosophy in a crusading spirit. Unlike the new generation of crude materialists, he had some conception of the possibly radical implications of his neo-Kantianism and of the progressive role of philosophical criticism. Immersed as he had been for years in German, French, and English literature, Lavrov was also fully aware of the philosophical poverty of his homeland. The numerous authorities cited by him in his essays, though important figures in the history of European thought, were with few exceptions either unknown to the younger generation or lightly dismissed by them. Thus his first characteristically learned and historical essays on philosophy did not establish him as a favorite author of the new intelligentsia generation. Quite to the contrary, when he did at last attract some of their attention, it was either as a well-intentioned but somewhat muddled academician or as an irrelevant "scholastic."

But Lavrov's reputation in the St. Petersburg literary world continued to grow. His articles for *Biblioteka dlia chteniia* had been solicited by an editor of the periodical because by 1859 Lavrov was considered to have the most encyclopedic mind in St. Petersburg in matters of philosophy, the exact sciences, history, and the social sciences.[17] Another symptom of Lavrov's growing stature was his association with the Literary Fund (the informal title of the Society for Aid to Indigent Writers and Scholars), which was founded in November 1859 and included among its members some of the most prominent Russian belletrists. Through the Literary Fund Lavrov met Turgenev, who helped to arrange a series of lectures which Lavrov delivered under the auspices of the Fund.[18] During the period 1859–62 Lavrov faced several audiences, and he soon discovered that it was impossible to please some without offending others. He reached the peak of his public career as a proponent of

17. P. D. Boborykin, *Za polveka* (Moscow, 1929), pp. 298–99.
18. P. L. Lavrov, "I. S. Turgenev i razvitie russkogo obshchestva," *Vestnik Narodnoi Voli* 2 (1884): 88.

anthropologism in Russia at a time when the liberal and radical groups that had united temporarily around basic reform goals were becoming bitter and irreconcilable opponents. During 1859–60 he gained the respect and admiration of a fundamentally liberal audience and attracted the attention and criticism of the radical publicists. In 1860–61, when he was forced to clarify his own position relative to the "progressive" forces around him, he became increasingly involved in radical causes. By 1862 Lavrov was identified by conservatives and some liberals as a member of the radical camp.[19] This change of public identity occurred less as a consequence of Lavrov's explication of his doctrine of anthropologism in lectures and articles, than as a result of his translation of the doctrine into personal support of radical individuals, groups, and causes.

Lavrov's first major work devoted to his own doctrine of anthropologism was *Ocherk teorii lichnosti* (Sketch of a theory of personality), which first appeared serially in *Otechestvennye zapiski* toward the end of 1859 and then in 1860 as a brochure entitled *Ocherki voprosov prakticheskoi filosofii* (Essays on questions of practical philosophy).[20] It was also the source of his first direct literary engagement with the radical publicists of *Sovremennik* and *Russkoe slovo*. There is little question but that *Sketch of a Theory of Personality* is a seminal treatise for Lavrov, for he cited it often in later works, long after he had become a revolutionary socialist and abandoned "preparationism" for the political strategy of Narodnaia Volia.

In *Sketch of a Theory of Personality* Lavrov engaged in the kind of speculative reconstruction of human moral evolution that seems to be practiced mainly by anthropologists today. His authorities were philosophers and philosophes, many of them perpetuators of the English and French tradition of speculative psychology. He pro-

19. Shtakenschneider attributed the most uncompromising nihilism to Lavrov, although she was more fully aware than most of the psychological complexities that existed alongside his logically derived nihilism. Actually, Shtakenschneider used the label "nihilist" in 1871, after Lavrov's arrest. In any case, all of the terms applied to Lavrov—liberal, radical, nihilist—were quite vague.
20. This treatise was dedicated to Alexander Herzen and Pierre Proudhon, who were identified by their initials.

posed to unite in a single theory the essential elements of the most advanced teachings in the area of "moral-political" science. In keeping with a basic tenet of anthropologism, Lavrov used human consciousness as his theoretical point of departure and posited individual self-consciousness as the first moment in the development of human personality.[21] From there he moved to the pleasure principle, relying on the studies of the German physiologist-psychologists, as well as on those of the English utilitarians, in order to establish the psychological source of motivation toward action in the individual. The pleasure principle, which underlay all human motivation in Lavrov's scheme, led him to reject the idea that men pursued knowledge for the sake of knowledge alone, or creativity for the sake of creativity alone. Both knowledge and creativity were instruments that the individual employed in his pursuit of pleasure and avoidance of pain. The human capacity for knowledge satisfied the human striving to grasp things as they are, while the human capacity for creativity (*tvorchestvo*) permitted men to transform reality in accordance with some idea of harmoniousness, wholeness, beauty—in keeping with a conception of things as they ought to be.[22] This latter capacity permitted man to create an ideal self and to strive constantly for self-development and self-perfection. Lavrov's sizable treatise traced the evolution of the ideal self through several stages of lower development, beginning with the self-centered individual and his egoistic striving for self-development and freedom. He divided the individual into three areas—body, thought, and character—and showed how, through the process of idealization, each of them inspired in the individual a sense of personal dignity, which in turn generated self-respect and the need for the respect of others. Finally, Lavrov established a set of duties corresponding to his tripartite division. Although men pictured their self-dignity in different ways, they all developed a duty towards it—an obligation not only to preserve it but to increase it to the furthest possible extent. Conceptions of sin and virtue arose from the con-

21. *Ocherki voprosov prakticheskoi filosofii,* in P. L. Lavrov, *Filosofiia i sotsiologiia,* ed. A. F. Okulov, 2 vols. (Moscow: Akademiia nauk, institut filosofii, 1965), 1:358.
22. Ibid., pp. 360–63.

cept of duty towards one's self-dignity. Sin consisted of acts or thoughts which affronted one or another aspect of the individual's ideal self, or in a failure to engage in activities which would further its development. Three moral rules issued from the foregoing: develop your body and respect it; develop your thought and respect it; develop strength of character and respect it. These rules gave rise to correlative rights and duties, among which were. the rights to personal liberty and the inviolability of one's person, the right and duty to develop one's critical faculty, and the right and duty to express one's opinions freely and publicly.[23]

Lavrov's *Sketch of a Theory of Personality,* especially when focusing upon the problem of individual development and freedom, relied heavily upon John Stuart Mill's recently published *Essay On Liberty,* Jules Simon's *La Liberté,* and Pierre Proudhon's *De la justice dans la révolution et dans l'église.* Mill's idea of a handful of individuals who were especially original, gifted, and endowed with strong character—the "salt of the earth"—confirmed Lavrov in his belief in the work of a creative minority at every stage of human development. Unquestionably, however, Proudhon's three-volume magnum opus, which appeared in 1858, was one of the most important permanent influences upon Lavrov. The ethical problems posed by Proudhon became the framework for Lavrov's own ethical thought, and the "realism" which Lavrov espoused was spiritually closer to Proudhon's than to that of any other major socialist thinker. One might say that Lavrov acquired his ethical psychology from Proudhon, applying it to the deontological foundation provided by Kant. Proudhon's deontological ethics contained a much more concrete psychological foundation for individual morality than did Kant's and Lavrov's, and Lavrov borrowed much from Proudhon in this area without, however, abandoning his fundamentally Kantian resolution of the problems of free will and determinism. As for Lavrov's left-wing Hegelianism—that, too, easily accorded with Proudhon. One simply converted critical thought from an abstract principle into a concrete function of willful, ethical actors. To put it in simplest psychological terms, every major intellectual system which influenced Lavrov was ultimately pressed into the service of

23. Ibid., pp. 377–88.

his superego. The logic of reason and the logic of conscience simply merged.

In *Sketch of a Theory of Personality,* as in other writings, Lavrov avoided existential questions and the possibility which they might present of unfettered egoism and self-assertion. Preeminently civic in his approach, he quickly moved away from the agonizing questions of existential and individual morality that Dostoevskii, his contemporary and fellow habitué of Shtakenschneider's salon, set forth with extraordinary power in his novels of the 1860s and 1870s. In effect what Lavrov was doing was creating an ethical model for his contemporaries to follow: that of a disciplined, self-reliant, and self-motivated individual—a "positive hero" of the type that Chernyshevskii later promoted in his novel *What Is to Be Done?* Much more of Lavrov's essay was devoted to establishing the duties of the individual toward society and to larger questions of social justice than to defining the limits of individual liberty. Like Chernyshevskii, whose hero, Rakhmetov, later became a revolutionary paragon for a significant portion of the new intelligentsia generation, Lavrov began with the concept of egoism and ended with the idea of social justice and useful social labor. He provided elaborate arguments to demonstrate that in the "developed" individual, egoism and the desire for social justice were in harmony rather than in conflict with one another, concluding that "the egoistic striving for pleasure at the expense of others in this becomes converted into the experience of pleasure in engaging in one's own activities which are useful and excellent to others."[24]

Nor was it enough simply to hold this philosophy, for Lavrov further demanded that the developed individual embody his conception of justice in life—if need be, through struggle and sacrifice.[25] He could not reveal exactly what that ideal of justice was, due to the conditions of censorship under which he wrote. But the treatise was dedicated to Herzen and Proudhon, and while Lavrov would neither mention Herzen nor present Proudhon's views without criticism, he did defend some of the latter's views vigorously. The note on which Lavrov ended his involved and abstract treatise

24. Ibid., pp. 456–57.
25. Ibid., p. 457

was one of left-wing Hegelianism. He sketched out the historical process through which justice would gradually embrace all of
humanity:

Criticism of the present [social, political, and economic order], recognition of the injustice of that which appeared to be just is the beginning
point of the process. It appears in separate individuals as thought,
consciousness. Consciousness little by little is disseminated, preparing
the ground for individuals who are not only conscious of the new principle, but also are gifted with the decisiveness to embody it. These are
the true heroes of humanity, the true movers in the development of
justice, the salt of the *earth,* according to Mill's expression. They do not
create, do not discover new thought, but they *resolve* to embody it, resolve to engage in struggle with that which they recognize to be unjust.
Once the struggle has begun, independent of its success, consciousness of
justice expands further and further; the resoluteness of some inspires
others. A new party grows up; criticism prevails; the new ideal becomes
the dominant one.[26]

The ideas of the historical role of criticism and of a resolute,
creative minority remained with Lavrov throughout his life. At this
stage in his writing, he emphasized criticism (*kritika*), which gradually replaced the idea of creativity (*tvorchestvo*) as the dynamic
principle in his theory of historical progress. As he became more
and more uncompromisingly revolutionary, he began to employ the
concept of criticism as a device to explain social dynamism. In
ethics, it explained the process by which the individual assessed
desire and motives and established a hierarchy of pleasures, rele-
gating short-term pleasures to a low position and durable pleasures
to a high position. The ascendance of kritika in Lavrov's system
was the preliminary step in his movement toward acceptance of what
Herzen called the only truly progressive contemporary doctrine:
socialism. How far he had committed himself to socialism in particular by 1860 is difficult to determine. Like Herzen, Lavrov was
too critically sophisticated to surrender to any single doctrine un-
reservedly or to believe in the inevitability of historical progress.
Perhaps even more than Herzen, however, Lavrov believed that
once a developed man had settled upon a progressive doctrine, it
was his duty to act consistently as if the chosen doctrine were ab-

26. Ibid., pp. 459–60.

solutely true and as if progress depended upon his resolute action. In 1856, in his letter to Herzen, he had used the term "rational religion" to describe his "faith" in the gradual and inevitable perfection of humanity, and had characterized the fundamental elements of that faith as "dogmas." By 1860 he had abandoned this terminology completely yet had retained the outlook suggested by it.

Despite his acceptance of a historical, subjectivistic, and therefore relativistic, epistemology, Lavrov nonetheless found a way to justify an absolute commitment to the "scientifically" most advanced doctrine of his era. It is impossible to avoid the conclusion that Lavrov's need to commit himself absolutely to the cause of progress preceded the elaborate rationalizing contained in his doctrine of anthropologism. But Lavrov himself evidently knew this, for in 1859 he had written, "Unconsciously a man draws near to the theory which satisfies his moral and civic needs . . . and in the practical province of the psyche, Fichte's words are almost always justified: 'What the man is, such is his philosophy.' "[27] Throughout much of his adult life Lavrov found new "scientific" support for his own moral needs. However, his willingness to discard old authorities and to supplant them with new ones waned during the 1870s, when his commitment to socialism hardened. During the 1860s Lavrov was still groping for a doctrine to which he could commit himself. His philosophy of anthropologism was, more than anything else, a way of justifying that commitment, and the *Sketch of a Theory of Personality* a major step toward the full exposition of Lavrov's anthropologism.

Perhaps the most succinct statement of anthropologism for this period in Lavrov's career is contained in the article "Chto takoe antropologiia?" (What is anthropology?), published in *Russkoe slovo* in October 1860. Rather than calling his philosophy anthropologism at this point in his exposition of it, Lavrov simply referred to "anthropology as a philosophical system."[28] At this time Chernyshevskii was also using the term "anthropology" to describe his own philosophical position. Despite basic differences in their philosophi-

27. Lavrov, "Prakticheskaia filosofiia Gegelia," (no. 4), p. 6.
28. "Chto takoe antropologiia?" in P. L. Lavrov, *Filosofiia i Sotsiologiia,* 1:480.

cal thought—especially at the level of epistemology—both Lavrov
and Chernyshevskii reflected the influence of left-wing Hegelianism
in general and Feuerbach in particular. Questions about their peculiar rendering of "anthropological point of view" are purely academic.[29] In general outlook and as an aspect of civic practice their
philosophies were very nearly equivalent. Both men advocated an
anthropocentric philosophy of action in the cause of enlightenment
and social justice by means of science, and both drew upon left-wing
Hegelianism, utilitarianism, and French utopian socialism when it
suited their purpose. Anthropology placed man at the center of the
system. Being based on Kantian epistemology, however, Lavrov's
anthropological system was phenomenalistic and subjectivistic, while
Chernyshevskii's was materialistic and objectivistic.

Given the peculiar character of Russian radicalism in 1860, Lavrov's rejection of philosophical materialism opened him to mild cen-
sure by Chernyshevskii, to a severe attack by M. A. Antonovich,
Chernyshevskii's lieutenant, and to the sarcasm of Dmitrii Pisarev
of *Russkoe slovo*. Had the latter two taken the trouble to analyze
the reasons for the extraordinary complexity of Lavrov's system,
and had they traced in his writings the continual deemphasis of
form (so central to his earlier aesthetic-synthetic point of view) in
favor of substance, they would have realized that there was nothing
in Lavrov's system that contradicted radicalism. Above all, the radical publicists who criticized Lavrov were objecting to a style of expression that in itself exhibited the kind of historical patience and
academic scrupulousness that was so out of tune with their own
urgency about change and their need to express a few clear, simple,

29. For an interesting discussion of the Russian response to Feuerbach,
including descriptions of Chernyshevskii's, Lavrov's, and Herzen's positions,
see G. Shpet, "Antropologizm Lavrova v svete istorii filosofii" in *P. L. Lavrov,
stat'i, vospominaniia, materialy* (St. Petersburg: Kolos, 1922). This collection contains several major articles on Lavrov as philosopher, sociologist, and
historian; Shpet's article is excellent. In May 1886, more than twenty-five
years after he wrote "Chto takoe antropologiia?" Lavrov claimed in a post-
card to Engels that Feuerbach had always been his favorite philosopher.
("Feuerbach a toujours été mon philosophe favori." MS in IISH. A Russian
translation of this document can be found in A. K. Vorob'eva, ed., *K. Marks,
F. Engel's i revoliutsionnaia Rossiia* [Moscow: Institut Marksizma-Leninizma,
1967], pp. 536-37.) There is little evidence that the direct influence of
Feuerbach on Lavrov was more important than Herzen's and Proudhon's.

and indisputable truths. Thus in 1860 even the full exposition of Lavrov's anthropological point of view did not gain him entry into the radical camp.

The publication of Lavrov's brochure entitled *Essays on Questions of Practical Philosophy* attracted the attention of both radical and conservative thinkers.[30] Possibly the most noteworthy effect of the appearance of Lavrov's brochure was that it stimulated Chernyshevskii to write "Antropologicheskii printsip vo filosofii" (The anthropological principle in philosophy),[31] which is considered to be the most important exposition of Chernyshevskii's materialism. He barely mentioned the content of the brochure, much to Lavrov's chagrin.[32] It also must have been somewhat disconcerting for Lavrov, several years Chernyshevskii's senior and with a number of major publications to his credit, to be patronized as a neophyte advancing along the right path. Unfortunately for him, he began to acquire some prominence in the years when the growing hostility between radicals and liberals revealed itself mainly in philosophical and aesthetic debates. Anyone who occupied middle ground was a fair target for either side and was used by both sides to clarify their own increasingly polarized positions. However, the few and brief comments which Chernyshevskii directed toward Lavrov served to point up a fundamental difference between the two men. It was, in large part, a professional difference between the publicist and the pedagogue. Lavrov's intellectual scrupulousness, his attempt to air all points of view, even erroneous ones, disturbed Chernyshevskii. The *Essays on Questions of Practical Philosophy* were full of references to philosophers whom Chernyshevskii had neither read nor cared to read. Why cite mediocrities, men obvi-

30. For a bibliography of reviews see *Izbrannye sochineniia,* 1:496.

31. N. G. Chernyshevskii, "Antropologicheskii printsip vo filosofii," *Sovremennik,* 1860, nos. 4 and 5. This important essay has been reprinted in several collections of Chernyshevskii's writings, including (in edited form) Nicholas G. Chernyshevskii, *Selected Philosophical Essays* (Moscow: Foreign Languages Publishing House, 1953); and James M. Edie, James P. Scanlan, and Mary-Barbara Zeldin, eds. *Russian Philosophy,* 3 vols. (Chicago: Quadrangle Books, 1965), vol. 2.

32. In replying to N. N. Strakhov, one of his critics, Lavrov also replied to the critics of *Sovremennik.* See P. L. Lavrov, "Otvet g. Strakhovu," *Otechestvennye zapiski,* 1860, no. 12, p. 101.

ously outside the mainstream of contemporary philosophy? Since Chernyshevskii felt he had grasped the simple and perfect truths of modern German philosophy, namely those declared by Feuerbach, he could not understand Lavrov's concern with what seemed to be the pitiful lies and errors of reactionary philosophies. Even when Lavrov rejected them, he did not fling them off with sufficient vigor and decisiveness to suit Chernyshevskii. Nonetheless, the young radical found great merit in the brochure and lamented that its progressive features and opinions were sullied by an unfortunate admixture of obsolete ideas. It was Chernyshevskii who first labelled Lavrov an eclectic.

Chernyshevskii had no patience for Lavrov's tortuous and involuted cogitations. His own intellectual puritanism is expressed by Rakhmetov in *What Is to Be Done?* in the following reflections:

No luxury, no caprices; nothing but the necessary. Now, what is necessary? Upon each subject there are only a very few first-class works; in all the others there are nothing but repetitions, rarefactions, modifications of that which is more fully and more clearly expressed in these few. There is no need of reading any but these; all other reading is but a useless expenditure of time. . . . If I have read Adam Smith, Malthus, Ricardo, and Mill, I know the alpha and omega of this school. I read only that which is original, and I read it only so far as is necessary in order to know this originality.[33]

This passage recalls Chernyshevskii's admonition to Lavrov, in "The Anthropological Principle in Philosophy," about stale and second-rate philosophical theories.

Despite this difference in intellectual style, there were other traits drawing the two men together. Given the demands of radicalism as he saw them, Chernyshevskii played the role of the lean man with a few hard, simple truths attacking fat and suspiciously complicated pedants; but he himself was very much the pedant and no less obsessed by grand scholarly schemes than Lavrov.[34] And although Chernyshevskii's rough treatment of complex epistemologi-

---

33. N. G. Chernyshevskii, *What Is to Be Done?,* trans. B. R. Tucker (New York: Vintage Books, 1961), p. 231.

34. According to E. Lampert in *Sons against Fathers,* by the age of sixteen Chernyshevskii had written more than 200 essays, many of which were in German, French, Latin, Greek, Arabic, Persian, Tatar, and Hebrew. He was

cal questions might have offended Lavrov, it did not estrange him, for he recognized in Chernyshevskii a manifestation of the Russian Enlightenment. In Lavrov's case there was accommodation to, but not imitation of, the more objectionable features of the new radical style, forged largely by the *raznochintsy* (non-noble members of the educated class) writing for St. Petersburg periodicals.[35] At this time the raznochintsy, Chernyshevskii among them, had established themselves as a leading force in the cultural life of the two capitals, Moscow and St. Petersburg, and had become ardent proponents of materialism, positivism, utilitarianism, and, sometimes, socialism. In literature they were devoted to realism and to Belinsky's didactic mode of criticism. A great part of the new generation of the Russian intelligentsia, whether aristocrats or raznochintsy, were attracted by the simplicity, clarity, and purposefulness of the radical publicists. Lavrov, closer to the intellectual generation of the 1840s in both age and culture, had gone through the painful transition from passive to active philosophies and from romanticism to realism in literature. He was fully aware of the philosophical and critical deficiencies of the new intelligentsia vanguard. However, unlike some members of his generation, he was less angered and offended by the radical raznochintsy than he was attracted by their crusading zeal. The philosophical, generational, occupational, and, probably, psychological differences which separated Lavrov from Chernyshevskii were ultimately less significant for their relationship than the com-

---

also a busy translator of important foreign works. Lampert writes, "In more tranquil times such a man would perhaps have remained a scholar—a role which Chernyshevskii had chosen in the first place." While in prison and exile between 1862 and 1889, Chernyshevskii began many projects—novels, stories, translations—and even managed to complete some of them. His last major project, begun in Siberia, was the translation and annotation of Georg Weber's *Universal History*. See *Sons against Fathers: Studies in Russian Radicalism and Revolution* (Oxford: Clarendon Press, 1965), pp. 95, 119.

35. The raznochintsy were often sons of clergymen, minor officials, or quasiprofessionals who could not be easily classified under the traditional categories of estates. The changing uses of *raznochintsy* have been examined in C. Becker, *"Raznochintsy:* The Development of the Word and of the Concept," *American Slavic and East European Review* 18 (1959): 63–74. For a brief but illuminating discussion of the raznochintsy see Richard Wortman, *The Crisis of Russian Populism* (Cambridge: At the University Press, 1967), pp. 5–8.

mon ethical orientation that each recognized in the other. They were both fundamentally puritans, and both were devoted to the younger generation.

An examination of Chernyshevskii's *What Is to Be Done?*, published approximately four years after his review of Lavrov's *Essays on Questions of Practical Philosophy,* reveals that he had manipulated the pleasure principle in much the same way that Lavrov had. Rakhmetov, that *nec plus ultra* of rational egoism, could easily have based his extraordinary behavior upon Lavrov's moral rules in the *Essays on Questions of Practical Philosophy.* (The rules it will be remembered, were, Develop your body and respect it, develop your thought and respect it, and develop strength of character and respect it.) Chernyshevskii's description of the honest, rational egoist's attitude toward others is very similar to Lavrov's idea of egoism:

You see, my good penetrating reader, what sly dogs honest people are and how their egoism works. Their egoism is different from yours, because they do not find pleasure in the same direction that you do. They find their greatest pleasure, you see, in having people whom they esteem think well of them, and that is why they trouble themselves to devise all sorts of plans with no less zeal than you show in other matters. But your objects are different, and the plans that you devise are different. You concoct evil plans, injurious to others, while they concoct honest plans, useful to others.[36]

Chernyshevkii's doctrine of pleasure and happiness through self-development and social toil is almost identical with Lavrov's. They both were able to reconcile the pleasure principle with an ascetic, devotional existence, and they both believed that the best men in Russian society would follow their example. Finally, both men combined either philosophical belief in determinism or psychological fatalism with demands for voluntarism and social action. Although Lavrov and Chernyshevskii never agreed about basic philosophical issues, before Chernyshevskii's arrest in 1862 they worked together as advocates of free criticism and as supporters of the student movement.

Lavrov continued his own enlightenment activities in a new medium—the public lecture. Public lectures were something of a rarity

36. Chernyshevskii, *What Is to Be Done?*, pp. 257–58.

in St. Petersburg. In 1859 only fifteen were given; in 1860, thirty-eight; in 1861, seventeen; and in 1862, only three. The decrease in lectures in 1862 reflected the government's reaction to the radical movement in the period after the emancipation of the serfs, and its attempt to curb intelligentsia criticism. Lavrov evidently planned to exploit his impressive skills as a public speaker in several programs of public lectures, but only the series on contemporary philosophy was realized, in November 1860.[37] Philosophy had been all but excluded from the university curriculum in 1848 and had not yet been reinstated. Lavrov's appearance on a public platform for the benefit of the Society for Aid to Indigent Writers and Scholars was a symptom of prereform liberalization and caused some stir in educated society. It also pointed up a chronic problem in Russian high culture.

The needs of the Russian empire had traditionally determined both the nature of education and the function of the educated stratum of Russian society. Now, however, the peculiarities of Russian historical development, in which the values and aspirations of a portion of the state-educated public ultimately clashed with state policy, encouraged the formation of a community of extraordinarily versatile men playing distinct and sometimes antagonistic cultural roles simultaneously. By 1860 significant numbers of educated men had set themselves up as critics of the system, living precariously as teachers, writers and translators, mainly in the two capitals, St. Petersburg and Moscow. Though a colonel in the artillery, and a mathematician whose business it was to teach cadets to plot the trajectory of ballistic missiles, Lavrov aspired to the role of philosophical critic and enlightener. His inclinations impelled him toward the liberal academy and the literary periodicals. He had outgrown his earlier career, and his appearance in the auditorium of the Passage, where he read three lectures on philosophy, for the benefit of the Literary Fund in November, 1860, was simply another step in his tentative movement toward a new role. Lavrov undertook his

37. Lavrov had also submitted a program of lectures on literacy to the school authority of the St. Petersburg district in the spring of 1861. They were to be read for the benefit of the Sunday schools. Permission was not granted, however. See "Delo o publichnikh lektsiakh v 1860-kh godakh," in *Istoriko-literaturnyi sbornik* (Leningrad: Izdatel'stvo otdeleniia russkogo iazyka i slovesnosti rossiiskoi akademii, 1924), p. 25.

task solemnly, with the conviction that responsibility for the revival
of philosophical thought in Russia rested to some extent with him.

Elena Shtakenschneider, fearing that he would not be able to
pander to the superficial tastes of the St. Petersburg literary crowd,
had nervously awaited Lavrov's lectures and was surprised and
pleased by his commanding presence. He delivered his first lecture,
"What is Philosophy in Knowledge?," to a full auditorium on the
night of November 22. Contrary to intelligentsia fashion, Lavrov
appeared in officer's uniform, decorated with all of his medals and
awards. However, instead of speaking to the audience from his
commanding height, he chose to lecture from a sitting position.[38]
He also avoided the glittering phrases that ordinarily evoked applause on such occasions. Shtakenschneider perceived a fundamental
ambivalence in Lavrov—a sense of superiority existing side by side
with a democratic desire to destroy the conditions sustaining elite-
ness.[39] The manner in which he staged his talks no doubt reflected
not only this ambivalence but also his conviction that philosophical
criticism had to be brought down to earth and used to transform
knowledge, art, and the human condition in general. Lavrov's initial
success on November 22 brought out larger and increasingly enthusiastic audiences on November 25, when he spoke on philosophy
in creativity, and on November 30, when he concluded with a lecture
on philosophy in life.[40] Shtakenschneider could now write, "Lavrov
has now become some kind of hero outside our circle, where he had
always been one."[41]

The series, soon published under the title "Tri besedy o sovremennom znachenii filosofii" was something of a tour de force, in which
Lavrov exhibited his mastery of philosophy, science, and literature, treating topics ranging from mythology to contemporary developments. Still demonstrating a great debt to romanticism, he
offered, among other things, his analysis of human development:
creativity unified and harmonized the welter of knowledge within

38. *Dnevnik i zapiski,* p. 271.
39. *Ibid.,* p. 274.
40. The talks were published under the title "Tri besedy o sovremennom
znachenii filosofii," Otechestvennye zapiski, 1861, no. 1, pp. 91–142; also
see P. L. Lavrov, *Filosofiia i sotsiologiia,* 1:511–73.
41. *Dnevnik i zapiski,* p. 275.

the mind, giving birth to art, religion, metaphysical myths, and science—in short, to culture.[42] The philosophical element in the creative faculty, however, criticized existing forms and employed all of the knowledge and resources at its command to alter them.[43] Creativity was the formal principle in human culture, while criticism was the dynamic principle.

Just as he had done earlier in his *Sketch of a Theory of Personality,* Lavrov also demonstrated to his audience that the pleasure principle and the idea of brotherhood were not irreconcilable. Only ignorance and indecisiveness, weakness of the critical faculty and weakness of character, prevented humanity from achieving a just and progressive condition.[44] With criticism mankind could surmount material circumstances, old forms and traditions, and establish new ideals and goals. With strength of character and decisiveness men could embody their ideals in social relationships: progress was the concretization of ideals shaped by criticism.[45]

Although Lavrov pointed out that man is in large measure a product of his milieu, he nonetheless believed that human consciousness acquired a measure of autonomy by means of its critical faculty.[46] He was well on the path toward his doctrine of the critically thinking minority and its role as the prime mover in the historical process. His theory of historical progress was a typical expression of the self-esteem of a portion of the growing secular intelligentsia who became a proselityzing minority, trying to reshape society in their own image.

Lavrov's *Three Talks on the Contemporary Significance of Philosophy* brought down upon Lavrov the wrath of two youthful polemicists, Antonovich of *Sovremennik* and Pisarev, writing for *Russkoe slovo.*[47] Antonovich's immense article, "Dva tipa sovre-

42. Lavrov, "Tri besedy o sovremennom znachenii filosofii," pp. 107–22.
43. Ibid., pp. 122–23.
44. Ibid., pp. 128–32.
45. Ibid., pp. 139–40.
46. In his theory of education, for example, Lavrov had assumed that at a certain stage the individual might assume control over his own further development.
47. M. A. Antonovich, "Dva tipa sovremennykh filosofov," *Sovremennik,* 1861, no. 4, pp. 349–418; D. I. Pisarev, "Skholastika XIX veka," *Russkoe slovo,* no. 5, pp. 74–82. The latter article can also be found in Dmitrii Pisarev,

mennikh filosofov" (Two types of contemporary philosophers),
went much further than Chernyshevskii's earlier criticism of Lavrov.
In addition to charging Lavrov with eclecticism, Antonovich accused
him of vagueness, confusion, and extreme idealism. He clearly resented the appearance of this new phenomenon in the literary journals—this upstart who dared to speak against the truths of modern
German materialism. Lavrov was an opponent who had to be cut
down as quickly as possible. Antonovich assumed that anyone who
was against materialism was also opposed to the philosophical beliefs which underlay *Sovremennik*. However, Antonovich praised
Lavrov's moral rules, despite their "metaphysical" derivation. In
practical questions of morality Lavrov was quite close to *Sovremennik*.

Pisarev, too, in "Skholastika XIX veka" (Nineteenth-century
scholasticism), took advantage of the appearance of a new philosopher to propagandize his crudely pragmatic and materialistic views.
His antiformalism, extreme even for the new breed of philosophe,
displayed the same impatience with complications and subtleties
in thought and doctrine appearing in both Chernyshevskii's and
Antonovich's criticisms of Lavrov. Pisarev, however, went even
further than the others. While Antonovich had taken pains to examine Lavrov's thought at length (although not always intelligently
or carefully), Pisarev dismissed it as scholasticism, and even criticized Antonovich for engaging in useless subtleties. Antonovich had
praised Lavrov's moral conclusions, but Pisarev found them utterly
opposed to his own views. "Nineteenth-Century Scholasticism" was
one of the first expositions of Pisarev's nihilism, and his attack on
Lavrov's idealism was an adumbration of his later quarrel with
Sovremennik.

Pisarev's failure to grasp Lavrov's meaning is as much attributable
to the lack of radical rhetoric in Lavrov's essays as it is to Pisarev's
misperception of the substantive ideas in them: Once again, it was
Lavrov's style that offended the new breed of radical publicist. Had
he searched Lavrov's writings as diligently as had Chernyshevskii,

Pisarev would have discovered arguments to reinforce his own positions.

Was it not philosophy that brought about mass movements, shattered the old idols, and shook antiquated forms of civic and social life in the past? Consider the eighteenth century! Take the Encyclopaedists! No, say what you please, but what Mr. Lavrov calls philosophy has no roots, lacks flesh and blood, and boils down to mere playing with words. That is scholasticism, and idle play of intellect that can be indulged in with equal facility in England and Algiers, in the Celestial Empire and present-day Italy. What is the significance of philosophy today? What is its justification in real life? What are its rights to existence?[48]

It was easy enough for Pisarev and the new generation of radical publicists to present as self-evident truths what a handful of Russian thinkers in the 1840s, especially Herzen, had finally grasped and articulated after painful wanderings through several schools of philosophical and aesthetic thought, but Lavrov's essays had recapitulated in depth the intellectual experience of that period. Lavrov, following Herzen, wanted to bring philosophy into living, historical processes. He was far from embracing scholasticism or "Buddhism," as Herzen had described devotion to pure science and pure form. Pisarev, however, carried the antiformalist tendency to its extreme in his peculiar variety of intellectual democratism:

If the generality and not only the select are to study and meditate and wish to do so, it would be a good thing to eject from science everything that can be understood only by the few and can never become common knowledge.[49]

Pisarev's democratism should not be taken at face value. Like the other foremost thinkers of the Russian intelligentsia during the 1860s, he believed in the work of creative minorities. Pisarev himself was a precocious intellectual and highly accomplished aesthete, whose personal crisis had assumed the form of an attack upon aesthetics and abstract or esoteric knowledge:

And how can one refrain from calling one-sided and ill-proportioned the development of such minds that are steeped in abstractions during all

48. "Nineteenth-Century Scholasticism," in Edie, Scanlan, and Zeldin, *Russian Philosophy,* 2:74.
49. Ibid., p. 75.

their lives, juggle with forms that are void of content, and deliberately turn away from the attractive and gay variety of living phenomena, from the practical activities of other people, the interests of their country, and the joys and sorrows of the world? The activities of people such as these are simply an indication of some kind of disproportion in the development of the individual parts of the organism; all their vital forces are concentrated in their heads; for these individuals their cerebral urges, which satisfy themselves and find their aims within themselves, have replaced the variegated and complex process that is called living. To give this phenomenon the force of law would be just as strange as seeing in the ascetic or the castrate the highest phase of man's development.[50]

Pisarev's angry demand for simple, accessible, exoteric laws and truths is one of the symptoms of the self-repudiation that individuals within the literary intelligentsia expressed in anti-aesthetic, crudely utilitarian, positivistic, and materialistic doctrines. In repudiating what they recognized as their own one-sidedness and ineffectiveness they also rejected the cultural forms and disciplines that they believed were responsible for their stunted development in other areas of human expression. They turned to these new areas with the exaggerated enthusiasm of converts. Thus Pisarev, a hyperaesthetic litterateur, became a propagandist for laboratory science and industrial enterprise and saw in scientists and entrepreneurs the new heroes of culture and society.

   Unlike Pisarev, Lavrov did not feel any compulsion to reduce the complexity of culture, nor did he feel the need to repudiate aesthetics and literary culture. Although he agreed with Pisarev's demand for full development of the individual and expansion of the educated class of society, Lavrov could not agree with Pisarev's rejection of ideals and goals. For Pisarev, ideals and goals were externally imposed abstract formulations which merely restricted the developing individual and impeded his instinctive response to living processes. Left to themselves, men were naturally kind and would help others for their own satisfaction rather than for the sake of some moral rule. Pisarev did not explain how egoism led to natural kindness or why men enjoyed helping each other. Lavrov, on the other hand, had tried to demonstrate that ideals, goals, and duties were natural

50. Ibid.

products of psychological development and neither violated natural egoism nor impeded human development. They were, in fact, both symptoms and causes of higher human development.

Lavrov defended himself against Pisarev and Antonovich in a lengthy article, accusing them of distorting his ideas. Without surrendering his phenomenalistic anthropologism and its emphasis upon ideal constructs, Lavrov tried to make it clear to his opponents that he shared their general concrete goals: "This quarrel is all the more unpleasant to me since I look upon it as internecine war. My critics and I have the very same practical goals, the very same enemies, the very same difficulties."[51] He considered Pisarev and Antonovich to be members of the embattled minority of intellectuals which strove for enlightenment and progress, and he tried to be conciliatory rather than to engage in polemics. This need to conciliate radical critics was a symptom of Lavrov's increasingly visible commitment to the causes of the younger generation of the intelligentsia, as well as a sign of growing estrangement from his own.

Between 1860 and 1862 the split within the intelligentsia widened. During this period Lavrov extended his associations with the left, and in doing so probably destroyed whatever chance he might have had for a new career in the academy. Since he was still an ambiguous figure, his actions on behalf of radical students and publicists did not convince all of his colleagues that he was a dangerous thinker or actor. However, the academic bureaucracy and the Third Section (secret police), in reacting to the student movement and the radical press, whether legal or underground, took no chances. Much to Lavrov's misfortune, his candidacy for the vacant chair in philosophy at the University of St. Petersburg was put forward in an atmosphere of fear of a "red" takeover of the faculty. Konstantin Kavelin, the historian and legal scholar and one of Lavrov's admirers in the liberal academy, could not prevail over the conservative opposition.[52] Both Lavrov and N. N. Bulchin, a professor at Kazan

51. P. L. Lavrov, "Moim kritikam," in *Sobranie sochineniia,* ed. N. Rusanov, P. Vitiazev, and A. Gizetti, 1st ser., no. 2 (Petrograd, 1917), p. 195. This article was first published in *Russkoe slovo,* 1861, nos. 6 and 8, pp. 48–69 and 88–108.

52. A. V. Nikitenko, *Dnevnik,* 3 vols. (Leningrad: Gosudarstvennoe izdatel'stvo khudozhestvennoi literatury, 1955-56), 2:175.

University, were regarded as too radical, and both were defeated. Lavrov had even prepared a conspectus of lectures.[53] He had chosen for himself the role of philosophical critic, had been certified by some of the foremost representatives of the Russian intelligentsia as one of the ablest and best equipped minds for that role, yet had been prevented from pursuing this new career. Inevitably, he sought other platforms.

The government's use of force against student demonstrators, and the arrest, detention, and imprisonment or exile of some of Lavrov's literary acquaintances in 1861 and 1862 converted him into an outspoken and active member of the opposition. But an attempt to apply to Lavrov the political nomenclature of the 1860s and 1870s leads to some confusion. In the vague manner in which the terms were employed at that time he could have been, and was, simultaneously labeled a liberal, a radical, and a nihilist. His contemporaries, of course, assessed him from their own special points of view. Kavelin evidently saw in him a kindred spirit, and therefore believed that he was a liberal of some sort. Nikitenko believed that he was a dangerous variety of radical, while Shtakenschneider found in Lavrov a number of contradictions, but finally concluded that he was a nihilist. In his autobiography Lavrov depicts himself as something of a pessimist during the early 1860s, with a very modest program.

But from the very beginning of his literary activity the necessity for political and social revolution was evident to him, and it is easy to find indications of this in his written works, especially in his poems. Nonetheless, at this time he did not see the basis for social revolution, nor even for political activity besides the slow preparation of minds.[54]

From an examination of his behavior after September 1861 it is quite clear that Lavrov included in the "slow preparation of minds" a wide variety of activities. Lavrov became a kind of activist, whatever his beliefs about the political and social possibilities of the moment. Some of his public actions can be described as a philanthropic support for individuals and groups whom he believed had been persecuted by the authorities; others can be taken as agitation for political, social, and cultural reform; and still others, as attempts

53. P. L. Lavrov, "Biografiia-ispoved'," *Izbrannye sochineniia,* 1:79.
54. Ibid., p. 103.

at reform through organization of and participation in clubs and societies.

The arrest of M. I. Mikhailov in mid-September was the first in a series of events which brought Lavrov even closer to the radical camp than he had been. Mikhailov—poet, translator, distributor of an illegal proclamation entitled "K molodomu pokoleniiu" (To the younger generation)—was one of the radical writers associated with *Sovremennik*. He was a central figure in the postemancipation agitation and also the first prominent literary martyr of the 1860s. Lavrov knew Mikhailov and had worked with him on the editorial board of the *Encyclopedic Dictionary*. Mikhailov's arrest caused considerable alarm in literary circles, and Lavrov was among the first to protest, to no avail.

Speeches, petitions, and collections by the liberal and radical intelligentsia were common tactics during 1861 and 1862, but Lavrov distinguished himself in these ventures by his fervor. At times he acted like a militant constitutionalist. In April 1862 he and fourteen other members of the Chess Club, a short-lived organization described by the agents of the Third Section as a hotbed of revolutionary plotting, signed a petition demanding a constitution from Alexander II.[55] In September 1862 he was a pallbearer in the funeral procession of Baron V. I. Shteingel, the Decembrist. Lavrov, intending to hold a commemorative service, stopped the procession in front of Peter Paul Fortress, near the spot where the leaders of the Decembrist movement had been hanged, but the authorities would not permit it.[56] This again was an unmistakable demonstration by Lavrov in support of constitutional government. As a founder of the Chess Club, as treasurer of the Literary Fund, and as a member of the editorial board and at that time editor-in-chief of the *Encyclopedic Dictionary,* he did everything within his power to support the radicals.[57] In May 1862, after Mikhailov had been sentenced to penal servitude in the Siberian mines, Lavrov wrote him

55. A. Shilov, "N. G. Chernyshevskii v donoseniakh agentov III otdeleniia," *Krasnyi Arkhiv* 14, no. 1 (1926):118. See also P. Vitiazev, ed., *Materialy dlia biografii P. L. Lavrova* (Petrograd: Kolos, 1921), p. 85 (hereafter cited as *Materialy*).

56. *Materialy*, pp. 85–86; also see n. 1, p. 86.

57. *Izbrannye sochineniia*, 1:79–80.

a poem very much in the spirit of his verse in the period following the Crimean War.[58]

Shortly after Mikhailov's arrest Lavrov became involved in the student movement, mainly as a sympathetic adviser who wanted to prevent bloodshed. The student movement that occurred in the autumn and winter of 1861–62 was provoked by new university legislation destroying autonomous student organization and discriminating against the poorer students who had poured into the universities after 1855.[59] The relative freedom of the period 1855–61 and the support of influential professors like Konstantin Kavelin had created the expectation that the rich and varied corporate life led by the students in the university cities would, if anything, continue to diversify and radicalize academic institutions. Issued without publicity during the summer of 1861, the new rules threatened to remove several of the conditions which supported the existence of the flourishing radical subculture in the university communities. Students returning in the autumn of 1861 refused to matriculate until the university administration clarified the rules. In the face of student intransigence and mass meetings, the authorities closed St. Petersburg University and decided to use troops against demonstrators. (Students from other institutions in St. Petersburg joined the university students in protesting the new rules and closure of the university.) Members of a student deputation that had forced General G. I. Filipson, university curator, to accompany them on their march from his house to the university and that had tried to negotiate with him were arrested during the night after the demonstration of Monday, September 25. On the following evening Lavrov discussed the situation with his study circle of young artillery officers. He had evidently learned that force would be used, and believed that the presence of military officers among the students would inhibit the troops. Following his advice, on Wednesday morning some of his students stationed themselves at strategic points leading into the

58. P. L. Lavrov, "Poslanie M. I. Mikhailovu," in Bikhter, *Poety-demokraty*, p. 75.

59. For a recent study of this period in Russian education, see Patrick L. Alston, *Education and the State in Tsarist Russia* (Stanford: Stanford University Press, 1969), pp. 45–50.

center of St. Petersburg and informed students with military rank that their presence was needed at the University. Several hundred students and their sympathizers gathered in the courtyard of the university, whose street entrances were guarded by a battalion of soldiers from the Finland regiment. It was a cold, damp, overcast day. During the late morning and early afternoon curious crowds gathered outside, while in the courtyard the students circulated a petition to Admiral Putiatin, the reactionary minister of education. The meeting disbanded without serious incident.[60]

The bureaucracy, however, refused to yield and in the course of the next two weeks succeeded in dividing the student body. More students and a few professors were arrested, among them Lavrov's colleague and friend, A. N. Engel'gardt. A manifestation in favor of the arrested students was planned for October 1, but it amounted to no more than attending Mass at the Kazan Cathedral on Sunday morning and then thronging on Nevsky Prospect,[61] and on October 11 the university opened its doors to those who accepted matriculation. Of potentially greater significance were the meetings and demonstrations planned by the students during the two- to three-week period after the closure of the university, but they had no serious issue. Lavrov watched the events of late September and early October 1861 with both apprehension and expectation. At one moment it seemed to him that some kind of revolutionary uprising might be imminent.[62] During this period an agent of the Third Section was assigned to Lavrov, who had been warned by General-Adjutant D. V. Putiata, chief officer controlling the military schools, that any further involvement in the student movement might lead to dismissal. Although the reports of the agent probably contain embellishments and inaccuracies about the extent of Lavrov's activities, and though it is difficult to ascertain how much of a role he played in the student

60. This account is based upon Shtakenschneider's description in *Dnevnik i zapiski,* pp. 296–98, and N. V. Shelgunov, *Vospominaniia* (Moscow: Gosudarstvennoe izdatel'stvo, 1923), pp. 126–30.

61. *Dnevnik i zapiski,* p. 300.

62. L. Panteleev, "Iz vospominaniia proshlogo," in *P. L. Lavrov, stat'i, vospominaniia, materialy,* p. 426. It is possible that Lavrov was describing the day of "society's" manifestation (1 October 1861), according to Shtakenschneider's account, above.

meetings that occurred, there is no question but that he actively took
the part of the students who refused to matriculate.

On the morning of October 12 the "matriculationists" and "anti-
matriculationists" gathered at the university, which had been reopened on October 11. Mounted troops stationed at the university
intervened in the struggle between the two groups, seizing students
and dragging them away or beating them with rifle butts. One student's ear was severed by a sabre stroke, while another's skull was
fractured. Almost 300 students were eventually taken to the Peter
Paul Fortress.[63] After these events, and more demonstrations, the
authorities once again closed the barely functioning university in
December 1861.

In retrospect, neither the student rebellion nor "society's" initial
support of it appears to have been a genuine threat to the government, but contemporary accounts describing the atmosphere in St.
Petersburg reveal that the government was alarmed and those sympathetic to revolution, hopeful. To Alexander Herzen, the student
rebellion was the beginning of a national uprising, and in the pages
of *Kolokol* he welcomed it with the slogan *v narod! k narodu!* ("to
the people!").[64] Expectations that had risen and fallen feverishly
in the years between the Crimean War and the emancipation of
the serfs in February 1861 rose once again. It was one of those
historical moments when men on the edge of rebellion are encouraged to assert themselves, whatever the suitability of their tem-
peraments for genuine revolutionary activity. Throughout this period younger men, mostly university students, pushed the older
members of the intelligentsia—Herzen, Ogarev, Chernyshevskii,
and, to some extent, Lavrov—toward more radical positions. The
publicists had played a central role in creating the atmosphere of
rebellion, but the students seized the initiative in the course of 1861,
sometimes entangling their reluctant and diffident mentors in revolutionary projects.

At this point in the development of the student movement, despite

63. *Dnevnik i zapiski,* p. 301; Shelgunov, *Vospominaniia,* pp. 130–31; also
Ocherki istorii Leningrada, 6 vols. (Moscow-Leningrad: Izdatel'stvo "Nauka,"
1955–70), 2:248–54.
64. *Kolokol,* 1861, no. 110, p. 918.

a great deal of ideological bitterness and personal antipathy, liberals and radicals could still make common cause. Several liberal professors resigned over Admiral Putiatin's university policy and over the brutal handling of the students. Liberal society in general sympathized with the students, encouraging them to carry on their rebellion. The government was forced into a defensive position after its initial blunders, and could neither severely punish the students seized in October nor destroy the movement for student autonomy. The movement reached its peak in the winter of 1861–62, when certain students and professors formed the Free University in St. Petersburg.

Lavrov was invited to lecture at the Free University but, along with Chernyshevskii, A. N. Pypin, and V. V. Bervi-Flerovskii (who was arrested shortly before the Free University collapsed), was not granted permission by the government. Although the committee that had organized the Free University contained radical student leaders who later formed the underground revolutionary organization Zemlia i Volia (Land and Freedom), the professors invited to lecture by the committee were not all radicals. As is often the case, the students attributed to professors whom they admired radical views similar to their own, and only later discovered that the teachers were moderate or even conservative in general outlook.

The collapse of the Free University shortly after its inception (it was organized at the end of January and collapsed in March) occurred largely as a consequence of dissension over the demand by some students that all lectures be suspended to protest the arrest of a liberal professor, P. V. Pavlov. On 2 March 1861 several prominent literary figures had participated in a program organized by the Literary Fund ostensibly for the purpose of raising funds for the exiled poet, Mikhailov, but also to serve as a forum for oppositional sentiment. Pavlov's speech made the greatest impression upon the sizable audience. He was arrested three days later and exiled to a provincial town. On March 8, N. I. Kostomarov, a historian on the faculty of the Free University, refused to accede to the radical students in their demand for cessation of lectures, provoking a stormy scene in the auditorium of the town council, which served as a lecture hall for the Free University. The disturbance on March 8 was the first important event in the process of breakdown of the liberal-radical front that had formed because of the new university legislation. Liberal professors who had sympathized with the students up to this point began to have second thoughts, while radical supporters of the students rushed to defend them.[65]

In the April issue of *Sovremennik,* Chernyshevskii "unmasked" the anonymous author of an article entitled "To Study or Not to Study?" appearing in *Sanktpeterburgskie vedomosti* on 1 May 1862. The staff of *Sovremennik* believed that A. V. Eval'd, the author of the article, was an agent of the Ministry of Education, for his article described the students as "blind tools" of radical agitators, themselves responsible for the failure of the Free University. In his article Chernyshevskii challenged the author of "To Study or Not to Study?" to a literary duel to determine the truth or falsity of the accusations against the students. He chose as his seconds G. Z. Eliseev and Lavrov. Lavrov too had defended the students against Eval'd in an article entitled "To Study, but How?" appearing in *Sanktpeterburgskie vedomosti* on 16 May 1862. Lavrov accepted the commission but was not able to accompany Chernyshevskii on the day of the duel and was replaced by Antonovich.[66]

At least in Chernyshevskii's eyes, Lavrov was an ally of the radical camp. Some of the associations with radicals that Lavrov formed in 1861–62 became quite important for him in later years. Eliseev, for example, served as his literary agent in the 1870s, when Lavrov was in exile and trying to get his works published in Russian periodicals. But, on the whole, circumstances did not encourage the development of stable relationships. Lavrov and Chernyshevsky met only two or three times before the latter's arrest in July 1862.[67]

65. *Ocherki istorii Leningrada,* 2:258–61.
66. For an account of this controversy and Lavrov's relationship to it, see *Izbrannye sochineniia,* 1:30–31; P. Vitiazev, "P. L. Lavrov v epokhu 60-kh godakh i ego stat'ia 'Postepenno'," pp. 12–13; M. A. Antonovich and G. Z. Eliseev, *Shestidesiatye gody* (Moscow: Academia, 1933), pp. 101–24. For a brief description of Lavrov's articles defending the students, see *Izbrannye sochineniia,* 1:500–501; also, R. A. Kimball, "The Early Political Career of P. L. Lavrov, 1823–1873," (Ph.D. diss., University of Washington, 1967), pp. 134–39.
67. Panteleev, "Iz vospominaniia proshlogo," p. 423; P. L. Lavrov, *Narodniki-propagandisty 1873–1878 godov* (St. Petersburg, 1907), p. 54; M. A.

Antonovich, though invited by Lavrov to write for the *Encyclopedic Dictionary,* never really believed that Lavrov belonged to the radical camp. Far more narrowly sectarian than Chernyshevsky, Antonovich failed to find in Lavrov the integral vision of his comrades. Antonovich's instincts were sound. Although Lavrov openly cultivated the radicals, he chose the role of adviser and teacher rather than that of comrade or leader. He had only tenuous connections with the student underground. In the early 1860s, when activists began to form circles, and when men like N. A. Serno-Solovevich and Nikolai Utin tried to create a genuine revolutionary organization, Lavrov remained something of an outsider.[68] In fact, when L. Panteleev tried to bring Lavrov into the first Land and Freedom group in St. Petersburg, he was rebuffed by younger members of the organization, though there is evidence that early in its existence Lavrov had established contact with Land and Freedom through A. N. Engel'gardt, who was one of his close friends. Evidently Lavrov had requested the right to attend the organization's meetings without, however, accepting the responsibilities of a full member. This was probably before the arrest of N. A. Serno-Solovevich and S. Rymarenko, also a friend of Lavrov's. Younger elements gained control of Land and Freedom in 1862 after the arrests, and to them Lavrov was a discredited member of the older generation. P. I. Bokov, influenced no doubt by Chernyshevsky's and Antonovich's criticisms of Lavrov in *Sovremennik,* opposed him on the grounds

---

Antonovich, "P. L. Lavrov v vospominaniiakh sovremennikov," *Golos minuvshego,* 1915, no. 9, p. 132.

68. The network of secret organizations in St. Petersburg, and Lavrov's relationships with individuals in them, are examined in E. S. Vilenskaia, *Revoliutsionnoe podpol'e v Rossii* (Moscow: Nauka, 1965), and in Panteleev's memoirs. Lavrov described his role in the "revolutionary underground," such as it was, as too insignificant for comment. I. S. Knizhnik-Vetrov disputes this in "Lavrov o Chernyshevskom," *Literaturnoe nasledstvo* 7–8 (1933), pp. 109–10. Knizhnik-Vetrov exaggerates Lavrov's involvement in Land and Freedom, which proved to be a rather abortive organization in any case. The general tendency in Soviet writing on Land and Freedom is to depict it as a significant phenomenon, embracing subsidiary organizations like the Chess Club, and involving the efforts of numerous important intelligentsia figures. One must discount much of this, for it is based upon flimsy evidence and excessive inference.

that he was a cabinet scholar and metaphysician and would be useless for the purposes of the organization. N. Utin supported Bokov,
and Panteleev's proposal failed.[69] Lavrov did not get a second
chance in Land and Freedom, and even if he had it is doubtful that
he would have exploited it. At approximately this time, in July 1862,
he was planning a trip abroad to visit his wife, who was in Germany.[70]

His wife's illness may have had a moderating effect on Lavrov,
although in his retrospective assessments of his activity during this
period he fails to mention it as a factor. The years 1861–62 must
have been unhappy ones, for in addition to the disappointments in
his career, he suffered the death of his twelve-year-old daughter,
Elizaveta, in 1861.

Lavrov's activities during the feverish and confused events of
the early 1860s are understandably ambiguous. He, along with other
members of the oppositional intelligentsia, experienced the rapid
growth and collapse of what had appeared to be a promising revolutionary movement. Against a background of rumors about a vast
peasant uprising, seditious pamphlets appeared, the students rioted,
mysterious fires broke out in St. Petersburg, the movement for
Polish independence grew increasingly serious—finally ending in
1863 in a bloody but unsuccessful rebellion—and militant constitu-
tionalists in Russia demanded that Alexander crown his reforms
with parliamentary government. The government and a considerable
portion of educated society believed that a radical conspiracy lay
behind these events. The authorities were able to deal with each of
the elements in the incipient revolutionary front separately: suppressing peasant riots; pacifying the students by appointing a liberal
minister of education, A. V. Golovnin, in January 1862 and issuing
a liberalized university charter; arresting the leading radical publicists and student agitators; and, finally, exploiting both the liberals'

69. Panteleev, "Iz vospominaniia proshlogo," pp. 425–26.

70. MS in Arkhiv Oktiabr'skoi Revoliutsii, Moscow (hereafter referred to
as AOR). Arkhiv III-ogo Otdeleniia, ekspeditsiia 1, no. 230, chast' 141, 19
July 1862. Antonina Khristianovna was in Germany, taking mineral waters
to cure the illness to which she evidently succumbed several years later.
Lavrov's association with S. Rymarenko, a member of Land and Freedom
and one of the leaders of the student movement, caused the authorities to
refuse Lavrov's request for a six week leave of absence.

fear of violence and the chauvinism of the conservative majority after the St. Petersburg fires and the Polish rebellion. Taken together, the events of 1861–63 revealed the weakness and disunity of the groups which opposed the government.

Sometime during the course of 1862, before the final stage of the reaction set in, Lavrov wrote a brief essay, one of the best clues to his vision of the conflicts in the Russian intelligentsia over the reforms. He had written it for *Sanktpeterburgskie vedomosti,* but it had been rejected, and Lavrov had then sent it to Eliseev for publication in *Vek* (The Century).[71] This time the censor forbade publication. The essay, "Postepenno" (Gradually), reveals that Lavrov was examining the models of historical progress put forward by both liberals and radicals, and was rethinking his own views. He accepted the idea that, like organic development, historical development entailed the consecutive unfolding of necessary stages, which, if tampered with, might lead to something "unnatural" or diseased. "Gradually" is dominated by the model of organic growth. However, rather than drawing conservative and gradualistic implications from the model, Lavrov came to a seemingly radical conclusion. While rejecting the idea of a forced great leap forward, or of skipping stages of development, he pointed out that the advocates of gradualism were in fact exponents of *uneven development.* That is, they were willing to take only a piecemeal approach, and violated their own organic principles by refusing to criticize openly and simultaneously all social ills.

Social consciousness matures gradually. But when it is aroused, then not *gradually* but rather *simultaneously* it directs its corrosive critique at all points accessible to it, and at all points the irrepressible need for renewal and development begins. There are only two possibilities here: either unnatural distortion or *simultaneous* development.[72]

Lavrov clearly understood the plight of his liberal friends, and he was possibly describing his own dilemma in the following passage:

You concerned yourself with the old order; you recognized that there

71. MS in AOR, fond no. 75, opis' 1, ed. khr. 324. Upravlenie Sanktpeterburgskogo Komendanta, 11 June 1866. Zapiski po delu o Lavrove, listed as point 2. Also see P. Vitiazev, "P. L. Lavrov v epokhu 60-kh godov i ego stat'ia 'Postepenno'."

72. Lavrov, "Postepenno," in *Izbrannye sochineniia,* 1:131.

was some kind of injustice in it; from this moment the entire old order is subject to criticism; independent of your will, it [criticism] begins to undermine all of its bases.[73]

But the "gradualists" did not want to destroy everything at once, because of this behaved rather ambiguously, and ended by suppressing criticism and development in some areas. Lavrov thus expressed something like Trotsky's law of combined development in the area of critical thought, though if we are to believe Lavrov's autobiographical statement about his political and social program during these years, he meant only the free play of critical thought simultaneously over all issues, and not necessarily a revolution that would destroy the social and political structure of the old order all at once.

The nihilism that Shtakenschneider had perceived in Lavrov was the end product of the "merciless" criticism which had led him to accept the essential features of utopian socialism. His sympathies lay with the radicals, and by the beginning of 1863 he had begun to see serious defects in the liberal mentality and posture. Even if he himself did not advocate revolution in the period 1861–63, and possibly felt that revolution would be premature, Lavrov experienced the high expectations and bitter disappointments of the period and felt the acute resentment that sometimes radicalizes men who usually believe in striving for the possible. In short, while not actively promoting revolution, he was apparently ready to welcome it.

The semiprofessional agents of the Third Section did not make distinctions between sympathizers of revolution and genuine revolutionary organizers in this period, and it is not difficult to understand why. The professional revolutionary did not yet exist. Measured by later standards, most of the names on V. A. Dolgorukov's (the head of the Third Section) list of chief suspects probably would not even qualify as revolutionaries. By 1863 most of the leaders of the radical opposition, both publicists and leaders in the student underground, had been arrested or had fled abroad. Though he had been under surveillance since the autumn of 1861, and under strict surveillance since April 1863, Lavrov was neither searched nor arrested during the reaction of 1862–63. He continued his work of enlightenment.

73. Ibid.

3.
Arrest and Internal Exile

During the years 1861–63 Lavrov devoted most of his literary efforts to Kraevskii's *Encyclopedic Dictionary*. He was appointed editor of the philosophical section early in 1861 and became general editor of the project after publication of the first volume later in 1861. Lavrov quite consciously exploited his post, transforming the *Dictionary* into a vehicle for what can be broadly termed rationalistic thought, and more particularly, for his anthropologism. In an attempt to attract as allies the materialists of *Sovremennik,* Lavrov invited Antonovich to write for the *Dictionary* even after the latter had written a scathing criticism of the first volume. Lavrov still believed that the materialists, though philosophically unsound, were attacking the very evils that he attacked, and that their struggle led in the same direction as his—toward human dignity and human development. Not unexpectedly, the *Dictionary* was attacked by the clerical press, and in 1863, after publication of the sixth volume, the government withdrew its subsidy from the enterprise, which closed down for lack of support.[1] In most respects, Lavrov's work on the *Dictionary* was a great waste of time and energy. Although he deepened his own knowledge of the history of philosophy and religion and, more generally, of the "phenomenology of the spirit," he did not reach a significant audience. The *Dictionary* did not play the role in the Russian Enlightenment that Lavrov had envisioned. In fact, it was only the first in a series of abortive projects begun by him in the years 1861–66.

The second major project was the journal *Zagranichnyi vestnik,* financed by a prominent St. Petersburg bookseller, M. O. Wolf. Lavrov was offered the editorship after his friend P. M. Tseidler went abroad and gave up the post, but in December 1863 the Third Section informed the Censorship Committee that the Ministry of

1. *Izbrannye sochineniia,* 1:79. A list of Lavrov's articles in the Dictionary can be found in Knizhnik-Vetrov's bibliography.

the Interior had refused to confirm Lavrov's appointment.[2] Instead, A. S. Afanas'ev-Chuzhbinskii became official editor of the journal, while Lavrov collaborated clandestinely.[3] *Zagranichnyi vestnik* offered the reading public translations of current European belles lettres and scientific, historical, and political thought. The selection of articles reflected Lavrov's involvement in the feminist movement and his growing interest in anthropology. Although he had intended to bend the journal in a radical direction, he was hampered by his coeditor, by fear of censorship, and possibly by his own inability to propagandize a single point of view. The pessimistic opening words of *Zagranichnyi vestnik* reveal his mood in the mid-sixties: "Both our society and our literature have suffered many disappointments. The present is gloomy; the future is not appealing."[4] Perhaps the most provocative editorial comment that Lavrov managed to insert into the journal was that which prefaced the article "Protsess Dzhona Brauna" (John Brown's trial). It stated that John Brown was a hero for all Russians who had sympathized with the destruction of serfdom in Russia.[5] Historical articles on European and American political institutions were also meant to be tendentious. Nonetheless, the journal seems relatively detached, almost academic in tone. The closure of *Zagranichnyi vestnik* in 1866 demonstrates the extreme wariness of the government more than Lavrov's skill as a firebrand. There is no reason to believe that the journal had a following in the youthful radical intelligentsia. Full sets of *Zagranichnyi vestnik* could be purchased at a reduced rate at Wolf's bookstore in the 1880s.

Lavrov wrote several articles for *Sanktpeterburgskie vedomosti* and *Biblioteka dlia chteniia* in 1863. However, a review of John

2. On 10 December 1863, Lavrov wrote to the Committee on Censorship requesting confirmation in his post as editor. He was turned down because of his record with the Third Section. See "Iz materialov o P. L. Lavrove," p. 222.

3. According to an agent of the Third Section in a report of 18 June 1864, the official editor opposed Lavrov's attempts to give the journal "a vaguely fanatical bent." Some of Lavrov's annotations to articles had attracted the censor's attention. See *Materialy,* p. 81.

4. Lavrov, "Ot redaktsii," *Zagranichnyi vestnik,* 1864, no. 1, p. i.

5. Editor's introduction to the article "Protsess Dzhona Brauna," in ibid., no. 2, p. 141.

Stuart Mill's *Utilitarianism* which Lavrov wrote in 1864 was not published.[6] The review reaffirmed Lavrov's admiration for Mill and utilitarian ethics, although Lavrov disagreed with Mill's explanation of the origin of social justice and offered instead the analysis set forth earlier in *Essays on Questions of Practical Philosophy.* The primacy of ethics in Lavrov's developing theory of progress, so readily observed in his earlier articles, now appeared in its newest form in this review. In *Three Talks on the Contemporary Significance of Philosophy* he had described progress as the concrete embodiment of ideals shaped by criticism. It was now clear that, above all, he had in mind ideals of justice. Once again Lavrov discussed ideals as if they were disembodied or autonomous forces which had to correct defects in the historical process:

Social forms are a means for achieving the good of each man. But they grow up not only logically from moral needs, but, in addition, *historically* [*italics mine*] from conditions completely alien to any kind of morality and justice. Men must struggle with them in order to embody justice in them, just as they struggled with other individuals in order to protect their dignity. The latter struggle led to conciliation on the basis of the ideal of justice; the former leads to conciliation on the basis of the ideal of *social utility,* according to the definition of utilitarianism, that is, on the basis of a gradual decrease in the amount of pain and an increase in the amount of pleasure for individuals. But this idea, too, is still only a way of becoming reconciled to historical necessity; it satisfies the needs of the moment and for that reason, while containing within itself the urge towards progress, it does not, in addition, contain the basis for it— the moral motivation of the individual to further its realization as his cause. Its realization occurs in the name of the moral idea of *social justice,* containing within itself the need for the gradual development of individual dignity and the subordination of the various historical social forms to the logical developments of moral ideas. *The progress of society*

6. MS in Tsentral'nyi Gosudarstvennyi Arkhiv Literatury i Iskusstva, fond 285, opis' 2, ed. khr. 5, "Novaia kniga Dzhona Stuarta Millia." Lavrov's signature appears on the first page. The manuscript is in Lavrov's hand. A marginal notation by Lavrov reveals that the article was written for *Sankt-peterburgskie vedomosti*: "Please send me two copies of the proofs, just as I asked for with the preceding article about 'Mori,' but didn't receive." "Mori" is the Russian transliteration of Murray. Lavrov had reviewed Alfred Murray's history of the Paris Academy of Sciences for the journal in November 1863. The manuscript of the article on Mill is dated 1864. Another heretofore unpublished article, "Liudvig Feierbakh, istoricheskii etiud," dated 1868, is included in P. L. Lavrov, *Filosofiia i sotsiologiia,* 1:637–75.

consists more and more in the embodiment of justice within it; social utility is only a consequence of this embodiment.[7]

This interesting mixture of utilitarianism, Proudhon's ethics, and left-wing Hegelianism once again demonstrates Lavrov's affinity for the revolutionary rationalistic tradition. History was to be assaulted by ideals, and ideals themselves issued logically from the phenomena of human consciousness. But Lavrov believed that only the enlightened minority, with its highly developed critical powers, was capable of forming higher ideals. Only they could assault history, overcome the inertia of tradition, and embody within social forms their ideals of social justice. Hence, the pleasure principle worked one way for the masses and another way for the intelligentsia. Mill's analysis suitably explained the behavior of the masses, but Proudhon's was a more satisfactory guide to intelligentsia morality. This division of society into two distinct groups, operating on different intellectual and moral levels, became more and more explicit in Lavrov's later work.

In the mid-sixties Lavrov must have kept pen and notepad constantly within reach, writing commentaries and criticisms of foreign literature in all fields. His writings reveal the enormous impact of the great mid-nineteenth-century advance in the biological sciences, psychology, sociology, and anthropology. Technical philosophical questions were no longer his central concern, as they had been in the late 1850s. There was, however, no sudden break in his development, but a gradual shift of emphasis from philosophy to psychology, anthropology, and sociology. The major tenets of Lavrov's subjective sociology were already worked out in his practical philosophy of the late 1850s. In fact, one might say that his exposure to Comte —to whose works the botanist A. N. Beketov introduced him in 1864[8]—and to Spencer merely converted him into a self-conscious sociologist and provided him with a new vocabulary. (The impact of Comte and Spencer upon Russian thought in the 1860s can hardly be exaggerated.)

Lavrov's intellectual development is an excellent mirror of some

7. Lavrov, "Novaia kniga Dzhona Stuarta Millia," conclusion.
8. Rusanov, "P. L. Lavrov," p. 257.

of the major features of nineteenth-century European thought. Even if he was slow to discover some of the most important theories of the epoch—those of Darwin and Marx, for example—he eventually incorporated them into his sociology. It is clear, too, that Lavrov was inevitably attracted to the most abstract problems in any given field, those most removed from the gathering of concrete data. He had always evinced interest in the philosophy of science, in new attempts to define and classify the methods of the sciences, and in essays on the organization of knowledge. The writings of Comte, Mill, Spencer, Renan, and Berthelot stimulated him to varying degrees in the mid- and late 1860s and, as was his habit, Lavrov attempted to synthesize the discoveries of even the most synthetic thinkers. He decided to write a vast history of science, a project which may have been encouraged by the appearance of G. H. Lewes's *Aristotle* in 1864. Lavrov was also acquainted with William Whewell's work in the methodology of science. References to the work of both men appear in Lavrov's writings in the mid 1860s.

There is reason to believe that some of his labors in 1865–66 were undertaken for the sake of money as well as for his own edification and the enlightenment of others. In October 1864 an agent of the Third Section enigmatically reported that Lavrov had suffered "various reversals caused by the liberal cast of his thought and activities."[9] In any event, Lavrov offered to read public lectures on the history of physical-mathematical sciences for a fixed fee. These lectures, read from 1864 until his arrest in 1866, served as the basis for his *Ocherk istorii fiziko-matematicheskikh nauk* (Essay on the history of the physical-mathematical sciences), which was published in serial form in 1865 and 1866, and in book form in 1866.[10]

While Lavrov actively continued to seek journalistic and organi-

9. *Materialy,* p. 82. Report of 24 October 1864. The agent suggested that more students would be attracted to hear Lavrov's liberal views than to learn about science.

10. In his own short autobiography Lavrov claimed that he read the course in 1865–66. However, it seems from the report of the agent of the Third Section that the series of lectures began on 30 October 1864. Since the autobiography was written twenty years or more later, the error is understandable. Lavrov's history first appeared in two journals: *Artilleriiskii zhurnal,* 1865, nos. 4–8, 10–12, and 1866, nos. 1–4; and *Morskii sbornik,* 1865, nos. 1, 3–5, 7–12, and 1866, nos. 2–3.

zational outlets for his ideas about enlightenment and social change in the mid 1860s, the major radical intelligentsia organs of the 1860s continued their propaganda. After Chernyshevskii's arrest, *Sovremennik* lost its earlier ideological clarity. Inspired largely by G. Z. Eliseev and the poet N. A. Nekrasov, it became an early organ of the populist tendency, in that it extolled the virtues of native Russian peasant institutions—the agricultural communes and workers' cooperatives—and opposed large-scale industrialization. Pisarev, like Chernyshevskii, writing in prison, still propounded his peculiar mixture of utilitarianism and elitism, and *Russkoe slovo* continued to offer the younger generation a vision of progress through science, enterprise, and self-development. *Russkoe slovo* was the chief organ of proindustrial Westernism. Lavrov did not participate in either of these journals, though he knew Eliseev. On the other hand, he did establish some tenuous ties with the nihilist subculture, which, with the decline of political ferment after the repression of 1862, became the major expression of intelligentsia opposition to the existing order. Followers of the radical publicists were attempting to fulfill utopian socialist programs in communal experiments and through the feminist movement. In a way, they were belatedly trying out the Fourierist ideas which had dominated the Petrashevskii circle in the 1840s and had been silenced during the reaction to the revolutions of 1848–49, but which were later elaborated and popularized by Chernyshevskii in his novel, *What Is To Be Done?*

A. V. Nikitenko, censor and professor of Russian literature at St. Petersburg University, noted in his diary in May 1864 that "Lavrov is busy . . . converting women and girls, for the most part quite young, into nihilists, for which purpose he has opened a course of materialist philosophy for them."[11] Nikitenko associated radicalism with materialism and was completely ignorant of Lavrov's real position. Lavrov did indeed lead study circles comprised of both men and women, but Nikitenko may have been referring to discussions leading to the formation of the Society for Women's Labor, a short-lived group which Lavrov helped to organize between the spring of 1863 and the winter of 1864–65. The society held its first

11. Nikitenko, *Dnevnik,* 2:442.

meeting in February 1865 (some fifty members attended), but signs of dissension appeared immediately when Lavrov, as chairman, proposed Countess V. N. Rostovtseva as one of the managers.[12] The nihilists, many of them evidently recruited by Lavrov himself, opposed Rostovtseva, demanded that an equal number of working-class women take part in the management of the society, and proposed as their candidate one Nagornova, a cleaning woman.[13] Later attempts to conciliate the aristocrats and nihilists failed. The aristocratic faction, convinced by A. K. Krivoshein that Lavrov was trying to seize power, tried to rescue the organization from him and his nihilist friends. (Lavrov had also invited Antonovich to join the organization.) By means of a devious maneuver, the aristocrats questioned the right of a large number of "unfamiliar" individuals, whose names appeared on Lavrov's list of subscribers, to attend a general meeting. Lavrov, in protest, withdrew from the organization, which did not survive its opening sessions.[14]

Lavrov's numerous ties with radical youth eventually involved him in one of the ephemeral publishing *arteli* (cooperatives or communes) that appeared in the 1860s. The *artel'* was conceived by I. A. Rozhdestvenskii, a former student of St. Petersburg University who had been arrested for participating in the demonstrations of 1861.[15] Members were to buy shares in the artel' and pay an entrance fee as well. Although forty to fifty persons joined the artel', only one of them paid the full entrance fee (thirty rubles), and no one bought a full share (1000 rubles). Most of the members paid only a token sum. Presumably the artel' would both publish and sell translations of scientific works, thus avoiding the profit-taking middlemen. Lavrov, of course, was an expert on foreign scientific literature. Beginning in October 1865, the artel' met in the reading room of V. V. Iakovlev's bookstore, a popular meeting place for nihilists. Lavrov, who had been elected to the editorial board, chaired one of the several general meetings.[16] Of course, agents of the Third Sec-

12. *Dnevnik i zapiski,* p. 351.
13. Antonovich and Eliseev, *Shestidesiatye gody,* p. 246.
14. *Dnevnik i zapiski,* pp. 351–56. For a bibliography of articles on the Society for Women's Labor, see *Materialy,* p. 87 n 1.
15. Vilenskaia, *Revoliutsionnoe podpol'e v Rossii,* p. 363.
16. Ibid., p. 366.

tion had from the start been alerted to the artel', which had never received official clearance from the authorities. Many of the members of the commune had been involved in the student movements of the 1860s and later had joined revolutionary organizations, so it is not surprising that the Third Section suspected the artel' of being a center of radical activity. According to Shtakenschneider, who evidently learned about it through Lavrov, it was actually a rather amorphous enterprise, whose members were largely incompetent to carry out their work, and Lavrov did not take it very seriously.[17] Ironically, his membership in the artel' served as the excuse for searching his apartment and arresting him in April 1866. One can speculate that the artel' may have been planned as a cover for an underground organization of a different sort, and that its publishing activities were not serious ventures. It may be that Lavrov was not taken into confidence and that he was being used by the artel' to help establish its front. There is no evidence that the artel' ever achieved its underground goals, if it indeed had any, or that Lavrov played a significant role in it.

During this period Lavrov continued to exercise philanthropic efforts on behalf of persecuted colleagues. As noted earlier, he had belonged to committees, collected money, and signed petitions hoping to mitigate the plight of students and publicists arrested during the postemancipation furor. Many of them were detained for several months in prison before being released; some were exiled to provincial towns and placed under police surveillance; and the most unfortunate were sent to penal servitude in Siberia. The poet Mikhailov died in August 1865 after three years in the Siberian mines. Chernyshevskii, who was exiled to Siberia in 1864, spent much of his first year there in an infirmary. Rumors about his condition reached St. Petersburg, and in January or February 1865 Lavrov urged the Literary Fund to petition the authorities about Chernyshevskii. The matter was dropped.[18] The Chairman of the Literary Fund, E. P. Kovalevskii, was evidently not inclined to involve the Fund in a possibly dangerous maneuver. His reluctance is

17. *Dnevnik i zapiski,* p. 386–87.
18. Sh. M. Levin, "Predlozhenie Lavrova Literaturnomu Fondu khoda-taistvovat' o Chernyshevskom," *Literaturnoe nasledstvo* 67 (1959): 137–40.

good evidence of the extent to which the government had cowed liberal society.

Though he could hardly have derived much satisfaction from it, Lavrov also participated in the newly created St. Petersburg provincial *zemstvo,* which, he asserted, should act as an independent institution rather than as a mere local extension of the central administration. Lavrov attacked the government's monopoly on the sale of spirits and opposed a government-proposed forest conservation program on the grounds that the central administration might not serve the interests of a given region. During his brief career in the zemstvo Lavrov exercised whatever opposition he could, but his oratory yielded nothing but material for the Third Section.[19] In later years, no doubt recollecting the futility of early zemstvo proceedings, he expressed contempt for the organization as a vehicle for change.

Alongside these abortive or futile projects, Lavrov continued to pursue a life of scholarship. His *Essay on the History of the Physical-Mathematical Sciences* was merely the beginning of his lifelong effort to embrace scientific, ethical, and social thought in a vast historical synthesis. It is one of the pioneering works in the history of science in Russia. Lavrov was interested not merely in historical changes in the character of scientific thought but also in cultural, social, and political conditions which either furthered or impeded the development of scientific thought. In this respect he was quite an advanced thinker in the history of science, and his work on Greek and Alexandrian science probably deserves more attention than it has received. However, in spite of his relatively sophisticated analysis of the elements of the historical environment affecting the development of science, Lavrov continued to believe in the creative role in history of individuals who not only bore the imprint of the spirit of their epoch, but also exhibited unique personal characteristics. Thus, he wrote:

The universal law of the development of humanity is realized by means of human individuals, and it is impossible not to take them into account when discussing it. Therefore, the biographical element necessarily enters into the history of science.[20]

19. *Materialy,* p. 88.
20. *Ocherk istorii fiziko-matematicheskikh nauk,* in *Artilleriiskii zhurnal,*

Lavrov had his own heroes of science, among them Archimedes and
the French scientists who during the French revolution had played
a civic role as well as a scientific one. *Essay on the History of
Physical-Mathematical Sciences* is one of the first expressions of
what was to become Lavrov's major concern during the late 1860s—
describing the origins, development, survival, and extension of scientific elites and their ideas. This concern undoubtedly reflected his
sense of the precariousness of the Russian intelligentsia's position
in Russian society, and he was struck by the similarities between
ancient Alexandria and modern St. Petersburg. In both conception
and design this set of essays is a symptom of Lavrov's long-range
commitment to historical scholarship and of the Russian intelligentsia's continuing devotion to the Encyclopedic tradition. In Siberia Chernyshevskii, too, dreamed of writing an ambitious history
of human thought. But Lavrov was in a position to carry out his
project. Given the temporary lull in his publicistic career—a lull
which was associated with the period of reaction and the general
subsidence of intelligentsia opposition after 1863—scholarly projects seemed to be his only real alternative in 1865–66.

During this period Lavrov's domestic life also must have affected
the nature and extent of his activities. In 1865 he spent four months
in Germany with his ailing wife. She died after an extended illness
either late that year or early in the winter of 1866.[21] According to
V. S. Kurochkin, who confided the information to Shtakenschneider
(Kurochkin also attended Shtakenschneider's salon), Lavrov had
lived a virtually monastic existence during the years of his wife's
illness, plunging even deeper into intellectual work than usual, and
avoiding any kind of entertainment.[22] This account, combined with
the fact that a young and beautiful girl named Josephina Antonovna
Riul'man had joined the household during the last two years of
Antonina Khristianovna's illness, and examined in the light of Lavrov's courtship of the girl shortly after his wife's death, suggests that

1865, no. 4, p. 13. Lavrov's book appeared serially. My reference is to the
first installment.
21. Curious though it may seem, there is almost no information about her
death in the memoir literature. See *Materialy,* p. 88.
22. *Dnevnik i zapiski,* p. 369.

Lavrov must have experienced a sense of liberation early in 1866. One can also assume that he felt a great deal of guilt. This guilt, probably associated both with his ambivalent feelings about his wife's death and with his precipitate and maladroit behavior towards a bewildered girl more than twenty years his junior, surely underlay some of the strange and self-defeating behavior which led to his incarceration and exile in April 1866. Shtakenschneider wryly and astutely observed:

Not even Faust went directly from his laboratory to Gretchen, but first dropped in to see a sorceress, got himself transformed, learned a few things, and forgot a few things. Lavrov did not take these precautions.[23]

Lavrov only succeeded in frightening the girl with his theatrically romantic performance. She finally told her brother, a medical student who tutored Lavrov's eldest son Mikhail, and the brother decided to seek the advice of Dr. P. K. Konradi, a physician who had attended Antonina Khristianovna toward the end of her illness and whose wife had done translations for *Zagranichnyi vestnik*. Presumably acting in Lavrov's interest, the Konradis succeeded in creating a small scandal in Lavrov's family and circle of acquaintances. He accepted it all as a just punishment for his behavior,[24] but the Konradis evidently decided that a match was possible and redirected their efforts toward that end.

Meanwhile, an unexpected event issuing from the revolutionary underground touched off a new wave of reaction that eventually reached Lavrov. On 4 April 1866 a suicidal young man named Dmitrii Karakazov, acting "in the name of the Russian people," fired a pistol at Alexander II. Like the Polish uprising of 1863, this event produced a great public reaction. The government cleverly exploited the claim of a St. Petersburg capmaker named Komissarov, who had been in Karakazov's vicinity during the attempt, that he had jolted the would-be assassin's arm and had saved the tsar. Kommisarov was a peasant, and, according to tradition, his native province of Kostroma was the birthplace of Ivan Susanin, a semi-legendary folk hero who had presumably saved Michael Romanov

23. Ibid.
24. Ibid., pp. 370–71.

from the Poles in the seventeenth century. In 1836 the Russian composer Glinka had written *A Life for the Tsar* (renamed *Ivan Susanin* in the postrevolutionary period), an opera based on the legend, and this thirty-year-old work was now played to enthusiastic crowds. Fact and legend merged in the somewhat hysterical atmosphere of both fear and celebration that pervaded St. Petersburg in April 1866, and it was widely believed that Karakazov was a Pole. While attending a performance of Glinka's opera with Lavrov, Shtakenschneider noticed that he refused to join in the stormy applause. He feigned laughter, but his eyes filled with tears.[25]

The harsh reaction that followed Karakazov's attempt, and the cowardly manner in which Lavrov's own liberal friends and colleagues behaved, remained vivid memories for Lavrov. Twenty years later he would write about

[the] political panic which seized the naïve and cowardly Russian liberals, when in the theatre they burst out in loud ovations to Komissarov, when the actors who played Poles in the opera *A Life for the Tsar* were forced to doff their helmets and to sing the official hymn, when . . . denunciations poured down like hail, brother repudiated brother, and whoever kept in a drawer copies of *Molodaia Rossiia, Velikoruss,* or copies of the abundant manuscript literature of the 1850s hurried, fingers trembling with fear, to burn all of this.[26]

It is very likely that much of the contempt that he later felt for Russian liberalism can be traced to the aftermath of the Karakazov affair. The affair was simply another symptom of the development of a distinct revolutionary subculture. Each reaction drove it deeper underground and estranged it even further from the liberal intelligentsia. Judging from Shtakenschneider's observations of Lavrov's behavior in the period after the Karakazov affair, and from Lavrov's own retrospective remarks, he probably shared Herzen's view, expressed in *Kolokol* in September 1866:

25. Ibid., p. 372.
26. Quoted in *Ocherki istorii Leningrada,* 2:290, from Lavrov's eulogy written after the arrest of his friend German Lopatin in 1884. See P. L. Lavrov, *German Aleksandrovich Lopatin* (Petrograd, 1919), p. 19. *Molodaia Rossiia* (Young Russia), written by P. A. Zaichnevskii, was a radical pamphlet circulated in St. Petersburg in the spring of 1862; *Velikoruss,* a less radical pamphlet series, began circulating in St. Petersburg in June 1861.

People of weak faith thought that the terrible blows struck by the government against the younger generation for everything—for the fires [Herzen is referring to the St. Petersburg conflagrations of 1862], which they did not set, for the Polish rebellion, for the Sunday schools [shut down as centers of subversion in the spring of 1862, shortly after the fires], for ideological ferment, for reading books which are read all over Europe, for holding current opinions, for their universal aspirations for humanity, even for their desire to work—had put an end to the movement which had begun after the Crimean War. Not in the least. It only rooted itself more firmly.[27]

But Herzen opposed individual terror as a self-defeating strategy and was repelled by conspiratorial types. In the 1860s Lavrov shared this aversion too and accepted terror as an aspect of revolutionary struggle only after his earlier visions of revolutionary development and strategies for social revolution had been frustrated several times. Like Herzen, Lavrov detested the "men of weak faith" who had deserted the revolutionary youth during the several stages of reaction that followed 1861. At each stage, however much he regretted the tactics employed by young revolutionaries, Lavrov found himself increasingly isolated from his liberal friends.

Thus in April 1866 Lavrov was troubled by painful dilemmas in both his personal life and his relationship with the revolutionary movement. It was a moment of crisis. Until 1866 the reaction had been softened by the government's attempt to placate public opinion and to pacify the universities. Now, under the guidance of M. N. Murav'ev, who earned himself the sobriquet, "Murav'ev the Hangman," the government decided to dispose of the radical subculture altogether. Murav'ev's plan included rounding up individuals who had played even peripheral roles in the earlier phases of the revolutionary movement, such as it had been in the early 1860s, and closing down once and for all the journals that had inspired revolutionary youth.[28] In the hysteria that followed the attempted assassination on April 4, rumors about Lavrov's arrest reached Shtaken-

27. Quoted in Sh. M. Levin, *Obshchestvennoe dvizhenie v Rossii v 60–70-e gody XIX veka* (Moscow: Institut istorii akademii nauk, Sotsekgiz, 1958), p. 255.

28. Lavrov was high on the list of suspects, largely because of his prominence and his wide connections in both radical circles and "society."

schneider at her country home near Gatchina.[29] Even before departing for the country she had offered to take with her any incriminating papers that Lavrov had in his possession, but he had given her only some old letters and his adolescent diary. When she returned to St. Petersburg, Shtakenschneider found that the rumors about Lavrov's arrest were false. He had recently been warned by an unidentified young man that his arrest was imminent, and that he had better leave Russia. The mysterious young man, who had approached him just as he left the skiff that transported him to the bank of the Neva where the Artillery Academy was situated, offered Lavrov a false passport and money for the flight. Lavrov had refused and had continued on to the examination scheduled for that morning. Nothing had happened. However, while describing his situation and recounting this event to Shtakenschneider, Lavrov displayed considerable agitation. Shtakenschneider noted something strange in his attitude.

Listening to Lavrov this morning I became convinced with each passing minute that he was to some extent ready to be arrested. He felt so thoroughly derailed, without self-control, and powerless to get a grip on himself again, that he spitefully wished for some external force to seize him.[30]

Her intuition about Lavrov proved to be quite correct. His personal affairs were swiftly reaching the crisis stage, thanks to the matchmaking of Evgeniia Ivanovna Konradi. The Konradis had arranged a meeting between Lavrov and Josephina Antonovna for April 21. The ill-matched couple was first to visit the Hermitage and afterwards to join the Konradis and Shtakenschneider.[31] Shtakenschneider sensed that Lavrov's awkward imitation of Faust was inevitably leading either to humiliation or possibly to a family tragedy. Lavrov himself no doubt realized this, yet he had gone too far to extricate himself gracefully.

April 21 arrived. Lavrov began the day inauspiciously. He decided to present the Konradis with a small gift, a crystal butter dish. After having the dish filled with four pounds of butter at a shop on

29. *Dnevnik i zapiski,* p. 372.
30. Ibid., p. 373.
31. Ibid.

the way to Shtakenschneider's house, he marched out into the spring sun, holding the dish with its melting contents stiffly before him, clutched in both hands. Following Shtakenschneider's advice, he took a cab to the Konradis apartment, where he deposited the gift, and then went on to pick up Josephina Antonovna for their day at the Hermitage. Evidently the day turned out to be a failure. When Shtakenschneider arrived at the Konradi apartment, Lavrov was gloomy and the young girl even sadder-looking than usual. The company included Josephina Antonovna's brother, a friend of his, and two friends of the Konradis. Despite the incongruousness of the situation, the party kept going. Shtakenschneider described the scene in her diary:

We sat down to supper at two. The new butter dish perched splendidly on the table. We sat at the table a long time. The white night peered in at all the windows, and we might have extinguished the candles, but no one noticed. We talked about *Belle Hélène,* which everyone in St. Petersburg was mad about the entire winter. I was the only one who hadn't gone, because I had been in mourning. Suddenly, the doorbell rang! The doorman was already asleep. Konradi got up with the words "very likely to the sick person" and went with a candle into the dark entrance hall. Spurs jingled, and we heard a strange voice: "Is colonel Lavrov here?" Konradi's face was pale, and the candle shook in his hand when he announced to Lavrov that a gendarme officer was asking for him. Lavrov got up slowly and went out, but not a minute had passed when he returned to us and announced that he had to go home with a gendarme officer sent by Murav'ev. He was not pale like Konradi; quite to the contrary, his face was animated, he looked as though he had grown taller and younger instantly.[32]

In view of the excruciating circumstances into which he had fallen, it is not difficult to understand why Lavrov suddenly came to life and visibly regained stature. The long-awaited knock on the door both confirmed him as a kind of hero and rescued him from an intolerably undignified situation. The drama of it all could not fail to impress Josephina Antonovna, while at the same time relieving Lavrov of the responsibility for carrying on the farcical courtship.

Lavrov was placed under a rather lax form of house arrest, judging by his comings and goings between early morning, April 22,

---

32. Ibid., p. 375. *La Belle Hélène* refers to Offenbach's operetta.

when the officer appeared at Konradi's apartment, and April 25, when he was relieved of his sword—as was customary with a military prisoner—and placed in a military prison. During that time Lavrov didn't lift a finger to save himself. His oldest son, Mikhail, took advantage of the lax police surveillance and managed to smuggle several bundles of papers out of the house for safekeeping with Shtakenschneider, while Maria, Lavrov's laconic nihilist daughter, infuriated her father's friends with her imperturbability.[33] Although Lavrov's bookshelves were littered with incriminating documents (given the nature of political crimes as defined by the existing regime), he himself expressed more concern over the personal documents that he had given Shtakenschneider earlier.

Lavrov's association with the publishing artel' described earlier served as the pretext for his arrest on 25 April 1866. The artel' was illegal because its charter had not been approved by the authorities. However, Lavrov's political poems of the mid 1850s and his activities, writings, and social activities of the period 1861–65 proved to be more important evidence against him.

At some point between April 25 and April 29, Lavrov emerged from the self-punitive mood which Shtakenschneider had observed before his arrest. He decided to try to save himself, to exert some effort on his own behalf. Any number of considerations—among them, perhaps, concern for his family—might have influenced him in this decision. In any case he began to smuggle correspondence out to Shtakenschneider and his family by concealing notes in his socks, which, with his other undergarments, he was allowed to send out for cleaning.[34] He also sent a plea for clemency to Grand Prince Konstantin Nikolaevich, who had been an idol of the liberal intelligentsia at the beginning of Alexander II's reign. During the late 1850s rumors had circulated that Konstantin Nikolaevich was in contact with Herzen himself. At that time Lavrov had been quite skeptical about anything of a revolutionary nature coming from the Grand Prince. But now he wrote him a long letter, asking that he be permitted to continue his work on the history of science.[35] In his

33. Ibid., pp. 377–78.
34. Ibid., p. 381.
35. Lavrov to Grand Prince Konstantin Nikolaevich, letter in *Golos minuvshego,* 1915, no. 7-8, pp. 219–22.

subsequent pleas for clemency he tried to convince the authorities that he was not a political criminal but a scholar, whose work could bring great honor to Russian letters. Almost three years later, in a letter to Prince A. A. Suvorov, Lavrov claimed that his projected history of science would be a major work, superior to any theretofore completed.[36]

Although Lavrov may have fabricated what he thought were the strongest arguments in his own behalf, he may have expressed his true intentions as well. Far more than most members of the radical intelligentsia, Lavrov was equipped to engage in interpretations or critiques of ideas originating in Europe. There is no question but that he, like other members of the Russian intelligentsia, struggled continually against a deep sense of national cultural inferiority, while simultaneously expressing great hopes for Russia's cultural future. By the 1860s Russian belles lettres had received European recognition, but Russian science—in the broadest sense of that word—still had not fully emerged; the Russian Enlightenment had not developed uniformly. Lavrov had already experimented in several areas of enlightenment—in pedagogy, in the phenomenology of the spirit, in ethics, in the transmission of the most advanced European thought to Russian readers, in the feminist and nihilist movements for autonomy and self-education—but he had been consistently thwarted. There is no evidence that he was an innovator in his own profession, mathematics.[37] His essential strength lay in his grasp of first principles and disciplinary structure, and, more importantly, in his historical approach. Ultimately his most significant scholarly contributions lay in the area of intellectual history, and in the mid- and late-1860s he was just beginning to define for himself the "scientific" approach to a history of thought. Arrest and imprisonment only forced him to clarify his intentions as a scholar and thinker, and it is improbable that he misrepresented his intentions in his petitions to the authorities.

36. Ibid., 1916, no. 12, pp. 126–31.
37. Lavrov's courses in mathematics were never published, nor did he ever publish any treatises or papers on mathematical problems. Unlike his predecessor, M. V. Ostrogradskii, Lavrov did not achieve European renown as a mathematician.

After four months of imprisonment Lavrov appeared before a military tribunal. All of his activities and associations had been carefully watched by the Third Section since his participation in the student riots. His connections with and sympathy for political criminals were easily established. During the search of his home the police found several poems disrespectful to the royal family and seditious in tone, the galley proofs of "Postepenno," the "Letters on Various Contemporary Questions" (published anonymously), and a number of other articles and poems attacking religion, the secret police, and Russian domination of Poland, while praising opposition to authority. One of the most serious pieces of evidence adduced by the prosecution was a letter to N. L. Tiblen, in which Lavrov had discussed plans to resurrect the *Encyclopedic Dictionary* and had outlined a method for introducing tendentious material while circumventing censorship. Lavrov acknowledged authorship of the poems, claiming that they had been evoked by the general frustration and bitterness which had prevailed in Russian society in the mid 1850s, but that they had not been accompanied by any intention to act. He also claimed that his unpublished article, "Postepenno," did not disparage Alexander II's reforms, but rather called for their rapid extension.[38] And so it went with each accusation of propagating or possessing harmful ideas. He had intended no disloyalty and had collected subversive materials because of his interest in the history of thought. There was more than a little truth in all of this, but it was a truth called forth in a moment of painful pressure when Lavrov had to choose between a life of scholarship, for which he was eminently suited, and imprisonment. Behind it lay an even deeper psychological truth, one which Lavrov knew about himself and which other perceptive observers understood—he had little or no capacity for the kind of passionate and total commitment to a cause that would permit him to act ruthlessly in its behalf. The neo-Kantian outlook did not encourage such commitment. Anyone who could achieve the fictive perspective required by neo-Kantian-

38. MS in AOR, fond 95, opis' 1, ed. khr. 324. "Zapiski po delu o Lavrove," 11 June 1866. Also see V. N. Nechaev "Protsess P. L. Lavrova 1866 goda," in *Sbornik materialov i statei,* 1921, no. 1, pp. 45–72; "K protsessu P. L. Lavrova," *Byloe,* 1906, no. 8, pp. 35–38; *Izbrannye sochineniia,* 1:39–43.

ism could not be truly sectarian and was therefore an unlikely candidate for lifelong involvement in the revolutionary underground. Furthermore, Lavrov simply did not feel like a renegade and was incapable of acting like one. Although his poetry of the 1850s had bravely called for the destruction of idols and for the ruthless extirpation of corruption, he himself had never ceased to use persuasion, nor did he sever his ties with official society.

It took an external shock to break those ties and to force Lavrov to transfer his discipline, sense of duty, and loyalty—qualities of character that had been inculcated in him from earliest childhood— to wholly new objects. The Russian nobleman's sense of duty at least partly explains Lavrov's attraction to Kantian ethics in the 1850s and his unswerving devotion to science, socialism, and *partiinost'* once the government forced him altogether out of an official career as a servant of the state. It was at first inconceivable to him that his many years of umblemished service, for which he had earned several medals of distinction, and his contribution to Russia's cultural progress would count for nothing. Actually, Lavrov's high rank and official post probably increased official resentment against him.

Lavrov was finally sentenced for writing and possessing criminal materials, for plotting to print harmful ideas, and for participating in an illegal organization. He was dismissed from the service and removed from his teaching posts. Nine months after his arrest the liberal minister of the interior, Peter Valuev, decided that he should be exiled to Viatka, an "inner" province, but instead, in February 1867, he was sent to the town of Tot'ma in the bleak northern province of Vologda. The military auditor-general, V. D. Filosofov, was responsible for the severity of the sentence. It is possible that Filosofov harbored a grudge for Lavrov's role in the collapse of the Society for Women's Labor. His wife, A. P. Filosofova, had been one of the organizers of the society, and blamed Lavrov for the anguish that she had experienced when the society split into hostile camps.[39] Quite clearly, Lavrov's family and friends were no match for his enemies in high places, and the numerous petitions of Elizaveta Karlovna Lavrova, Lavrov's seventy-eight year old mother, were either pigeon-holed or rejected. Elizaveta Karlovna chose to

39. *Dnevnik i zapiski,* pp. 356, 382–97.

live with her son in Vologda, but the model family which Shtakenschneider had described in the pages of her diary virtually disintegrated during his years in exile.[40] Only his mother and surviving
daughter, Maria, remained loyal to him, and the financial difficulties
experienced by the entire family strained even their loyalties.[41]

Lavrov's life in Tot'ma was far from unendurable. S. F. Khominskii, the governor of the province, was a relatively humane man,
well disposed toward the community of exiles. Under Khominskii's
regime the exiles were able to write articles and to place them in the
legal press. However, A. E. von Merklin, the chief of the gendarmerie in Vologda, was a meticulous and wary policeman who
had some psychological leverage over Khominskii because the latter
was of Polish origin and therefore automatically suspect.[42]

In the six months in which he lived in the little town of Tot'ma
(population 3,500), Lavrov met two people who played quite significant roles in his life. The first was Anna Chaplitskaia, who had

40. The history of the disintegration of the family can be reconstructed
from the correspondence between Lavrov and his children, preserved in the
Nicolaevsky Collection in the Hoover Institution's archives. It is the history
of the transformation of a formerly well-established dvorianstvo family into
a group of déclassé individuals, each pursuing a separate path. Lavrov's two
sons were bitter disappointments to him. The eldest, Mikhail, held a respectable post in the Bureau of Railways in St. Petersburg. He was, according to
his sister Maria Negreskul's accounts, a cold and formal bureaucrat. Lavrov's
younger son, Sergei, never finished his gymnasium course. He worked for a
while as a mechanic, later serving as a junior officer in the Russo-Turkish
War. Sergei married a peasant woman from Simbirsk province, and in the
early 1890s returned to Velikoliutskii district, where he became a farmer.
Maria's life, as revealed in her letters, was quite melodramatic. She lost her
first husband shortly after their marriage, and also her first-born son. She
and her second husband, Emmanuel Negreskul (her first husband's brother),
suffered police persecution for their radical connections. Eventually Maria
Negreskul joined her father in Paris and lived with him during his declining
years. See Vl. Vilenskii-Sibiriakov et al., eds., *Deiateli revoliutsionnogo dvizheniia v Rossii,* 5 vols. (Moscow: Vsesoiuznoe obshchestvo politicheskikh
katorzhan i ssyl'no-poselentsev, 1927–34), vol. 2, ed. A. A. Shilov (1931),
pp. 1012–14.
41. For example, even Maria, closest to him in character and conviction,
was piqued by her father's anxiety about the money realized from the sale
of redemption settlements and the family's use of it. (Maria Negreskul to
Lavrov, 22 April 1870, MS in Nicolaevsky Collection, Hoover Institution.)
42. See P. Vitiazev, *Ssylka P. L. Lavrova v vologodskoi gubernii i ego
zaniatiia antropologiei* (Vologda, 1915); *Dnevnik i zapiski,* p. 544 n 385.

been involved in the Polish revolutionary movement, and who became Lavrov's mistress. The unhappy affair with Josephina Riul'man was evidently forgotten. Lavrov was still waiting to be tried when he learned that Josephina had become engaged to Ia. P. Polonskii, the poet, whom she married in July 1866. Although he continued to express solicitude for her welfare in his correspondence with Shtakenschneider, Lavrov had sufficiently recovered by 1867 to enter enthusiastically into his new relationship with Anna Chaplitskaia, though this too was soon to end tragically.[43] The second person who was to play an important part in Lavrov's life was Alexander Longovich Linev, who had been exiled to Tot'ma in 1866. In the 1870s Linev would become a major collaborator on Lavrov's *Vpered!*

Lavrov's lodgings in Tot'ma became the social center for the intelligentsia in the area. Nonetheless, he requested a transfer to Vologda, the capital of the province. The most prominent intelligentsia exiles lived in Vologda, and Lavrov longed to make contact with them.[44] His request was granted, and in August 1868 he was permitted to resettle in the provincial capital for reasons of deteriorating health. However, on the day of his departure from Tot'ma, the local intelligentsia injudiciously arranged a rousing sendoff for him, which compromised him in the eyes of the Gendarmerie. Thirteen members of the exile community and some local officials contributed three rubles each toward champagne, food, and the rental of four troikas to see Lavrov off in proper fashion.[45] Von Merklin was sufficiently alarmed by the manifestation to set into motion the bureaucratic machinery to transfer Lavrov out of Vologda and into a less dangerous place as quickly as possible. In his eyes Colonel Lavrov was the most dangerous political criminal in the province.

Meanwhile Lavrov was settled in Vologda, where the exile com-

43. A letter to Josephina Riul'man is published in *Materialy,* pp. 33–34. For Lavrov's relationship with Anna Chaplitskaia, see M. P. Sazhin, *Vospominaniia* (Moscow, 1925), p. 23, and Sazhin, "P. L. Lavrov v vospominaniiakh sovremennikov," *Golos minuvshego,* 1915, no. 10, pp. 16–17.

44. M. P. Negreskul, "Vospominaniia," *Golos minuvshego,* 1915, no. 9, p. 140.

45. Sazhin, *Vospominaniia,* p. 29; D. G. Venediktov-Beziuk, "Pobeg P. L. Lavrova iz ssylki," *Katorga i ssylka,* 1931, no. 5, p. 186.

munity included such prominent figures as N. V. Shelgunov, M. P. Sazhin, and V. V. Bervi-Flerovskii. The latter's *Polozhenie rabo-chego klassa v Rossii* (Position of the working class in Russia) is often named with Lavrov's own *Istoricheskie pis'ma* (Historical letters) as one of the most popular and influential books among the radical intelligentsia in the 1870s. The presence of these two pro-fessional figures in exile once again points up the government's severe treatment of renegade academicians. Shelgunov and Sazhin found a five-room apartment for Lavrov and his mother.[46] (Lavrov complained about the number of windows in his new lodgings in Vologda, saying that the sun pursued him from one place to another in his study.) The new arrival intended to enter fully into the greater opportunities for intellectual and social life in Vologda. In addition to the exile community Vologda had a pedagogical seminary and a gymnasium, which attested to the wide dissemination and appeal of radical thought. Many of the students were strongly influenced by Pisarev and Chernyshevskii.

But Lavrov soon discovered that even here in the wilderness mem-bers of the intelligentsia displayed the same divisiveness and hostility toward one another that he had witnessed in St. Petersburg. Sazhin, a typical *raznochinets* firebrand, and his radical circle regarded Lavrov as a "gentleman liberal." In their eyes, the older exiles—Bervi-Flerovskii, Shelgunov, and Lavrov—were members of the older generation politically, although Shelgunov was more accepta-ble to them than either of the other two. Sazhin and Shelgunov tried to discourage Lavrov's desire to fraternize with the administration and local landlords. During his short stay in Vologda Lavrov arranged literary gatherings for the local intelligentsia. However, hardly anyone came except Sazhin, N. V. Kedrovskii, and Shel-gunov. Lavrov's sociability with the administration and the local landlords was interpreted by Sazhin as an attempt to ingratiate him-self with officials in order to facilitate his pardon, though it was more probably a symptom of his need for intellectual comradeship and the stimulation of discussion. Furthermore, Lavrov did not regard

    46. Sazhin, "P. L. Lavrov v vospominaniiakh sovremennikov," p. 116; "Pis'ma Lavrova vologodskoi ssylki," *Katorga i ssylka,* 1931, no. 6, pp. 165–78.

himself as a social outcast and didn't intend to behave like one. The younger radicals were sectarian, viewing people outside their circle with suspicion and hostility, while he continued to cultivate wider associations. Sazhin correctly observed that Lavrov expected the authorities to repent for their injustice.[47] To the new radical generation, who neither expected nor demanded any kind of fair treatment, this seemed a peculiar attitude indeed.

Much to Lavrov's dismay, he was transferred in October 1868 to the dismal little town of Kadnikov, where he was the only exile. The situation was becoming desperate. Lavrov's health was deteriorating rapidly, and his petitions for better living conditions were ignored.[48] Despite the fact that part of his vast library had accompanied him into exile, he found that he could not satisfactorily continue his scholarly work on the history of thought.

However, neither failing health nor lack of research materials caused any perceptible diminution in his literary output during his years in northern exile. He wrote numerous articles and reviews for *Knizhnyi vestnik, Zhenskii vestnik, Sovremennoe obozrenie, Bibliograf, Otechestvennye zapiski,* and *Nedelia.* He employed the younger exiles and radical seminarists as copyists for his almost illegible manuscripts. Although the articles appeared under the pseudonym P. Mirtov, or under the initials P. L. or P. M., literary St. Petersburg knew very well who had written them. But Lavrov still dreamed of a magnum opus, and chafed at the government's refusal to review his case. He considered even the Historical Letters, first printed serially in *Nedelia* in 1868–69, to be light essays which would not help to advance his reputation as a scholar.[49] His work in anthropology, sociology, and the history of thought were his major concerns.

47. Sazhin, *Vospominaniia,* pp. 29–30.
48. At least that is what he claimed in several letters written during this period. One begins to suspect that Lavrov suffered from a mild form of hypochondria, given the very frequent references to failing health in the larger body of his correspondence. They contrast with the comments of memoirists who usually were struck by his robust appearance until about 1889.
49. This is Sazhin's contention (see *Materialy,* p. 11). It is upheld by D. N. Ovsianiko-Kulikovskii, a more impartial source. Lavrov's remarks to Ovsianiko-Kulikovskii could not have been made earlier than 1878. See D. M. Ovsianiko-Kulikovskii, *Vospominaniia* (St. Petersburg, 1923), p. 150.

Kadnikov was not so remote from the provincial capital that Lavrov could not occasionally drive in by sleigh for clandestine meetings with Anna Chaplitskaia. (The distance was forty *versty*— a *verst* being equivalent to about two-thirds of a mile.) He could still manage to get his manuscripts copied by local students. But as early as October 1868, after being resettled in Kadnikov, Lavrov had begun to entertain the idea that the authorities were not going to repent. The idea of flight from internal exile began to take shape in his mind, but he decided to give the authorities three years from the time of his arrest to permit him to return to St. Petersburg or to settle abroad.[50] Meanwhile, he acquired a son-in-law with radical connections when his daughter Maria married Mikhail Fedorovich Negreskul on 2 February 1869. Lavrov's son-in-law was his major collaborator in the early attempts to arrange his escape in 1869.[51]

Through Negreskul, Lavrov became associated with the short-lived journal, *Bibliograf*. Other old friends continued to help Lavrov by placing his articles in their journals. N. L. Tiblen published *Sovremennoe obozrenie* (The contemporary review), one of the several journals which appeared in the years after the government permanently closed down *Sovremennik* and *Russkoe slovo,* and which tried to perpetuate their general ideological tendencies. *Nedelia* (The Week) was another such journal, on which Lavrov collaborated with the help of several intermediaries, including his friend Konradi who was the editor. *Otechestvennye zapiski* became the major organ of the still-inchoate *narodnik* tendency under the editorship of the poet Nekrasov, the brilliant satirist M. E. Saltykov-Shchedrin, and the publicist G. Z. Eliseev, who was Lavrov's major intermediary on that journal. The several reviews mentioned above, along with *Zhenskii vestnik* (Women's herald), served as major outlets for Lavrov's ideas after the collapse of *Knizhnyi vestnik* (Book herald) in 1867.[52] the latter journal had been dominated by young writers who, like Lavrov, were admirers of Proudhon.[53]

50. This is Lavrov's claim in "Moi pobeg iz ssylki," MS in AOR, fond 1762, opis' 1, ed. khr. 3; Negreskul, "Vospominaniia," p. 141.

51. Lavrov, "Moi pobeg iz ssylki."

52. Lavrov wrote three major articles for *Zhenskii vestnik* in 1867.

53. For a description of this group see James H. Billington, *Mikhailovsky and Russian Populism* (Oxford: Oxford University Press, 1958), pp. 21–24.

Among them was Nicholas Mikhailovksii, who later joined *Nedelia* and *Otechestvennye zapiski*. Mikhailovksii became a major proponent of "subjective sociology"—one of the theoretical bases for the narodnik movement—and although he and Lavrov disagreed about several important theoretical issues, he is usually depicted as Lavrov's ideological partner in the founding of "subjective sociology." Another young writer on the staff of *Knizhnyi vestnik,* N. V. Sokolov, author of a Proudhonist study of historical rebels called *Otshchepentsy* (usually translated as The refractories or The refractory ones to approximate *Les Réfractaires,* the title of the book of Jules Valles that had inspired Sokolov), became an opponent of Lavrov's faction in Zurich in 1873 when the Russian colony there split into Bakuninist and Lavrovist segments. Through all of these journals and their editorial boards Lavrov established stronger ties with the radical subculture than he had previously enjoyed. Life in exile only furthered his education in radicalism.

It is clear from his own programmatic statements in 1868–69 that Lavrov considered himself to be a continuator of the critical tradition represented by Herzen, Belinsky, Chernyshevskii, Dobroliubov, and Pisarev. He viewed the Russian school of realistic criticism as only one aspect of a pan-European cultural phenomenon. He used *realism* as a generic term denoting the scientific world view which had spread from Europe's learned societies in the seventeenth century and had begun to permeate all of modern life.[54] The struggle between idealists and materialists over epistemological questions no longer appeared important to him compared to the struggle between the scientific world view and outmoded philosophies. Both idealists and materialists could be realists.[55] Realism was therefore an orientation rather than a specific philosophy. Positivism, utilitarianism, and anthropologism all belonged to the category of realism. Lavrov valued Feuerbach, Proudhon, Mill, and Comte above all other contemporary philosophers because they were realists of one stripe or another. However, he criticized other realistic doc-

54. Lavrov, "Pis'mo v redaktsiiu," *Bibliograf,* 1869, no. 1, p. 8. For a thorough discussion of Lavrov's relationship to *Bibliograf,* see N. Bel'chikov, "*Bibliograf,*" in V. Polianskii, ed., *Russkaia zhurnalistika, 60-e gody* (Moscow, 1930).

55. Lavrov, "Pis'mo v redaktsiiu," p. 12.

trines from the point of view of his own anthropologism. Of the three doctrines mentioned, he found positivism the least satisfying because he believed that it had subordinated practical questions to theoretical ones. Lavrov described the anthropologist's view of positivism in this way: "He does not recognize it as a philosophy, but accepts its aspirations as his guide, and views his own philosophy as an attempt to solve the problems, perfectly correctly set forth by positivism."[56] While in exile in Russia and abroad, Lavrov clung to this position and demonstrated once again that ethics dominated his own system. All scientific discoveries had to be examined with an eye to their ethical implications, all artistic and scientific work undertaken with social goals in mind.

One of Lavrov's great problems in the late 1860s was that of incorporating recent scientific authority into his world view without endangering his own conception of ethical behavior. Rapid advances in physiology, embryology, geology, and paleantology had helped to increase the popularity of evolutional-organic models in mid-nineteenth-century thought. Lavrov recognized the conservative implications of the evolutional-organic model. He had struggled with them in his article "Postepenno" in 1862 before his exposure to Darwin. *The Origin of Species* complicated matters even further. It made survival of an organism in the struggle for existence prima facie evidence of its fitness. When applied to political systems the evolutional-organic model could be used to justify the existence of Tsarist Russia or the Second Empire. This was tantamount to right-wing Hegelianism and, of course, wholly unacceptable to Lavrov.

In order to overcome the difficulties of the evolutional-organic model, he drew on his conception of the ethical scientist: The ethical scientific observer posits a range of possibilities for the organism. All possibilities are labeled better or worse, healthy or harmful, according to a subjective scale of values—the observer's ideals. Having determined the condition of the organism by observation, one should not sit idly by but should actively intercede in the process of change. Lavrov encouraged the sociologist to practice social

56. P. L. Lavrov, "Zadachi pozitivizma i ikh resheniia," *Sovremennoe obozrenie,* 1868, no. 5, p. 154.

"medicine." In the article "Herbert Spencer and his Essays" he wrote:

Since the sociologist deals with an organism comprised of feeling, desiring, and suffering elements, he can and is perhaps dutybound to ask: Within the limits of the inevitable laws of the action of life's external conditions, which forms of organization are better suited to the elements of a social organism? Among various possible processes of transition from a primitive, more homogeneous social order to a more perfect one, which process involves less suffering for individuals, more justice in their mutual relationships?[57]

In short, when dealing with the condition of being human (*chelovechnost'*) the scientist cannot avoid ethical considerations. This is perhaps the cardinal rule of Lavrov's sociology, often called subjective sociology.

The term *ethical sociology* is an accurate description of Lavrov's position. Though based upon a subjective method, it is presented as a rigorous and demanding discipline. Lavrov never exalted the subjective ideals of lonely, heroic individuals. He sometimes sounded as though he were validating all rigorously worked out convictions, however individualized. But his writings of the late 1860s reveal that his historical, subjective approach did not lead to an atomistic relativism. Lavrov believed in something similar to what Karl Popper in *The Open Society and its Enemies* calls the "intersubjectivity of scientific method." Despite his strong aversion for dogmatic authority, Lavrov never failed to search for scientific authority within a community of men who shared a rigorous, critical methodology for he believed that a scientific community of ethical sociologists could shape scientific ideals. The hortative side of his publicistic work, in which he demanded that "developed" individuals endowed with critical thought and critical convictions display the strength of character to engage in civic action, is usually emphasized at the expense of the rather cool, socio-historical aspect of his writings. From his essays and reviews of the late 1860s one can infer the beginnings of a socio-historical theory of limited possibilities, a statistical approach to the problem of achieving social

57. P. L. Lavrov, "Gerbert Spenser i ego 'Opyty'," *Zhenskii vestnik,* 1867, no. 6, p. 55.

change through the action of a group of willful individuals. He assumed that there were historical factors which set limits to a movement for progressive social change at any historical moment, but that at any given instant something progressive might be achieved. The ethical sociologist had first to determine the maximum possibilities for social progress in a given situation and then try to achieve them. However, Lavrov only sketchily developed these ideas as part of his rather general and abstract anthropologistic critique of the writings of Comte and Spencer. In *Historical Letters* he further clarified both his conception of scientific ethics and the proper role of the critically thinking vanguard in Russia at that historical moment, and provided compelling arguments for the social service function of ethical sociologists.

The answers to burning questions about the role of the intelligentsia, which Lavrov worked out during his exile in Vologda, became his most significant contribution to the Russian revolutionary movement, but they were only one aspect of the extraordinarily broad range of problems that Lavrov was investigating. Studies in anthropology and religious history replaced those in the history of science, and these new areas of inquiry in turn were incorporated into Lavrov's larger vision of a history of human thought, beginning in prehistory and ending with the most advanced contemporary scientific thought. His work in anthropology heightened his awareness of the distinction between human groups that had undergone dynamic change and therefore were historical—and those that had simply reexperienced unchanging cycles. Increasingly, he treated religion as a pathological phenomenon. His own devotion to a historical and scientific world view led him into the kinds of dichotomous formulations that often accompany a clarified radical commitment.

One can find an abundance of such dichotomies in one of Lavrov's most complex and difficult essays of the late 1860s, "Neskol'ko myslei ob istorii mysli" (A few thoughts on the history of thought), which was published in a volume of essays assembled by the group that ran *Knizhnyi vestnik*.[58] Civilization and culture, historical life and anthropological life, critical thought and habit, science and dogma, understanding and feeling, knowledge (*znanie*) and skill (*umenie*),

58. *Nevskii sbornik* (St. Petersburg: V. S. Kurochkin, 1867).

the critically thinking minority and the backward masses—all represented higher and lower development, dynamism and stagnancy. This kind of analysis confirms Lavrov's kinship with eighteenth-century rationalism. He pictured history as the record of the struggle between the forces of reason and those of tradition: since only the critically thinking minority possessed reason, it followed that history was the record of their struggle against the hostile forces, both natural and cultural, which limited their activities. To maintain his dichotomy Lavrov had to provide critical thought with a measure of autonomy from cultural influences. He had confronted this problem before in slightly different form in his theory of intellectual ontogeny and in the *Three Talks on the Contemporary Significance of Philosophy*. Although he could not deny the influence of the cultural milieu upon thought, he distinguished certain areas of thought which he presumed were less influenced by the milieu than others: Thought which contained *feeling* as one of its elements— religious thought, for example—was more likely to be influenced by culture than more abstract forms of thought, such as scientific thought. Scientific thought was the attainment of a small minority, but it could be inculcated in others:

The element of science . . . comprises, of course, the attainment of a minority, and by its very need for understanding (*ponimanie*), enters into a struggle with the element in which feeling (*chuvstvo*) predominates. Before the pedagogical activity of the scientifically developed minority, the number of people with knowledge increases and the process of knowledge accelerates; the general background yields, and the process of development proceeds all the faster.[59]

In spite of his elaborately drawn distinctions between types of thought, one can discern the traditional dichotomy of reason and feeling in Lavrov's analysis. Feeling dominated in areas of thought which were characterized by dogma, habit, closed-mindedness, fanaticism, and faith. It was an enemy of progress.

Lavrov's distinction between culture and thought roughly corresponds to Guizot's two elements of civilization—the general material progress of society, and the intellectual and moral development of individuals. Just as Guizot had demonstrated that these

59. Ibid., p. 570.

two elements of civilization were intimately connected, Lavrov attempted to establish a dynamic relationship between thought and culture:

> Therefore it is understood that the development of thought, too, proceeds alongside of the development of culture, either lagging behind it or outstripping it; but in many instances, and even most frequently of all, the movement of thought occurs under the influence of change (*dvizhenie*) within the culture, and in turn influences cultural change.[60]

In *Historical Letters* Lavrov wrote, "The history of thought, conditioned by culture, in connection with the history of culture, changing under the influence of thought—this is the total history of civilization."[61] However, Lavrov tended to view cultural forms as obstacles to progress. By the late 1860s, the concept of *form* had acquired distinctly negative connotations, as it tends to do in theories of progress because it implies staticity or rigidity. Lavrov remained within the revolutionary rationalistic tradition in his belief that scientific (rational) thought, propagated by a creative minority, could set into motion and ultimately help to liberate the tradition-bound and authority-suppressed masses.

During the late 1860s Lavrov's critique of positivism, his inquiries into anthropological and religious phenomena, and his methodological reflections about a history of thought all provided materials for the *Historical Letters*. There was no essential difference between Lavrov's anthropologism of this period and that of the late 1850s. The philosophical bases of his system remained the same, from epistemology to ethics. What had changed was the nature of the demands that Lavrov made upon the intelligentsia, the critically thinking minority: his emphasis shifted from a program of self-development to one of social service, from the activity of acquiring scientific knowledge to that of disseminating it. In short, Lavrov had earlier concentrated his efforts on the problem of reforming, unifying, and expanding the intelligentsia. In *Historical Letters* he now shifted his attention to the problem of the relationship between the scientific vanguard and the backward masses. To be sure, he was not the first Russian thinker to approach this problem; it had been

60. Ibid., p. 572.
61. Lavrov, *Izbrannye sochineniia,* 1:244.

with the intelligentsia from the very moment that they had become conscious of themselves as a distinct subculture. But it was only one of the problems that issued from their peculiar response to imported culture. Until the publication of the *Historical Letters,* the problem of their relationship to the masses had remained in the background for all but a small segment of radical youth. By the late 1860s the reactionary regime of Dmitrii Tolstoi, who had replaced Golovnin as minister of education in 1866 after Karakazov's attempt to assassinate the tsar, had recreated the conditions that had existed in the universities in 1861. At that time in 1861—when the pursuit of higher education on the government's terms had seemed insufferable to the radical intelligentsia—Herzen had first put forth the slogan, Go to the people! However, the radical intelligentsia still had not achieved sufficient morale and a sufficient "critical mass" for significant portions of it to break away from the university cities. On the whole, their impulse toward rebellion was channeled instead into self-education and self-development—toward the further clarification of a valid life style and meaningful work. Now, when the *Historical Letters* were beginning to appear serially in *Nedelia,* the nihilist self-education movement was reaching its peak, and in St. Petersburg the technical institutes and the university were once more exploding into rebellion.

4.
Historical Letters

The middle and late 1860s was a period of incubation during which the nihilist movement nurtured the radical intelligentsia's belief in self-development, science, labor, and utility, without really altering or contradicting their profound need for social justice, and without satisfactorily answering the question of how one can live according to one's values. Service to a barbarous regime was unthinkable. A professional career fulfilled values of science, labor, and utility, but it was hardly the kind of immediate, heroic self-assertion in the cause of progress for which many longed. Impatient young *intelligenty* needed to demonstrate their virtue, to assume their rightful position as the best men in society. They were haunted by Rakhmetov's image. However, the regime had demonstrated its ruthlessness and strength, and the intelligenty were all too aware of their own weakness.

Pisarev had suggested a solution which appealed to many in the intelligentsia. By stressing science, labor, utility, and self-development, he had encouraged professionalism. His propaganda helped produce hundreds of agronomists, doctors, statisticians, and engineers. Ironically, he and other Westernizers probably strengthened the old regime by recruiting talent necessary for the new wave of modernization. Furthermore, in his effort to emancipate the new generation from any lingering romanticism, Pisarev had inspired behavior which in some ways resembled that of the romantic generation of the 1830s. The solitary intellectual exchanged Schelling for Darwin and traded ecstatic nights discussing poetry and philosophy under the stars for nightly labors over the severed members of laboratory specimens; nonetheless, he was as secluded as his romantic forebears. A new generation of superfluous men came into being. Many of them were urbanized, penniless, sickly, and overworked, but they had one solace—their faith in science and progress.

In a sense they were trying to withdraw into the future.[1]

Simultaneous with the development of what one might call romantic scientism, however, a different kind of underground intelligentsia was forming. It was led by men who perpetuated the conspiratorial tradition that had emerged in the early sixties and had produced Karakazov. These men, while pursuing the heroic discipline taught by Chernyshevskii, were quite willing to discard science, except insofar as it served their revolutionary purpose. Thus by 1869 two distinct and antagonistic tendencies had emerged, one emphasizing science, and the other action. Michael Bakunin, in emigration, had inspired the conspiratorial tendency which achieved its most extreme expression in "The Catechism of a Revolutionary" and which was propagated by Sergei Nechaev, the most zealous (and devious) leader in the conspiratorial underground. Nechaev's murder of Ivanov, one of his own recruits, in Moscow in November 1869 led to mass arrests and finally to a mass trial in 1871.

It was at this moment in the history of the Russian revolutionary intelligentsia that Lavrov's *Historical Letters* appeared, first serially, and then as a separate volume in 1870. That Lavrov was aware of the younger generation's worship of the natural sciences and their withdrawal into narrow, laboratory-bound work is quite evident from the very first letter. It is not certain when he first learned about Nechaev, but his first son-in-law, Mikhail Fedorovich Negreskul, had become a strong opponent of Nechaev after meeting him in Switzerland in the spring of 1869. Negreskul had visited his father-in-law late in the summer of 1869, and Lavrov very probably learned about Nechaev through him even before the Ivanov scandal.[2] Negreskul was one of the dozens of suspects arrested in December 1869 in the wake of Ivanov's murder, for the government did not distinguish between Nechaev's supporters and his opponents. Nechaev himself had purposely implicated some of his opponents by sending them his revolutionary proclamations. Negreskul was imprisoned in Peter and Paul fortress, fell ill with tuberculosis, and

1. For a brief discussion, see Philip Pomper, *The Russian Revolutionary Intelligentsia* (New York: Thomas Y. Crowell, 1970), chapter 4.
2. Lavrov, "Moi pobeg iz ssylki."

was placed under house arrest in St. Petersburg, where he died in February 1870.[3] The absence of any direct attack upon Nechaev or Nechaevism in the *Historical Letters* therefore should not be construed as a sign of ignorance or indifference on Lavrov's part. All of the major arguments in the *Historical Letters* militate against Nechaevism. Censorship, the design of the series, and the lateness of his discovery of Nechaev probably account for the lack of reference to him or his conspiracy. In a letter to Natalie Herzen dated 19 July 1870, shortly after the publication of *Historical Letters,* Lavrov wrote about Nechaev: "I don't know him personally, but I believe that he is one of the most harmful elements in our emigration."[4] Thus Lavrov offered the new generation of radicals an alternative both to the romantic scientism that Pisarev's followers were practicing and to the lurid conspiracies which had led to the decimation of the ranks of the revolutionary intelligentsia and to the educated public's disenchantment with the younger generation.

The use of the term *letter* to describe an essentially essayistic enterprise was, of course, not confined to Russia in the nineteenth century, but it is difficult to imagine a European nation, aside from France, in whose intellectual history the letter played such an extraordinary role. Some of the foremost figures in the Russian intelligentsia chose to express their strongest opinions in letters. The tradition began most clearly in 1836 with Chaadaev's first "Philosophical Letter," continued with Herzen's *Letters from France and Italy* (1847–50), Belinsky's "Letter to Gogol" (1847), which had circulated clandestinely in manuscript, and Chernyshevskii's *Letters without an Address* (1862)—to name some of the outstanding examples of this genre. Lavrov himself had resorted to it earlier in his career in the form of his letter to Herzen in 1856, followed by the "Letters on Various Contemporary Questions" (1857–58). All of Lavrov's earlier epistolary essays had served the same end. In them he had attempted to define the problems confronting the Russian intelligentsia and to prescribe a course of action for it. The

3. *Deiateli revoliutsionnogo dvizheniia,* vol. 1 (1928), part 2, p. 264.
4. *Literaturnoe nasledstvo,* 1959, no. 63, pp. 485–86.

Historical Letters fall within this tradition.[5] Taken together, the "Letter of a Provincial about the Problems of Contemporary Criticism," which appeared in *Otechestvennye zapiski* in 1868; the *Historical Letters,* published in 1868–69; and a "Letter to the Editor," published in *Bibliograf* in 1869, comprise Lavrov's program for the Russian intelligentsia in the late 1860s. An earlier theoretical article, "A Few Thoughts on the History of Thought," presents in briefer form many ideas which he incorporated into the *Historical Letters.*

Lavrov's mood when he wrote these letters was essentially one of bitterness and disappointment over the position of the intelligentsia in Russia. The new journals (or established journals, like *Otechestvennye zapiski,* under new guidance) were trying to assert their leadership of the radical intelligentsia. *Otechestvennye zapiski* had not yet established itself as the new guide for youth. The men who were to become the principal publicists of the nascent populist movement still scattered their efforts over several journals. Lavrov, for the first time enjoying a close relationship to a radical movement within the intelligentsia, grasped its need for a strong sense of unity, direction, and purpose. More than a decade of exposure to radical thought and, more particularly, to the rhetoric of realism, scientism, and utilitarianism had altered his techniques of argument, if not his fundamental philosophical orientation. His fundamental orientation was still a curious combination of neo-Kantian critical openmindedness and left-wing Hegelian militancy. But now he was able to combine the familiar demands of the radical leaders of the 1860s with his own peculiar demands for full commitment to progressive ideals worked out by critical thought. He never really proposed a specific doctrine or strategy, and never demanded more than what was possible in Russia. It was just the right mixture of realism and idealism, of firmness and indefiniteness, and of commitment and caution for the shattered but rapidly regrouping forces of the radical intelligentsia. Lavrov finally achieved the fortunate conjunction of the right journal, an acceptable style, and a timely

5. Most references to *Historical Letters* will refer to James P. Scanlan's excellent translation (see chap. 2, n 12).

message that transformed him into a major figure in the history of
the Russian revolutionary intelligentsia.

The *Historical Letters* actually deal with several distinct, though
related, problems. In keeping with his lifelong habit of starting with
first principles, Lavrov felt compelled in his first letter, "The Natural
Sciences and History," to distinguish history from other disciplines,
and to establish its relationship to them. He assiduously avoided
any separation of problems of knowledge from problems of practice—of moral action. He tried to demonstrate that history not only
was more immediately relevant to contemporary problems than such
natural sciences as physics, and chemistry, and physiology but also
provided essential data for the "higher natural sciences"—especially
for sociology.[6] He quite consciously made his appeal to the "thinking realists" in the younger generation who had so avidly responded
to crude materialism and had fallen into uncritical worship of the
natural sciences. In 1870 this appeal had deep significance for a ma-
turing generation of radicals. Having discovered that the life of science could be just as remote from the task of social revolution as the
life of art, they could now entertain a new approach to the question
of knowledge and morality. However, Lavrov did not ask them to
abandon their scientism and utilitarianism, for he opened up to them
new and more promising areas of scientific investigation while presenting his arguments in utilitarian terms. Indeed, one of the striking
features of Lavrov's approach is his ultra-utilitarian calculation of
social pleasures and miseries. He drew up a social balance sheet in
which everything was measured—the quantity of pleasure in society, the quantity of pain; the size of the masses, the size of the enlightened minority; the amount of progress, the price of progress. It
is an essay which contains none of the optimism about progress
which Lavrov had expressed in his letter to Herzen in 1856. Both
the historical balance sheet of progress and the prospects for further
progress were presented in a bitter and admonitory voice.

Lavrov explicitly rejected theories of historical recurrences, of
the inevitable collapse of civilizations, or of inevitable historical
progress according to objective laws. However, he did believe that,
inevitably, men who wrote history did so with a theory of progress

6. *Historical Letters,* p. 85.

in mind. This was the second stage of subjectivity in Lavrov's scheme. In the first stage, in keeping with the principles of his anthropologism, Lavrov assumed that historians must study the consciousness of historical actors—their conscious moral personality.[7] In the second stage the historian assesses the actors' motives from the point of view of his own ethical ideals. All historical writing was moralistic for Lavrov and inevitably involved value judgments.

Thus, willy-nilly, a man is bound to evaluate the historical process subjectively: that is, having acquired, in accordance with his level of moral development, one or another moral ideal, he is bound to put all the facts of history into perspective according to whether they have promoted or opposed this ideal, and to give primary historical importance to those facts in which this promotion or opposition is most vividly exhibited.

But here two further significant circumstances present themselves. First, from this standpoint all phenomena become identified as beneficial or harmful, as morally good or evil. Second, in the historical perspective set by our moral ideal we stand at the end of the historical process; the entire past is related to our ideal as a series of preparatory steps which lead inevitably to a definite end. Consequently, we see history as a struggle between a beneficent principle and a harmful principle, where the former—in unchanging form or through gradual development—has finally reached the point at which it is for us the supreme human good.[8]

The ideas described above appeared in Lavrov's first two letters. In the third letter, "Velichina progressa v chelovechestve" (The magnitude of progress in humanity), Lavrov offered the reader his own definition of progress: *"the development of the individual in physical, intellectual, and moral aspects, and the embodiment of truth and justice in social forms."*[9] There was nothing explicitly radical in these words, unless one began with the assumption that existing social forms did not permit any of the above. And of course, both Lavrov and his readers, informed as they were by the left-wing Hegelian tradition and by Proudhon's ethics, could only see the formula as a reproach to the economic, cultural, social, and political structure of the Russian empire. However, Lavrov could not attack

7. Ibid., p. 99.
8. Ibid., pp. 101–2.
9. *Izbrannye sochineniia,* 1:199.

Russia directly, and he had to make his points subtly by parading before his readers either the splendid civilizations of antiquity which had perished because of inequality and injustice, or contemporary European civilization. Since the 1840s, Russian journalists had used this ploy—exposing exploitation and social and economic misery in Russia by referring to fallen civilizations of the past, to the European proletariat, or to American slavery—and by the time that he wrote the letters in serial form, Lavrov was fairly accomplished at this device. (Even so, many of the changes made for the 1870 edition were in the direction of even greater obliqueness.) From his historical examples he drew the conclusion:

Thus, two dangers continually threaten every civilization. If it is confined to an excessively small and exclusive minority, it is in danger of vanishing. If it will not permit the critically thinking individuals who give it vitality to develop among the civilized minority, it is in danger of stagnating.[10]

Lavrov's mathematical and positivistic side showed through in his belief that the law of large numbers applied to social phenomena, and a brief statement added to a later edition of the *Historical Letters* summarizes fairly well his views about the fundamental conditions for social progress:

The law of large numbers will never be slow to demonstrate, with relentless rigor, what little historical significance there is in the development of a small group of individuals under exceptional circumstances. A majority must be placed in a position where its development is possible, likely, and firmly grounded before we may say that society is progressing.[11]

History and his own experience had impressed upon Lavrov the vulnerability of intellectual elites. Progress occurred somehow in spite of institutionalized oppression and exploitation. Implicit in his formula of progress is the dynamic relationship between thought and culture suggested by François Guizot's analysis of *l'état moral* and *l'état social*. (Lavrov believed that his own view of progress was very similar to that which Proudhon expressed in *De la justice dans*

10. *Historical Letters,* p. 127.
11. Ibid., p. 114.

la révolution et l'église.)[12] The existence of historical intelligentsias was proof to Lavrov that the first part of his definition of progress had been realized to a limited extent. Certainly, however, neither the first nor the second part of his definition had ever been realized for the downtrodden masses of humanity. Hence progress was nowhere secure, and never would be unless definite conditions to foster it were established.

The social reforms which Lavrov characterized as the "conditions of progress" in the *Historical Letters* are similar to the minimum program of social reform implicit in his activity in the late 1850s and early 1860s. This minimum program included better living conditions for the masses, universal education, full freedom of the press, and political institutions sufficiently flexible to permit social change in accordance with the ideas of critically thinking individuals. Above all, Lavrov wanted to insure fruitful contact between intelligentsia pedagogues and the unenlightened majority of society.

Lavrov's discussion of the nature of the progress and its precarious position set the stage for his central message—a definition of the role of the "developed" or critically thinking minority. His is the first systematically developed theory of the origins and role of the Russian intelligentsia—or any intelligentsia, for that matter. His were the first timely and compelling arguments that the intelligentsia, by virtue of its very existence and position, had a number of specific obligations to the larger society. In short, he told the intelligentsia how it had evolved, what it was, and what it ought to do. Lavrov's arguments were tinged with emotion, and the youthful intelligenty who read the letters brought their own powerful emotional needs to them. The meeting of the two signaled the development of one of the most important trends in Russian revolutionary history.

Lavrov employed two basic arguments to convince the intellectual that he should renounce his isolation from the masses. The first argument was the one mentioned above: that progress would be endangered if it were entrusted to small, isolated groups of men. The second and truly compelling argument was that the intelligentsia owed a debt to the masses, at whose expense they had gained the

12. Ibid., p. 105.

leisure and material comforts necessary for higher intellectual and
moral development.

A member of the small minority, experiencing pleasure from consciousness and his own development, from the search for truth and in the
embodiment of justice, should say to himself: Every comfort which I
enjoy, every thought which I had the leisure to acquire or work out, was
purchased by blood, by the suffering of or by the labor of millions. I
cannot correct the past, and no matter how dearly my development cost,
I cannot renounce it; it is the source of the very ideal which stirs me to
action. Only the weak and intellectually backward person falters from
the responsibility weighing upon him and flees from wickedness to
Thebaic or to the grave. Evil has to be righted, insofar as that is possible, and it has to be done only during one's lifetime. Evil must be healed.
I remove from myself responsibility for the bloody cost of my development if I use this very development in order to lessen evil in the present
and in the future. If I am a developed man, then I am obliged to do this,
and it is quite an easy duty, since it coincides with that which is a source
of pleasure for me: searching for and disseminating greater truth, clarifying for myself the most just social order. And in striving to realize it,
I increase my own pleasure and at the same time do everything that I
can for the suffering majority in the present and in the future. Thus, my
cause is defined by one simple rule: live according to that ideal which
you set for yourself as the ideal of a *developed* man![13]

It seems strange that Lavrov had to exhort the intellectual to do
that which was presumably innate to him. A "developed" man's
pleasures were supposed to be "higher" than those of ordinary men.
His needs were supposed to be different. Lavrov found it difficult
to understand how an educated man, an intellectual, could be immoral or amoral. This view led him to his third argument, which was
a kind of threat of excommunication from the intelligentsia, and
therefore from history, aimed at amoral and immoral intellectuals.
In essence an attack upon art for art's sake and science for science's
sake, it confirmed Lavrov's allegiance to the realistic tradition in
Russian criticism.

Neither literature, nor art, nor science saves one from immoral indifference. By themselves they do not include nor cause progress. They only
furnish it with tools. They accumulate strength for it. But only that
writer, artist, or scholar served progress who did all that he could to

13. *Izbrannye sochineniia,* 1:225–26.

apply his energies to the dissemination and strengthening of the civilization of his time, who struggled with evil, embodied his artistic ideals,
scientific truths, philosophical ideas, publicistic strivings in creations
which were fully infused with the life of his times, and in activities which
strictly corresponded to the amount of his energies. Whoever did less,
who because of selfishness [*lichnyi raschet*] stopped halfway, who because of a bacchante's pretty head, because of engrossing investigations
over infusoria, because of a prideful quarrel with a literary rival—
forgot about the immense amount of evil and ignorance, against which
he should have been struggling, might as well have been anything—a
skilled artist, an uncommon scholar, a brilliant publicist—but he excluded himself from the ranks of conscious actors of historical
progress.[14]

Lavrov was at least as concerned with the attitudes of artists, writers, or scientists as he was with the concrete products of their activities. If two scientists achieved identical results but one was motivated
by curiosity or sheer love of contemplation, while the other was
consciously thinking of the applications of his work and its wider
consequences, then only the latter really participated in progress.[15]
Pursuing this idea to its logical conclusions, in later years Lavrov
wrote that no man was capable of living a completely historical life
because the trials of the flesh—disease, personal problems, and the
like—diverted him from his conscious purpose.[16] This extraordinary
view dramatically illustrates both Lavrov's subjectivism and his
asceticism. He demanded that the intelligenty spend their entire
waking lives in moral, purposeful thought and behavior. Since few
could live up to his standards, he had more than his share of bitterness and disappointment.

Lavrov's subjectivism, as should be clear from the above discussion, demanded a total fusion of knowledge and ethics. Ultimately it required the subordination of knowledge to ethics, of
means to ends, of individuals to causes, of self to conscience. His
assumption that a group of critical thinkers could share an ethical
science did not contradict this, nor did his program of striving for the
possible in social reform. There was always a "scientific" authority

14. Ibid., p. 230.
15. Ibid., pp. 230–34.
16. Lavrov, *Opyt istorii mysli novogo vremeni*, 2 vols. (Geneva, 1894),
1:29–30.

to whom he could appeal to reinforce his ideals. Furthermore, since the "possible" was no less subjectively determined than the ideal, and since its limits were discovered painfully in action, the distinction between possible and ideal in Lavrov's thinking tended to fade, or to disappear altogether. The realm of the "possible" was the realm of strategy, and strategies needed testing in action.

In his eighth letter, Lavrov came closest to defining a strategy for the intelligentsia. Actually he provided a historical scenario for the development of a revolutionary party, rather than a real strategy. The terms that eventually had to be translated into strategy were *the individual, the historical environment,* and *the party.* Lavrov believed that in the first phase heroic and fanatical individuals would have to undergo martyrdom but would serve as an inspiration for those who would, in the next phase, become an organized social force:

> So that the force will not be spent in vain, it must be organized. The critically thinking, determined individuals must be determined not only to fight but to win; to this end it is necessary to understand not only the goal toward which one is striving but also the means by which it can be attained. If the struggle has been in earnest, those who are combatting outmoded social institutions will include not only individuals who are fighting in the name of their own suffering, which they have come to understand only through the words and thoughts of others, but also individuals who have thought through the state of affairs critically. They must seek each other out; they must unite, and stand at the head of the party and direct others. Then the force will be organized; its action can be focused on a given point, concentrated for a given purpose. Its task is then purely technical: to do the most work with the least expenditure of strength. The time for unconscious suffering and dreams has passed; the time for heroes and fanatical martyrs, for the squandering of strength and for futile sacrifices, has also passed. The time has come for cool, conscious workmen, calculated strokes, rigorous thinking, and unswerving, patient action.[17]

The perceptive reader would immediately understand that the first phase of Lavrov's scenario was already historical reality in Russia, and that the task ahead was to organize a unified party. Lavrov quite clearly came out for the subordination of individuality

17. *Historical Letters,* pp. 172–73.

to the party's cause, except in those instances where there was an essential clash between the party's program and the individual's ideals. He expressed for the first time a developed view of party solidarity and a sectarian spirit almost wholly alien to his earlier work. In fact, historians have found in the eighth letter, "Rastushchaia obshchestvennaia sila" (The growing social force) a Jacobin or even Bolshevik tendency. It would be wrong to dismiss the eighth letter as the product of an uncharacteristic and passing mood, for in the remaining thirty years of his life he repeatedly returned to themes of party solidarity and discipline, and even used military metaphors to describe them. On the other hand, he did not clearly belong to the Jacobin trend in the Russian revolutionary tradition. Despite some leanings in that direction, he is finally quite ambiguous. The history of his relationships with real revolutionary groups between 1870 and 1900 reveals so much flexibility that it is difficult to establish a strong bias for one or another revolutionary strategy in him. One must conclude that the idea of a unified and effective party was far more important for him than any strategic model, that he arrived at his conception of a party during the first two years of his exile in Vologda, and that it was an important turning point in his career.

It seems extraordinary that letters eight through fifteen could have been printed in tsarist Russia, for in them one can find not only the idea of a revolutionary party, but also the outlines of its goals, if not its strategies. They contain critiques of religion, the state, the family, contract, property—indeed of every existing economic, social, political, and cultural institution. It is almost impossible to avoid their socialistic and anarchistic implications. Yet the censors found them too abstract and oblique to prohibit their publication.[18]

Ultimately it is difficult to assign the *Historical Letters* to any well-articulated submovement in the Russian revolutionary tradition. As noted above, Lavrov's idea of a unified and disciplined party was not associated with a truly Jacobin or Bolshevik mentality

18. See S. A. Pereselenkov, "Ofitsial'nye komentarii k istoricheskim pis'mam P. L. Lavrova," *Byloe*, 1925, no. 30, pp. 37–41; and *Historical Letters*, pp. 38–39.

or strategy. On the other hand, it would be equally mistaken to assign the *Historical Letters* to the populist tradition of the 1870s. That would be anachronistic, attributing to his thinking in the 1860s attitudes that Lavrov acquired only in the 1870s. Lavrov's ideas about the role of the masses and the contribution of the intelligentsia changed in the 1870s as he became more aware of the strengths of the former and the weaknesses of the latter, whereas in the *Historical Letters* the masses were portrayed as victims and not as a vast and vital force. Members of the intelligentsia were depicted as repositories of critical thought, but Lavrov admonished them to relinquish their monopoly of it. He did not suggest that a handful of critically thinking individuals should reorganize society, but rather demanded that the few teach the many and inseminate society with critical thought. (If Lavrov glorified anything in the *Historical Letters,* it was critical thought.) Writing as he did for the legal press, he presented no well-defined program of action. It was quite easy for the reader to make his own substitutions and to assume that for all practical purposes "critically thinking individuals" were synonymous with socialists, and that the *Historical Letters* called for the formation of a united party of socialist *intelligenty.* Only a united and disciplined party of the intelligentsia could become a genuine social force. Hence Lavrov urged youthful intellectuals first to acquire critical thought; second, to unite with like-minded individuals for the struggle against the old order; and third, to spread critical thought among the masses. Lavrov's doctrine of limited possibilities demanded that the intellectual carefully assess the milieu. If reactionary forces were too great and the chances of success nil, then withdrawal from the struggle was not only honorable but imperative. Self-preservation became a primary consideration, since destruction of the socialist intelligentsia would interrupt the continuous development of the forces of progress. These ideas were the beginnings of the revolutionary strategy which Lavrov elaborated as editor of *Vpered!*

The letters received a mixed reception, as one might expect.[19] Herzen, who at first welcomed the letters, later wrote to Ogarev "Mirtov's [the pseudonym under which the letters appeared] let-

19. For a bibliography of reviews of the 1870 and 1891 editions of *Istoricheskie pis'ma,* see *Izbrannye sochineniia,* 1:505–6.

ters are getting more tedious—what abstract language."[20] Tkachev, later one of Lavrov's arch opponents, wrote a long negative review, in which he confusedly developed his own idea of progress. One of Lavrov's own relatives, who had reproached Lavrov for his radical activities in the early 1860s, attacked the *Historical Letters* in Mikhail Katkov's *Russkii vestnik,* a reactionary journal. Lavrov's comrade in exile, N. V. Shelgunov, reviewed the letters for *Delo* (virtually untranslatable without distortion, but probably best rendered as "the fact," rather than "the cause" or "the deed," given its journalistic aims). Shelgunov passed favorably upon Lavrov's intentions, his spirit, and even his style, but took issue with Lavrov's emphasis upon history and his calculated and remorseless moralism. Shelgunov wrote:

Taking obligation as his point of departure, Mirtov hangs over everyone's head a Damoclean sword of perpetual responsibility. . . . He commands everyone who considers himself to be a critical individual to pay back to humanity, to pay back incessantly, the large sum spent for his human development, and then, having taken upon himself this moral duty, to choose as wide an arena of social work as is possible for him.[21]

However, the very attitudes which troubled Shelgunov—a true man of the 1860s in his belief in the spontaneous philanthropic impulse of enlightened human beings—had great appeal for the younger generation. The *Historical Letters* became one of the gospels of the revolutionary movement in Russia, and Lavrov one of its leaders. Almost everyone had underestimated both the numbers and the mood of the new generation of activists among the intelligentsia. The resurgence of the student movement after 1867 was a symptom of their growing impatience and militancy. The older generation had interpreted reality for them; they themselves were prepared to change it. Thus it was the younger generation that converted the *Historical Letters* into a populist tract by testing its ideas in action and, ultimately, by forcing theorists like Lavrov to clarify their own ideas about revolutionary strategy.

20. Herzen to N. P. Ogarev, 12 October 1869, in A. I. Hertsen, *Polnoe sobranie sochinenii i pisem,* ed. M. K. Lemke, 22 vols. (Petrograd, 1919–25), vol. 21 (1923), p. 114.
21. N. V. Shelgunov, *Sochineniia,* 3 vols. (St. Petersburg, 1904), 2:419.

Lavrov himself remained a committed but doctrinally ambiguous figure. By 1869 he already exhibited a mature awareness of the relationship between bourgeois liberalism and workers' socialism, and indicated clear leanings toward socialism. In an anonymous letter published in *Bibliograf* he wrote:

Political injustice was only one of the symptoms of economic injustice. Political economy made it a law of nature. The socialists and communists presented their plans for its removal. In the middle of the century these theoretical views were seemingly near realization, but reaction was stronger. Little by little a realistic point of view penetrated to the proletarian masses; their knowledge grew, together with the consciousness of their material strength and their complete lack of organization. The idea reached them that they could become a political force, could produce thinkers, and hence could oppose a new civilization to the old one in the name of the very same realistic views which were held by their opponents. Political parties suddenly changed their character. So-called liberals and progressives were suddenly weak and even their label sounded inexact, just as . . . had occurred with the party of idealists in the province of theory.[22]

Lavrov viewed revolutionary socialism as only one manifestation of the age of realism, and the workers' movement as a symptom of the emergence of a scientific world view. His analysis of the workers' movement, however, was tinged with the same skepticism which pervaded the *Historical Letters:*

The workers' question will probably be decided with justice, but the opposing forces are still so enormous, and the obstacles to its correct solution so numerous, that an opposite solution is possible more than once. In the last analysis it will, of course, be solved correctly, but this can be put off to such a distant phase of history that the combination of all elements will change.[23]

Lavrov's open-ended historical vision did not permit him to think in terms of an immediate resolution of questions of social justice on the basis of existing social forces. He did not attempt to hide his doubts about the nearness of victory or indeed about the very theory of social progress which defined the evil to be combatted, the good to be pursued, and the social forces embodying each of them. In

22. *Bibliograf,* 1869, no. 1, p. 13.
23. Ibid.

fact, there is some evidence that Lavrov viewed the women's liberation movement as the truly significant movement of his day:

The workers' question will with its solution change all political and economic relations. But complete solution of the woman's question will not only introduce a new element into the aforementioned spheres of thought and life; it must change all of the manifestations of culture to its most intimate [*intimnyi*] forms; it must provide art with completely different forms; it must recast mankind into completely new forms of life, difficult for us to imagine.[24]

Lavrov's disciplined neo-Kantian relativism did not permit him to close the question. But his left-wing Hegelian militancy and Proudhonist righteousness forced him to commit himself to the struggle for human liberation and human dignity. Ultimately, another neo-Kantian approach—what Hans Vaihinger later called "the philosophy of 'as if' "—provided the solution. Although Lavrov never quite arrived at the concept of fiction—he always talked about hypotheses, ideals, convictions, and idealization—in effect he had to resort to fictions in order to avoid a soft and yielding relativism on the one hand and a hard, absolutistic positivism on the other. In his tenth letter, "Idealizatsiia" (Idealization), Lavrov had written:

The only idealization which is absolutely inevitable for man is the notion of *free will*, by virtue of which he cannot in any way rid himself of the subjective conviction that he voluntarily sets goals for himself and chooses means of achieving them. However convincingly objective *knowledge* demonstrates to man that all his "voluntary" actions and thought are nothing but necessary consequences of an antecedent series of events—external and internal, physical and psychic—the subjective *consciousness* that these actions and thoughts are voluntary remains a constant, inescapable illusion, even in the very process of demonstrating the universal determinism which rules both in the external world and in the spirit of man.[25]

Without this concept of free will, Lavrov's whole theory of moral action would be baseless. But according to Lavrov's own account of his life, throughout his adolescence he had been a "fatalist," and at other moments later in his life, even after he had formulated his concept of free will, he sounded very much like a fatalist. One won-

24. Ibid.
25. *Historical Letters,* p. 196.

ders if Lavrov ever really *felt* free. His freedom included strict duty, subordination, and the rigorous and vigilant quest for "scientific" rather than arbitrary authority. Ultimately it led to depersonalization in the name of one's ideal and one's party—to the transformation of the individual into an "organ," and the suppression of those elements of his individuality ("habits and customs") which clashed with "essential" aims. It was the kind of freedom that a man with a hypertrophied conscience might enjoy. If Lavrov never really felt free, then his theory of free will may have been a construct, a useful fiction which permitted him to fit into his anthropologism an idea which had no deep roots in his personality but which he believed was an essential component of progressive thought in the intellectual culture of his era. Like most ideas which lack deep psychological roots, Lavrov's idea of freedom visibly faded and shriveled once he finally committed himself to a "scientific" authority, a powerful social force, and to the party which presumably belonged to it. Finally, it took several external shocks—a combination of coercion and unforeseen personal losses—to emancipate Lavrov from his sedentary life of scholarship and to convert him into a revolutionary publicist. It is hardly an exaggeration to say that his fate was decided for him. And even after the decision to join revolutionary parties was, to a considerable extent, forced upon him, his relationships to the parties were always somewhat peculiar. He *served* them but never really fully or wholeheartedly joined them. He was always something of an outsider, as men of rigid conscience and cool words usually are when movements enter their activist phase. Like men of ideals in all times and places, Lavrov found the concrete circumstances and vehicles in which he had to pursue his ideals deficient and frustrating.

5.
Commitment

Lavrov's plan to flee internal exile took more definite shape as the remorselessness of the authorities became increasingly clear. Escape from internal exile in the *guberniia* of Vologda was evidently no unusual feat. Lavrov's mistress, A. P. Chaplitskaia, preceded him to Western Europe by several months.[1] His own plans were delayed by M. P. Sazhin's flight in June 1869, because the local gendarmes established stricter surveillance of political criminals. But the major reason for the long delay between his decision to escape and the escape itself was his dependence upon others for its planning and execution.

Lavrov was utterly helpless and clumsy in the world outside his study. He couldn't see without his spectacles and suffered from night blindness.[2] Obviously he could not manage the escape himself. His son-in-law, M. F. Negreskul, and another man named Frodberg went abroad early in 1869 and spoke to Herzen about Lavrov's plight. That summer Negreskul and Lavrov's eldest son, Mikhail, came to Kadnikov with the information that Herzen awaited Lavrov and would introduce him into radical circles in Paris.[3] Lavrov's huge library was to be shipped there before his escape. All of the details of the flight were worked out, and the escape was planned for early in the winter of 1869. But before matters came to a head, Negreskul was arrested.[4] In despair, Lavrov decided to attempt the escape himself and asked his Petersburg contacts to send him an internal passport.

1. Sazhin, "P. L. Lavrov v vospominaniiakh sovremennikov," p. 122.
2. A. A. Vinitskaia, "Iz prikliuchenii v Parizhe," *Istoricheskii vestnik,* 1912, no. 1, p. 136.
3. Lavrov, "Moi pobeg iz ssylki."
4. For a brief description of Negreskul's activities, see J. M. Meijer, *Knowledge and Revolution: The Russian Colony in Zurich, 1870–1873* (Assen: Van Gorcum and Co., 1955), pp. 42–43, and Franco Venturi, *Roots of Revolution* (New York: Grosset and Dunlap, Universal Library, 1966), p. 357.

No action was taken, however, until German Lopatin offered his services to Lavrov's daughter at the beginning of 1870. Ultimately it was Lopatin who engineered the flight. German Alexandrovich Lopatin, one of the most dashing figures in the revolutionary underground of the late 1860s, was an extraordinarily resourceful person and an accomplished escape artist, although his attempts to liberate Chernyshevskii from Siberian exile all failed. A product of the mid-1860s, when Chernyshevskii's *What Is to Be Done?* was still the moving force behind underground organizations, Lopatin in many ways resembled Chernyshevskii's Rakhmetov. Distinctly a man of action, Lopatin was one of the participants in the earliest phase of the populist movement—that of reconnaissance in the countryside—which existed side by side with the Nechaevist tendency. Through Lavrov's daughter, Maria, he had learned about the escape plans which had been laid for 1869 but which had collapsed because of difficulties with the disposition of Lavrov's estate and, more importantly, because of his son-in-law's arrest.[5] Now, with the help of Lopatin, new plans for Lavrov's escape took shape.

On the day of his flight, 22 February 1870, Lavrov's mother covered for him by pretending that he was in his room with a migraine headache. (Elizaveta Karlovna played her role well and joined her son in Paris in May 1870—only to die a few weeks after her arrival.) Lopatin disguised Lavrov by stuffing his cheeks with cotton to simulate a toothache and by binding up Lavrov's head in a handkerchief. The two men fled to Iaroslavl by sleigh, continued from there by rail to Moscow, and then to St. Petersburg. The only interesting incident occurred near Vologda, where a colonel in the gendarmerie approached them but did not notice anything suspicious.[6] While in St. Petersburg, Lavrov stayed at the apartment of a young artillery officer, one of his former students. He almost immediately boarded a train for Europe, this time accompanied by Emmanuel Fedorovich Negreskul, his son-in-law's brother. Lavrov lay in his coach feigning illness in order to disguise his impressive height—over six feet—which might have given him away. At one point in the trip he leaned out of the coach to ask a conductor for

5. G. Lopatin, "Vospominaniia," *Golos minuvshego,* 1915, no. 9, p. 137.
6. Ibid., pp. 138–39.

the time, not realizing that the figure in uniform was actually a gendarme.[7] Lavrov's myopia provided only this slight misadventure during the last phase of his escape from Russia, and he arrived in Paris without further mishap on 13 March 1870.

He reached Paris several weeks after the death of Alexander Herzen, the man whose writings had played such a significant role in converting Lavrov to a radical philosophy. One can only imagine what a blow Herzen's death was to Lavrov, what joint projects with Herzen he had contemplated in vain. Furthermore, Lavrov's arrival in France came during the struggle between Marx and Bakunin in the First International. Within a few weeks he witnessed the outbreak of the Franco-Prussian War, followed by the creation of the Third Republic and the rise and fall of the Paris Commune. All of these factors were to affect the formation of his radical program. But from the moment of his arrival until late in 1872 Lavrov remained on the periphery of the Russian socialist émigré community. However committed he was to the socialist movement, he was still unprepared to assume a central role in it.

Although it has been suggested that Lavrov had been liberated at the behest of radical circles and that he had intended to engage in revolutionary activity abroad, there is considerable evidence to support the argument that he fled internal exile in order to continue his scholarly research.[8] Despite his desire to keep alive the revolutionary spark among the Russian intelligentsia, he did not have much faith in the possibilities of a successful revolution in the late 1860s, but instead visualized a long struggle between the forces of enlightenment and reaction before the creation of a real basis for a revolutionary uprising. Furthermore, as noted above, Lavrov had expected the authorities to repent and at the very least to resettle him in a city where he might continue his scholarly work. He had finally asked permission to leave Russia for either Bonn or Heidelberg.[9] When

7. Negreskul, "Vospominaniia," pp. 142–43.

8. N. A. Morozov in his memoirs states that the Chaikovskii circle engineered Lavrov's escape. See *Povesti moei zhizni*, 2 vols. (Moscow: Akademiia nauk, 1962), 1:133. In view of Lopatin's memoirs this must be dismissed as erroneous.

9. Elena Shtakenschneider, "Vospominaniia," *Golos minuvshego,* 1915, no. 12, pp. 121–39.

this last request was refused, he saw no other choice but flight. The severity of the climate in Vologda was ruining his health and endangering his plans for a magnum opus. There is no reason to doubt the sincerity of Lavrov's statements in a letter to his son, Mikhail, written in Paris on 24 July 1870. He expressed righteous indignation about his unjust treatment but emphasized the reluctance with which he had acted:

I turned to Prince Suvorov . . . setting forth to him my position and asking him to petition the Emperor personally for a change from internal exile to exile abroad for the period of time the government considered it necessary to exclude me from Petersburg. In this way I could continue my work in the libraries of foreign capitals and university cities without breaking ties with Russia, awaiting the moment when I could return to her. I had very little hope . . . but considered it my duty to do everything . . . in order to avoid the final difficult measure—emigration.

I would be prepared to return to Russia if they permitted me to live quietly in Petersburg and to continue my scientific work by means of local libraries, since not one city in Russia besides Petersburg has sufficient materials for my work. But Petersburg is closed to me by the Emperor's command; upon my return they would immediately send me off to some remote corner of Russia; hence I must live abroad.

I remain Russian in spirit; the broadening of truth and justice in my fatherland was and is my sincerest desire and goal, whose fulfillment I am ready to further with all my strength. My future employment depends upon conditions which I cannot foresee, but at the moment the continuation of my scientific labors is the primary, if not the only, aim of my [present] activities.[10]

Lavrov's behavior during his first months in exile in Paris tends, if anything, to reinforce the impression gained from this declaration of intentions. The atmosphere of intrigue and suspicion in the émigré milieu repelled him. Arriving in the wake of the Nechaev episode, Lavrov at first refused to get involved with Russian émigré factions and regarded their schemes with skepticism, if not contempt. Bakunin was the most prominent émigré socialist after Herzen's death, but his reputation had been damaged and his authority challenged by Nechaev and Nikolai Utin. In Lavrov's eyes, socialism as a higher ideal had to be served wholeheartedly in a spirit of self-effacement. Intrigues, petty animosities, and factional struggles violated the dig-

10. *Materialy,* pp. 34–39.

nity and sweep of socialist aims. Furthermore, Lavrov was afraid of tarnishing his own reputation and was exceedingly careful not to involve himself in anything sordid. Therefore, he refused to join frenzied émigré attempts to organize journals and publish pamphlets.[11] He was mystified by the bitter struggle between Marx and Bakunin over control of the First International and, as usual, longed for a serene condition of unity. On 19 June 1870 he wrote to Lopatin:

Accusations and gossip are pouring down like hail. From Bakunin's letter I see that he regards Marx's political-social party (the German one, as he calls it) as one of the most hostile parties. Why do these gentlemen bear such malice towards one another? Couldn't you help, if not to conciliate these camps, then to mollify their hostility, since it positively harms the social cause? It seems to me that it is quite possible in some places to further the social cause by way of struggle with state principles, and in others—to use the political order as a tool for socialist conquest. The common foe of one and the other is the present economic-juridical state, and there is still time to quarrel about the rest.[12]

Lavrov had not worked out the details of a program of socialist development. During the 1860s he had tried to demonstrate that socialist ideals were scientific by examining the intellectual and moral ontogeny of "developed" individuals, but it is clear from his remarks to Lopatin that in June of 1870 Lavrov was still thinking in terms of a long, drawn-out struggle, and hadn't accepted any rigid developmental scheme along socialistic lines either for the near or distant

11. Sazhin visited Lavrov on 3 June 1870. He brought a letter from Bakunin inviting Lavrov to collaborate on a Russian émigré review, whose staff would also include Ogarev and A. A. Zhuk. Lavrov was still on friendly terms with Sazhin at that time. However, he did not have much faith in the future of Bakunin's journal. In a letter to Lopatin, Lavrov wrote, "Bakunin, Ogarev, Zhuk, and Sazhin are going to put out a monthly Russian review, and Bakunin is inviting me to participate. Of course, a review is not a political journal, and one can announce that one is not solidary with many of the opinions of the editors, so there is some possibility of collaboration, but I am nonetheless a bit wary because I don't think that the journal will be a success." (Lavrov to Lopatin, Paris, 19 June 1870, MS in IISH.) Also, see Meijer, *Knowledge and Revolution,* p. 67. In still another letter to Lopatin written several months later, Lavrov revealed his reactions to a new proposal for collaboration, this one by M. El'pidin. He wrote, "Have they all lost their minds?" (Lavrov to Lopatin, Paris, 3 September 1870, MS in IISH.)
12. Lavrov to Lopatin, 19 June 1870, MS in IISH.

future. Indeed, as late as 1872 he still believed that the resolution of the problem of women's liberation might ultimately be more important historically than the victory of workers' socialism.

That he was in no haste to devote his full time and energy to the struggle is confirmed in several of his letters to Shtakenschneider and Lopatin written during the summer of 1870. One of Lavrov's former students—a wealthy landowner, chemist, and banker—had tentatively promised to support him for five or six years, during which time he could devote himself to two major literary projects.[13] Lavrov was delighted and overwhelmed. The first project was to be a three-volume history of modern European thought, and the second an immense encyclopedic dictionary of theoretical and technical thought. Lavrov wanted Lopatin to act as his assistant, hoping that he would accept employment as translator and copyist after completing his work on the Russian translation of *Das Kapital*. On 3 September 1870 he wrote to Lopatin for his help, saying, "my long-standing, favorite project, set aside with such heartache, would still be realized in its best form and completely according to my conception."[14] With grandiose scholarly schemes such as these exciting his imagination, Lavrov must have pictured a very modest role for himself in the revolutionary movement.

On the other hand, Lavrov's enthusiasm over such projects may have been a smoke screen for the diffidence which he felt in general during his first months abroad. Even while in exile in Russia he had managed to lead an orderly, routinized existence, working steadily at voluminous manuscripts, presiding over the Thursday soirees at which his mother poured tea. Although Lavrov had always attacked "routine" thinking, he himself had led a highly regulated existence. He had spent most of his life in studies and lecture halls, where people and objects were readily accessible and easily controlled, where he could bend his thoughts and the thoughts of others in whatever direction he chose. It is likely that he was extremely disoriented in the circumstances in which he found himself in 1870. Moreover, given Lavrov's habitual reticence about personal matters, one can only speculate about the effect of his mother's death in July 1870, but it no doubt contributed to his sense of uprootedness.

13. Lavrov to Lopatin, 29 August 1870, MS in IISH.
14. Lavrov to Lopatin, 3 September 1870, MS in IISH.

These newest upheavals in his life forced him to face up to defects and incapacities which had never before caused him great problems because of his relatively sheltered, scholarly existence. His self-esteem, so very secure in the late 1850s, had suffered several severe blows. Lavrov now saw himself as an imperfect being. A clear manifestation of this attitude was his hero-worship of German Lopatin. Lopatin was cool, intelligent, yet decisive and daring. In a letter to Rosaliia Khristoforovna Idel'son[15] Lavrov wrote:

The kind of keen character which Lopatin possesses . . . is the essence of the man. I know that in my own youth I was never so secure [*ravnovesen*], so unbending before life's blows, and I think that you, too, lacked this character. Perhaps you were carefree in childhood but that is something else. He is not carefree; on the contrary, he is extremely careful about all details, extremely deliberate in everything that he does, and quite seriously disposed towards everything that is being done around him, and that which he himself does. His strength—and it is a very unusual strength—lies in that very joining together of seriousness and extreme care for detail with a cheerful but sober disposition, which doesn't permit him to inflate objects, people, and events to unreal dimensions. We never possessed this, and shall never possess it. . . . You are also spoiled by introspection [*reflektsiia*], which damaged me so much in my youth, but I am far less introspective than you.[16]

Without Lopatin's initial help Lavrov probably would have been completely adrift, and his offer of employment to Lopatin may have been an expression of his continuing insecurity and his need for a protector. Lavrov, completely helpless in practical matters, could not manage the details of life and was stunned by unforeseen adversity, while Lopatin somehow managed to ride the crest of any situation, however sudden and disturbing it might be. Lavrov felt that such a man was meant for a great role in life. Several years later, feeling that the younger man might accomplish what he him-

15. Rosaliia Khristoforovna Idel'son was of Ukrainian origin, Jewish, a member of the Russian colony in Zurich, and the wife of V. N. Smirnov. She was one of the earliest collaborators on the journal *Vpered!*, and Lavrov's steady correspondent during the 1870s. An important link in the early fund-raising activities of the *Vpered!* group, she remained one of its central figures, especially during the Swiss period of the journal's existence. (She remained in Switzerland when the journal moved to London, and studied medicine in Berne.) Lavrov's and Smirnov's letters to her reveal more about the history of the journal during the London period than does any other source.
16. Lavrov to R. Idel'son, 25 November [1873], MS in IISH.

self had failed to do, he encouraged Lopatin to assume a position of leadership in the socialist movement.[17]

Lavrov's state of mind in 1870 hardly let him picture himself as a leader in the socialist movement. Though he was undoubtedly interested in the Russian section of the First International and had received a full set of the group's journal, *Narodnoe delo,* in July 1870, there is no evidence that he ever tried to establish close ties with the group itself. Apparently he imagined that he would play a modest role as a collaborator on socialist journals but that his major contribution would be his work on the history of thought, written, of course, from a socialist point of view. Furthermore, Lavrov tried to maintain a lifeline with Russia, at first refusing to believe that all ties with his homeland and past life had been severed, that he could never return and continue his life of teaching and scholarship.[18]

The Russian legal press was Lavrov's primary source of income during most of his life in exile, and what would become years of frustrations and misunderstandings with intermediaries, editors, and publishers began almost immediately after he established himself in Paris.[19] He continued to write for *Otechestvennye zapiski* and after a short time contributed to *Znanie* (Knowledge) and *Delo.* His relations with all three journals were strained to the breaking point at one time or another because of delayed payments, intended or unintended slights, and difficulties with censorship. Extremely sensitive to criticism, Lavrov needed constant reassurance that his work was needed and appreciated. He also demanded punctuality and meticulousness from others to what was perhaps an unreasonable degree in view of the dangers and difficulties involved in publishing his articles and sending him his salary and author's copies. The articles themselves were aptly described by Saltykov-Shchedrin as "forests, the ends of which one might never attain."[20] G. Z.

17. Lavrov to Lopatin, 30 March 1876, MS in IISH.
18. A major proponent of this view is P. Vitiazev. See his "Na graniakh zhizni" in *Vpered!,* ed. Vitiazev (Petrograd: Kolos, 1920); and also his "P. L. Lavrov v 1870–1873 godakh," in *Materialy.* Also see German Lopatin, "K rasskazam o P. L. Lavrove," *Golos minuvshego,* 1916, no. 4, pp. 186–98.
19. Lavrov worked through a complex and highly unreliable network of intermediaries including Shtakenschneider, Ukrainian writer M. A. Marko-Vovchok, and Alexander Kropotkin.
20. *Literaturnoe nasledstvo,* 1934, nos. 13–14, p. 528.

Eliseev, however, encouraged Lavrov to send "serious" articles instead of the review of European literature and life which Lavrov had intended to write for *Otechestvennye zapiski*.[21]

If the first months of Lavrov's life abroad were marked by insecurity, exaggerated hopes, and painful concerns about money and steady employment, the period beginning in September 1870 marked a sudden reversal of mood. The fall of the Second Empire in France was the cause of great rejoicing and new expectations. On 12 September 1870 Lavrov wrote to Lopatin, who was traveling with a South American passport:

Well, sir, citizen of a South American republic (whose name I don't recall—Colombia, or maybe Uruguay or Paraguay), here am I living in a republic! Here I see with my own eyes the great day, and the manner in which the national guard decided the fate of a nation, and the falling eagles and all that. I was on the Place de la Concorde and on the steps of the Corps Législatif on the fourth of September, and shouted *"Vive la république"* with the others, and even offered my services to the besieged (not today—tomorrow) city and perhaps I'll receive my brassard today.[22]

During the siege of Paris and the Commune of March 1871, Lavrov was evidently so profoundly affected by the heroic behavior of the working class that he was moved to poetry. A poem written by Lavrov on Christmas Eve, 1870, reflects the influence of the First International. Louis Varlin had introduced Lavrov into the des Ternes Section of the International in November or December of 1870, and the vigor of the working class movement evidently had impressed him. He even resorted to biblical allusions in order to give color and dignity to his conception of an awakening force, a proletariat weaned from false religions and conscious of its own strength and role. He saw with his own eyes the emergence of a force which he had presumed to exist, but whose strength and courage he had never before felt.[23]

21. For Lavrov's correspondence with Eliseev, see P. Vitiazev, "P. L. Lavrov i ego korrespondenty," Ibid., 1935, nos. 19–21, pp. 261–62. Some of Eliseev's letters to Lavrov are preserved in the IISH.
22. Lavrov to Lopatin, 12 September [1870], MS in IISH. In another letter, written to Shtakenschneider, he repeated this message almost word for word (*Golos minuvshego,* 1916, no. 7-8, p. 114).
23. See pp. 160–63 for further discussion.

Even while in exile in Russia Lavrov had surmised from his study of the workers' movement that the "realism" of the age had begun to penetrate their midst and that they were a growing force in society. However, to confidants like Lopatin and Shtakenschneider, Lavrov revealed a skepticism which he felt constrained to hide from others. Publicly he was an optimist, but it is clear from his letters that he had doubts. In February 1872 he wrote to Shtakenschneider:

I have no hope for a quick victory. I don't even think that we'll live to see it, but I don't think that it will take five hundred years. If the twentieth century does not decide the question, it will mean that the question was badly put, and will be replaced by a new formulation.[24]

And in July, 1872:

The twentieth century will perhaps put it—the workers' question—another way, and our socialism will be for our posterity what the scholastic attempt to decide the question of nature on the basis of biblical text and Aristotle is for the naturalists of modern Europe.[25]

As a student of the history of thought Lavrov was alert to the dangers of reliance upon sacred texts or ultimate explanations.

Even while recognizing Lavrov's continuing doubts, one should not underestimate the effect of the Paris Commune upon Lavrov's philosophy of revolution. If it did not convince him that the socialist renovation of society was imminent, it at least demonstrated that the masses were able to produce their own leadership. His admiring discovery of the intelligent, responsible behavior of leaders from the masses during the Commune is reminiscent of Peter Kropotkin's admiration of the spontaneous social creativity of former convicts in Siberia and Paul Aksel'rod's discovery of the German workers' movement. For Lavrov the Paris Commune was direct proof that the common man could intelligently guide his own affairs. His letters of the period reveal a profound contempt for French political parties and their leaders. Emigration and life in France confirmed his rejection of traditional political solutions to social problems. He summarily dismissed "radical phrasemongers" like Gambetta, Louis Blanc, and Ledru-Rollin.[26] Lavrov, of course,

24. *Golos minuvshego,* 1916, no. 9, p. 118.
25. Ibid., p. 128.
26. Ibid., no. 7-8, p. 135.

strongly identified with the socialist intelligentsia, but their divisiveness and moral weakness forced him to turn to the Commune as the only other social force capable of furthering progress. There had always been some solace in the idea of a vast, potent force which the intelligentsia could educate and lead.

In a letter written in February 1872 to Shtakenschneider, Lavrov summed up his views on the positive aspects of the Commune.

Its positive results are the following: the political program of the workers' movement . . . is clearly set forth, that is, a federation of communes with the widest possible self-government; it has been shown that in everday affairs not only lawyers and bourgeois types can be administrators, but artisans straight from the workshop, and that administration will be none the worse for it; there now exists a bloody legend, which can be entered into the martyrology.[27]

Lavrov had already written some brief pieces on the Commune for the journal *L'Internationale* in March 1871, in which he had fully expressed his sympathy for the Central Committee of the National Guard and had also described his own perspectives on the fate of bourgeois society.

The socialist-thinker, studying the events taking place within the space of a few days, can confirm with ever greater certainty that this bourgeois society, which exploits and demoralizes the proletariat, has absolutely no basis for existence. It has behind it neither moral right, nor numerical strength, nor even the knowledge how to act. . . . It has behind it only routine.[28]

Lavrov's correspondence to *L'Internationale* reveals that he had formed his basic ideas about the Commune before the appearance of any of the contemporary works on the Commune—those of Marx and Lissagaray, for example. In March 1875, as editor of *Vpered!* Lavrov wrote a short piece commemorating the Commune in which he expressed views similar to those above, and in which he described the Commune as the first revolution of the proletariat. In a later work on the Paris Commune, he described 28 March 1871 (the day on which the Commune was officially proclaimed) as "the first, though quite pale, dawn of the proletarian republic." Lavrov him-

27. Ibid., no. 9, p. 117.
28. P. L. Lavrov, "Korrespondentsiia iz Parizha, 28 Marta 1871," in *Izbrannye sochineniia,* 1:455.

self had witnessed its birth in front of the Hôtel de Ville and had heard the Marseillaise thundered by 50,000 voices. But despite his presence as an eyewitness, when he retold the events of the uprising more than eight years later in *18 Marta 1871 goda,* his major work on the Commune, he chose to rely upon the accounts of G. Lefrançais, A. Arnould, P. Lanjalley, P. Corriez, P. Lissagaray, and others.

The impact of the Paris Commune upon Lavrov was supremely important for his conception of the role he would play in the socialist movement and, indeed, for his general theory of leadership in the movement. From the evidence we have, it seems that Lavrov had accepted all of the basic arguments of revolutionary socialism while still in Russia, but that he had no intentions of becoming a leader in the movement. Not even his involvement in the First International and his participation in the Commune fundamentally changed this attitude. Quite to the contrary, they only reinforced his own propensity for pedagogical and collaborative rather than leading roles. Now that he had seen that the masses could produce their own leadership, he could assert his belief that the socialist intelligentsia should concern itself with leadership of the revolution only to the extent that they were to be the first organizing cadre of the revolutionary party—the vanguard of a vanguard. In this way Lavrov moved toward the idea of the diminution of the role of the intelligentsia and the expansion of the role of the masses characteristically associated with Russian populism; however, he did not abandon his fundamentally rationalistic approach.

Lavrov had actually left Paris in mid-April 1871, during the Prussian siege and the turmoil of the Commune, in order to seek aid for the Commune from the General Council of the International. After an unsuccessful stopover in Brussels, he went on to London to consult Marx and Engels, with whom he established lasting, if not always cordial or friendly, relations.[29]

Contemporary Soviet historians have carefully examined the development of Lavrov's views on the Paris Commune, not only be-

29. There are a number of legends associated with Lavrov's trip to Brussels and London. Eduard Bernstein believed that Lavrov had carried a large sum of money from the general council of the International to the Central Committee of the Commune. (E. Bernstein, "Karl Marks i russkie revoliut-

cause they are strikingly similar to Marx's and, later, Lenin's, but because it is just possible that Lavrov's radical assessment of the significance of the Commune as a new form of proletarian government actually influenced Marx. However, they are naturally reluctant to give Lavrov priority in a theoretical assessment of such enormous weight, and can only hint at the possibility. Thus, in a recent study describing Lavrov's views on the Commune and his trip to London in late 1871, we find:

> What did Marx and Lavrov talk about [referring to Lavrov's first meetings with Marx and Engels]? Surely, above all, about the Commune. Lavrov was one of the few persons from whom Marx could gather fully reliable information about the events in Paris; Lavrov had reflected a great deal about the revolution on 18 March.[30]

It is true that Lavrov strongly relied upon Marx's *Civil War in France* in his later writings about the Commune, but mainly as confirmation and authoritative backing for his own views. However, he was evidently not favorably impressed by Marx after their first meetings, In fact, in letters to Elena Shtakenschneider, in which he previewed his later study of the Paris Commune he added a gratuitous slap at Marx:

> Marx would have been quite out of his place in Paris; he isn't the kind of man who could have influenced the masses in such a moment. One can accuse him (and I do) of other failings, but that's another matter.[31]

Is it possible that this oblique attack is a reference to Marx's use of Lavrov's views in *The Civil War in France* without acknowledging them? Or is it a comment on the manner in which Marx had responded to the anticentralists in the First International? Lavrov's own immediate experience with the Paris Commune, and especially

---

sionery," *Minuvshie gody,* 1908, no. 11, p. 2). An agent of the Third Section reported that Lavrov fled Paris in the company of Auguste Blanqui on 18 May 1870. According to the agent, Lavrov was trying to form a secret society for the purpose of assassinating all of France's highest government officials. The agent also reported that Lavrov was a member of the deputation of Communists presented to Gladstone. (*O begstve Lavrova,* a report of the third expedition of the Third Section, begun 24 February 1870 and completed 11 June 1871, MS in AOR.)

30. B. S. Itenberg, *Rossiia i Parizhskaia Kommuna* (Moscow: Nauka, 1971), p. 123.

31. *Golos minuvshego,* 1916, no. 9, p. 128.

his contact with leaders like Varlin, had inclined him toward the anti-centralist position. Like other Russian émigré participants in the First International, he had been under severe pressure from both sides. No doubt he had both irritated and amused Marx and Engels by his earnest effort to reconcile the warring camps. The First International did not survive the split between the centralists and anti-centralists, and, although it was not clear to Lavrov at the time, the First International was already less an organization than an idea. Consequently Lavrov found himself in the midst of a frustrating situation, in which the theoretical leaders of European socialism were able neither to provide aid and effective leadership for a spontaneous proletarian uprising, nor even to unify their own organization. The meaning of Lavrov's criticism of Marx, then, must remain an open question.

Lavrov, of course, felt his own incapacities as a leader during the turmoil of the Commune. But for a moment, at least, he had experienced the exhilaration of being present at a great historical moment. He had suffered with other Parisians during the Prussian siege, had carried provisions, eaten dogmeat, and had helped bear away the wounded after a massacre in front of the Hôtel de Ville. He had even offered his services as a teacher to the communards.[32] In short, Lavrov had stood with the forces of progress during a moment fraught with historical possibilities, for he believed that it would have been sinful for men with socialist convictions to remain outside the fray. Those who hadn't supported the Commune had possibly caused great harm:

The presence of one hundred or two hundred more developed and sincere men at the center of the movement might have considerably altered the course of events. I affirm that it was correct, just, and rational to stand under the banner of revolution on the 18th of March, to hurl oneself into the incipient but already inevitable movement, and to accomplish within it what could be accomplished.[33]

Mistakes were unavoidable in a complex revolutionary situation. Plans went awry, and there was a great deal of seemingly futile sac-

32. B. S. Itenberg has unearthed Lavrov's plan for a fifteen-booklet course in the sciences, written especially for the working class. The course never materialized. See *Rossiia i Parizhskaia Kommuna,* pp. 117–20.

33. *Golos minuvshego,* 1916, no. 9, p. 127.

rifice and bloodshed, but those who desired the progress of humanity and who believed that it could only be achieved through a social revolution were not alarmed at the thought of "a little blood and pus which flow beneath the lancet from humanity's wounds."[34]

In Lavrov's eyes the uprising of 1871 was of great value, despite the ultimate collapse of the Commune. It was almost a laboratory experiment in revolution. It proved that a federation of self-governing communes was practicable, and that the working class could create its own administration without the help of bourgeois lawyers.[35] Above all, it confirmed and strengthened Lavrov's own conviction that no revolution could succeed without careful preparation. Old political conceptions inherited from the revolutionary struggle of the eighteenth century had to be swept aside; the movement had to be purified and solidly founded upon the social-revolutionary principles of the International.[36]

One could write an interesting comparative history of the reactions of Russian émigré radicals to revolutionary events in a foreign setting. Herzen had witnessed the June days in Paris in 1848 and had reacted with *From the Other Shore,* which contained a brilliant and radical perception of the falseness of liberalism and bourgeois civilization in the mid-nineteenth century. Lavrov shared Herzen's contempt for bourgeois civilization, but he had none of Herzen's capacity to surmount the various "isms" which were offered as alternatives to it nor was he capable of Herzen's "existential egoism."[37] While the turmoil of 1848 had urgently brought Herzen's individualism to the foreground, the Paris Commune only confirmed Lavrov's sense of partiinost' and his hopes for the European proletariat. There is not the slightest ambivalence in his public and private correspondence. He had committed himself to the party of the proletariat.

Actually, Lavrov was applying to European conditions his idea of a "scientific" community of ethical sociologists, and he had be-

34. Ibid., no. 7-8, p. 135.
35. Ibid.
36. Ibid., p. 134.
37. Martin Malia, *Alexander Herzen and the Birth of Russian Socialism* (New York: Grosset and Dunlap, Universal Library, 1965), p. 382.

gun to search for the most authoritative doctrines in the socialist camp. Rather than fleeing the horrors of mass conflict caused by factions with opposing ideologies, he looked for the most secure ideological position from which to launch the proletarian struggle at the next opportune moment. That is what attracted him to Marx and Engels, for he accepted Marx's socioeconomic theory as a truly scientific analysis of the contradictions in the bourgeois economic and social orders. His relationship to the Russian radicals of the 1860s, and especially to Chernyshevskii, is called to mind. Never very interested in developing his own critique of political economy, Lavrov tended to defer to others in the area of economics; his own discussions of economics were largely a parading of the horrors of bourgeois competition and exploitation. Thus, despite occasional friction between Marx and Lavrov—usually brought on by Marx's overbearing hostility towards the "intriguers" in the Russian émigré socialist community—Lavrov exhibited an unusual degree of deference to Marx both during the latter's lifetime and after his death. Marx and Engels treated him with considerable condescension. He seemed to them well-intentioned, if somewhat eclectic and confused theoretically, and far less objectionable than most Russian émigré socialists, whose flamboyance and aggressiveness had irritated them. Relations between Marx and Lavrov were probably sustained more through their mutual friendship for German Lopatin than through any great esteem for one another. Although Lavrov's correspondence reveals both personal pique for Marx's coldness and serious objections to his handling of certain theoretical problems, he refrained from any public, frontal attack on Marx or Engels in an effort to help the cause of socialist solidarity.

Marx's socioeconomic doctrine provided an escape from the blind alley of competition, exploitation, and misery. Contradictions within capitalism indicated that it would inevitably fall. The theory of increasing misery predicted that the workers would inevitably rise against their oppressors. Here were well documented, convincingly argued doctrines, whose optimistic conclusions were an attractive alternative to Lavrov's own personal skepticism about progress, which he had succinctly expressed in a letter written to Shtakenschneider in September 1870:

You want to know in what I believe? Of course, not in the new republic or even in the inevitable victory of truth and justice, and not even in inevitable progress. I only know that this progress is possible, that this victory is possible, and it seems to me that I know by which paths one must pursue this goal.[38]

However, contact with Marx and Engels in 1871 did not suddenly convert Lavrov into an unqualified optimist. He was still swayed by doubts, distrustful of his own enthusiasm. In July 1872 he wrote to Shtakenschneider:

Have I indeed in my old age entered into illusions, against which I have always struggled so strenuously, whether in myself or in others? Have I erred? . . . It must be that it is my fate to be forever alone; I never strike the general note, now falling a half-tone lower, now a tone higher—what can one do? I must sing according to my voice.[39]

Notwithstanding the romantic pose which Lavrov sometimes struck, there is a great deal of truth here. Lavrov's theoretical acceptance of partiinost', like his theoretical commitment to a concept of free will, had no solid foundations in his personality. There was nothing in his past upon which to base any true optimism, either about a revolutionary party or about his own role within one. However, there is almost astonishing consistency in his progressive radicalization, first in the 1850s and 1860s, when he continually drifted toward the left, and then in the period 1870–1900, when he successively served the most active and militant groups within the Russian revolutionary movement. This *posledovatel'nost'* ("logical consecutiveness") of radical commitment became the most important thing in Lavrov's life as, one by one, his ties with his past life, both professional and personal, were destroyed by forces largely beyond his control. However, both the fiery young revolutionaries with whom he came in contact and liberal acquaintances sensed some kind of disjunction between Lavrov's personality and his commitment to radicalism. Turgenev summed it up well when he said:

He is a dove trying hard to pass himself off as a hawk. You must hear him cooing about the need for Pugachevs and Razins. The words are

38. *Golos minuvshego,* 1916, no. 7-8, p. 115.
39. Ibid., no. 9, p. 123.

terrible, but the glance is gentle, the smile is most kind, and even the enormous and unkempt beard has a tender and peaceful character.[40]

Because Lavrov's radicalism was fundamentally intellectual, it was also fundamentally unconvincing to those who knew him well—and to perceptive observers who had only passing contact with him.

Logical radicalism, even when combined with righteousness, does not quite ring true; without an inner core of anger and vindictiveness it is hollow, and sometimes fragile as well. Although Lavrov's radicalism was neither hollow nor fragile, it lacked real force. Despite occasional expressions of anger, he simply did not possess the emotional drive which propelled such radicals as Marx and Bakunin. Perhaps this is why Lavrov did not open any new paths and never really led a party, though he was endowed with great intellectual ability. For only the kind of sustained drive possessed by men like Marx and Bakunin (and harnessed to capable intellects) could simultaneously invent, convince, and inspire. That is not to say that Lavrov completely lacked drive and inspirational qualities. However, he could not but notice that he was a "half note lower" than the revolutionaries around him. They noticed it too.

Lavrov was also a half note higher than the amoral positivists and pure scholars with whom he became acquainted soon after his arrival in Paris. He derived little satisfaction from his scholarly associations with members of the Paris Anthropological Society, or from his work on the newly founded *Revue de l'Anthropologie*. He was disgusted at the calm, unconcerned manner in which his colleagues accepted the brutal suppression of the Paris Commune.[41] He never felt that he belonged in Paris' intellectual society in the way that he had belonged in St. Petersburg's. According to G. N. Vyrubov, a prominent Russian émigré scholar and positivist, Lavrov was never taken very seriously by his Parisian colleagues.[42]

40. Turgenev to P. V. Annenkov, Paris, 9 January 1879 in I. S. Turgenev, *Polnoe sobranie sochinenii i pisem,* ed. M. P. Alekseev et al., 28 vols. (Moscow: Nauka, 1966), 12:411.

41. *Golos minuvshego,* 1916, no. 7-8, p. 139. In a letter dated 8 December 1871, Lavrov wrote about a dinner celebrating the founding of the *Revue de l'Anthropologie*.

42. G. N. Vyrubov, "Revoliutsionnye vospominaniia," *Vestnik evropy,* February 1913, p. 61.

Something about Lavrov's attitudes and ideas evoked condescension from men of his generation both to the right and to the left of him, and he, no less critical of them than they were of him, felt isolated. Although in a new setting and with different men holding substantively different sets of ideas, he found himself in the same relative position that he had occupied in St. Petersburg in the 1860s. Furthermore, in the period 1870–72 he was experiencing the severing of a number of important ties without finding any satisfactory new ones. In his two years in Paris he hadn't formed any strong attachments. In fact, he had become something of a Francophobe. In January 1872 he wrote, "I avoid French society and am friendly mostly with German businessmen, to some extent with Jews, and a few Poles."[43] The only reason that he stayed in Paris at all was that the Russian colony there was larger than the one in London, and there were greater possibilities of finding people to copy his manuscripts and to translate them.[44] To further compound his problems, Lavrov's connections with Russian legal journals were, for one reason or another, foundering. In January 1872 he was contemplating severing relations altogether with *Otechestvennye zapiski*. *Delo* was having difficulties with the censorship, and the editor, G. E. Blagosvetlov, in several letters written between April 1872 and December 1872, cautioned Lavrov to avoid sending articles dealing with religion and politics.[45] Lavrov had never succeeded in finding a source of income in Paris. The two projects about which he had written so excitedly to Lopatin simply hadn't materialized. Hence, even though he was a sedentary individual who longed to settle down in one place as quickly as possible and build himself a comfortable nest of books and journals, Lavrov contemplated moving to London or to Zurich.

It would be a mistake to explain in purely negative terms Lavrov's movement toward involvement in émigré politics during the course of 1872. If anything, one might say that his final choice was "over-determined," and it is entirely possible that he would have become a revolutionary socialist journalist and scholar even in the

43. *Golos minuvshego,* 1916, no. 9, p. 114.
44. Ibid., pp. 124–25.
45. Blagosvetlov to Lavrov, 14 October 1872, MS in IISH.

absence of some of the factors mentioned above. Long-established needs were all the while narrowing his choices and guiding him towards the colony of Russian students in Zurich. Thoroughly disenchanted with the older émigrés, he naturally turned to the *molodezh'* ("youth"). The purity and zeal of the new generation, whether real or imagined, kept alive for Lavrov the spirit and meaning of the intelligentsia. Unlike other intellectual émigrés, such as Turgenev and Vyrubov, he could not lead a satisfactory existence outside the milieu of the Russian intelligentsia. Lavrov continually resolved the problem of his isolation in the same way—by moving forward to meet the new generation of the radicals within the intelligentsia. In doing this, however, he merely exchanged one set of personal problems for another. Eventually this practice led to a typically Lavrovian compromise in which he worked with the young radicals and socialized with men of his own generation—writers and scholars whose level of culture and whose life-styles were more like his own.

Lavrov's peculiar modes of adaptation alone were not to blame for this compromise. The position of the older émigrés had always been rather uncomfortable. While inspiring reverence from afar by their publicistic activity, they sometimes surprised their young followers by their ignorance of conditions in Russia, their devotion to stale conventions, and even by their outmoded dress. Herzen had continually affronted and been affronted by the young radical types who came on pilgrimages to London to see him during the heyday of *Kolokol*. Unlike Herzen, Ogarev and Bakunin had sometimes tended to go to the other extreme—to defer to the young activists to the point of self-subordination. This had been particularly true of Bakunin's relationship with Nechaev—one of the great scandals in the émigré community. The Nechaev affair and the collapse of Bakunin's *Alliance* were the beginning of the end of his active role in revolutionary politics, though he was still an inspirational figure despite it all. In any case, the role of émigré publicist and revolutionary theoretician was a peculiarly difficult one, and in 1872 the new intelligentsia circles were casting about for distinguished revolutionary émigrés who could play the part.

Lavrov's *Historical Letters* and other essays on science and morality appearing in *Otechestvennye zapiski* had attracted a considerable following among the younger generation. The disappearance in the 1870s of major intelligentsia ideologues of the 1860s had created a vacuum of leadership: Chernyshevskii was in exile in Siberia; Dobroliubov, Pisarev, and Herzen were dead; Ogarev was muddled, an intellectual ruin incapable of sound decisions. In the 1870s the only émigrés who had sufficient reputation and following to assume leadership of a genuine movement were Lavrov, Bervi-Flerovskii (who returned to Russia from Finland in 1873), and Bakunin. In 1872–73, quite independently of any developed intentions or schemes which either man may have had, both Lavrov and Bakunin were increasingly thought of as the titular heads of distinct revolutionary orientations that were emerging in Zurich, St. Petersburg, and other centers of ferment in the intelligentsia. Both of them were encouraged by young followers to assume leadership of the movement from abroad.

Bakunin fell under the influence of M. P. Sazhin, who had fled Vologda shortly before Lavrov and had traveled to the United States under the name of Armand Ross. In 1870 he had returned to Europe and had become involved in the Nechaev affair, the Bakunin-inspired Lyons uprising, and the Paris Commune. Sazhin was also an important figure in the Zurich colony, where he intrigued with the help of several other Bakuninists, among them Zemfiri Ralli (a Rumanian émigré who had participated in the student disorders of 1868–69 in Russia), A. L. El'snits, and V. A. Gol'shtein—all veterans of the student movement and the Nechaev conspiracy. These younger men, and others, were the real leaders of Bakuninism. Bakunin himself played a very small role in the Zurich colony. He was an international revolutionary, and his ties with the Russian movement as such were not especially strong in 1872. In the course of 1872–73, his expulsion from the International, the collapse of his fragile and semifictitious revolutionary organizations, his failing health, and the extradition of Nechaev from Switzerland led Bakunin to "withdraw from the lists," as he himself put it.[46]

By 1872, Lavrov was preparing to enter the lists. He had, for reasons discussed earlier, resisted previous efforts by young radicals

46. See E. H. Carr, *Michael Bakunin* (New York: Random House, Vintage Books, 1961), chapter 32.

to entangle him in émigré journalism or pamphleteering. In March 1872 he was approached by emissaries from St. Petersburg who wanted him to head an émigré journal. Lavrov presumed that the journal would be an outlet for ideas which Russian radical publicists could not express in the legal press, and that its editor would not create policy, but would only serve to promote general socialist aims.[47] The plan was acceptable to him, since at this stage he still did not have any fixed notions of socialist strategy or development, and he wrote out his initial program, which he believed expressed the ideology of the radical publicists in St. Petersburg who were trying to keep alive the traditions of the 1860s.[48] It was a tentative program, which he assumed would be examined by the groups in Russia that were commissioning the journal. They were to express their opinions about it, correct it according to their views, and help him to formulate a final program. However, against Lavrov's wishes, the tentative program was lithographed and circulated among radical circles in Russia, where it evoked a negative reaction.[49] Accord-

47. This episode has never been completely clarified, not even by Lavrov himself. Meijer's explanation, based upon documents in the IISH, is that a group of St. Petersburg Lavrovists approached Lavrov in March 1872 (Meijer, *Knowledge and Revolution,* p. 115). According to recent accounts, based upon documents in the AOR, Lavrov was visited by A. A. Kril', S. N. Kril' (his wife), and P. F. Baidakovskii. See G. M. Lifshits, "O trekh variantakh programmy 'Vpered'," in *Obshchestvennoe dvizhenie v poreformennoi Rossii* (Moscow: Nauka, 1965), p. 241; B. S. Itenberg, *Dvizhenie revoliutsionnogo narodnichestva* (Moscow: Nauka, 1965), p. 198; N. A. Troitskii, "Osnovanie zhurnala P. L. Lavrova 'Vpered!'," in *Iz istorii obshchestvennoi mysli i obshchestvennogo dvizheniia v Rossii* (Saratov: Saratov Univ. Press, 1964), pp. 98–118. Itenberg disputes both Lifshits's and Troitskii's conclusions. In a more recent study, Boris Sapir accepts Troitskii's evidence but not his conclusion that the Chaikovskii circle was involved. See Boris Sapir, ed., *Vpered! 1873–1877,* 2 vols. (Dordrecht, Neth.: International Institute for Social History, 1970), 1:238–50 (hereafter cited as Sapir, *Vpered!*).

48. See Boris Sapir, "Unknown Chapters in the History of *Vpered!*," *International Review of Social History* 2 (1957):52–77. Lavrov explained the reasons for his three programs in *Narodniki-propagandisty 1873–1878 godov* (St. Petersburg: Tip. T-va Andersona i Loitsiankago, 1907), pp. 56–61; also see Lifshits, "O trekh variantakh programmy 'Vpered'," and Sapir, *Vpered!,* 1:251–63.

49. V. N. Smirnov to A. S. Buturlin, March or April 1873, typed MS in Nicolaevsky Collection, Hoover Institution Archives. Also see Itenberg, *Dvizhenie revoliutsionnogo narodnichestva,* p. 202; he believes the letter was written in October 1873.

ing to Sazhin, hardly an unbiased observer but probably accurate in this account, some members of the Chaikovskii circle, the most important socialist organization in Russia, reacted by saying, "Why do we need a *Vestnik evropy* (Messenger of Europe) abroad when there is already one in Petersburg?"[50] The implication was quite clear: to some radicals Lavrov's tentative program was indistinguishable from a liberal, constitutional program.

The legalism of the tentative program can be traced to Lavrov's belief that he was serving the legal populist tendency represented by Eliseev, with whom he corresponded and whose ideas were well known to him. Only several weeks later did he learn that Eliseev had no connection at all with A. A. Kril' and P. F. Baidakovskii, the "delegates" who had approached Lavrov in March 1872.[51] Thus the program proved to be a tactical error, although it is impossible to measure how many potential supporters Lavrov alienated by his initial misstep. Lavrov had written that four types of legal party might exist in Russia: a government party, supporting the autocracy; a party of constitutional liberals of the European type; a Slavophile party; and a new agrarian socialist party. Formation of an agrarian socialist party had been the immediate practical goal of Lavrov's first program:

Self-government of the commune and secular science—these are the simple principles which must be the motto of the new party. . . . We invite sympathetic readers to help form this political party . . . as the most immediate specific aim, an aim which is far from the full realization of our true social ideal, but which is a step along the road to it and can serve as the basis for future political and social victories.[52]

This kind of emphasis on working within the existing legal framework, combined with his prescription for an exhaustive process of education and his warnings against the use of self-defeating means which could lead to an even harsher reaction—in short, his empha-

50. Sazhin, *Vospominaniia,* p. 38.
51. Certainly a letter from Eliseev to Lavrov on 7 July 1872 clarified Eliseev's position (MS in IISH).
52. Lavrov, quoted in Sapir, "Unknown Chapters in the History of *Vpered!,*" p. 73.

sis upon the possible—created an impression about his program that forced him into a defensive position from the very outset of his career as a revolutionary journalist.[53]

Meanwhile, Lavrov was undergoing another personal crisis. Sometime during the summer of 1872 Anna Chaplitskaia, who had been living and working in Brussels, died.[54] There is scant reference to his life with Anna in his correspondence. In 1870, in several letters to Lopatin, Lavrov had conveyed the regards of "A. P." (her initials) or of "sa petite majesté," no doubt his pet name for her.[55] Sazhin is the only other source on this subject, and he claimed in his memoirs that Lavrov loved her deeply. Certainly her death "shocked him terribly."[56] Deeply fatalistic—in psychological antithesis to his doctrinal voluntarism—Lavrov took Anna's death as an admonition. His personal life with her was the only thing that had stood between him and his duty, and it now seemed to him that fate was forcing him to submit to that duty. Shortly before Anna's death he had been debating the wisdom of accepting the role of revolutionary leader for the young radicals who had approached him. He was now fully aware that he would be more than a mere collaborator or overseas agent of legal publicists in Russia. Some of his old acquaintances had strongly advised against the undertaking. In July 1872 Eliseev had written:

53. Lavrov seemed to call for an extended period of formal education: "The first and necessary condition consists in their [the critically thinking propagandists of the new party] *own* preparation, in the clarification of their own ideas through serious scientific studies. . . . A careful assimilation of all judicial, economic, intellectual, moral, and individual peculiarities of the area in which they work is obligatory." (Ibid., p. 74.) Lifshits agrees that the text published by Sapir is indeed the first program. According to Lifshits's analysis, the first and second programs were quite similar in their emphasis upon peaceful solutions and their cautiousness about means.

54. *Materialy,* p. 21; also see, *P. L. Lavrov, stat'i, vospominaniia, materialy,* pp. 507–8, where it is claimed that she died in Holland. According to Knizhnik-Vetrov, she had earned a living by making artificial flowers for ladies' hats. See *Izbrannye sochineniia,* 1:488 n 363; and "P. L. Lavrov o Parizhskoi Kommune," *Katorga i ssylka,* 1931, no. 10, p. 49.

55. See, for example, letters of June 19 and September 12 (MSS in IISH). At some point between the autumn of 1870 and the summer of 1871, Chaplitskaia left for Brussels.

56. Quoted in *Materialy,* p. 21.

To all appearances the government is satisfied with you. They no doubt expected that having fled abroad you would begin to act like Herzen. . . . After a year or two, or maybe even less, they will agree to your return.[57]

In another letter written shortly after the one quoted above, Eliseev had questioned the right of the molodezh' to make any demands on Lavrov, and had even argued that it was wrong to assume that the group which had approached Lavrov truly represented the views of the younger generation.[58] In short, there had been considerable pressure against him from some of the veterans of the 1860s—men whose opinion he valued highly. Anna's death several weeks later may very well have resolved the question. Lavrov decided to go to the molodezh' in Zurich. In a letter to Shtakenschneider written shortly after his first trip to Zurich, Lavrov wrote:

To you and even more to others not knowing my psychological state, it may seem as though I am sacrificing all to an idea . . . but I have already told you that this is an illusion, that I am not sacrificing anything, because I approach the altar with empty hands. . . . They approached me with this moral duty at the very moment that an implacable and unconscious law of nature severed all the threads which could interfere with and partly countervail against my attraction for that duty. . . . I even believe that I am acting reasonably from a purely egoistic point of view; perhaps this shall rouse me. . . . Besides this, there is nothing.[59]

Lavrov himself was aware of the interesting parallel between this sudden reversal in his personal life and the earlier disastrous episode with Josephina Riul'man, which had coincided with his arrest in 1866.[60] In each case an external force interceded, and latent guilt feelings broke to the surface, appearing as a kind of submissiveness to whatever fate had prepared in the way of punishment.

Anna Chaplitskaia's death came at a moment when Lavrov was already contemplating some sort of move, and it is probably not an exaggeration to say that his decision to go to Zurich was overdetermined. However, this personal tragedy unquestionably altered the nature of Lavrov's commitment, and added sufficient motivational

57. Eliseev to Lavrov, 7 July 1872, MS in IISH.
58. Eliseev to Lavrov, 13 July 1872, MS in IISH.
59. Quoted in *Materialy,* pp. 22–23.
60. *Golos minuvshego,* 1916, no. 9, pp. 135–37. Lavrov suggested that he might have lived out his life as an armchair scholar if he hadn't been arrested in 1866.

force to partly overcome the diffidence which he felt about himself as a leader and a man of action. He now traveled to Zurich fully intending to do his duty, to submit to the molodezh', and to lead them. It was a rather strange kind of commitment, and the style of "leadership" which issued from it was never fully convincing.

During the summer and autumn of 1872, even before Lavrov left Paris for Zurich, he had been contacted by Sazhin, who continued to act as Bakunin's watchdog and who intended to assert Bakuninist control over any promising publishing venture conceived by the colony of Russian émigré socialists.[61] Lavrov already had the reputation of a muddled and eclectic thinker because of his unwillingness to support fully either side in the dispute in the First International. Though clearly leaning toward the federalist position, he nonetheless refused to accept a fully anarchistic program, adopting instead an antinationalist position with provision for political forms of an intermediary nature. In the program written in March 1872, he had supported the idea of a European federation modeled on the United States.[62] Nothing that Lavrov wrote in 1872 about the gradual disappearance of the state was inconsistent with the position that he had taken in the *Historical Letters* or in his interpretation of the Paris Commune. Later (1875–76) he wrote a lengthy treatise on the subject, called *Gosudarstvennyi element v budushchem obshchestve* (The state element in the society of the future). In the autumn of 1872 Lavrov did not believe that the Bakuninists were that far from his own position, and when he discovered that they were interested in a joint journal, he drew up a second program, one which presumably would uphold the unity of the First International and at the same time conciliate the Bakuninists. Actually, the differences in revolutionary temperament and intellectual style exhibited by Lavrov and Bakunin proved to be at least as significant as substantive issues, and hopes for reconciling the two were doomed from the start, as Bakunin himself sensed.

The Lavrovist-Bakuninist split was developing before Lavrov

61. Sazhin to Lavrov, 20 June and 1 August 1872, MSS in IISH.
62. According to Lifshits, this idea had been further developed in the second program (Lifshits, "O trekh variantakh programmy 'Vpered'," pp. 254–55).

had even arrived in Zurich or had begun to lay the foundations for his journal. Lavrov was served well by several followers, especially by S. A. Podolinskii, a medical student in Paris who acted as a Lavrovist agent and transmitted to Lavrov communications from the Lavrovist circles that were forming in Zurich and St. Petersburg. It was Podolinskii who did most during the summer and autumn of 1872 to promote Lavrov's cause. He established the first tie between Lavrov and L. S. Ginzburg, the leader of the Lavrovist faction in St. Petersburg.[63] However, Lavrov's appearance in Zurich in late November (sometime between November 21 and 24) was the final precipitating factor. Bakunin had retired to Locarno and had left the prosecution of his cause in the hands of Ross, El'snits, and Ralli.

Lavrov won for himself an important ally in Valerian Nikolaevich Smirnov. Another veteran of the student disorders of 1869 and of the Nechaevist organizations in Moscow, he was one of a number of students who had been released into their parents' custody, and had eventually found his way to Zurich. He had been associated with the Bakuninists V. A. Gol'shtein and A. L. El'snits. In August 1872, several weeks before Lavrov's arrival in Zurich, Smirnov had written to A. S. Buturlin that he did not find much to choose from between Lavrov and Bakunin.[64] Now, under the impact of Lavrov's presence, he underwent a kind of conversion. Lavrov organized a series of lectures and *Konversationstunden* for the Zurich colony which produced both favorable and unfavorable responses: the Bakuninists, of course, found him tedious and pedantic; but the colony as a whole was quite sympathetic to Lavrov's rationalistic approach and style. Smirnov, for example, was impressed by Lavrov's ability to produce rational arguments and evidence about even "details," while simultaneously projecting to his audience a passionate commitment to the social cause.[65] In short, Lavrov appeared to be the perfect combination of reason and feeling, and Smirnov found him much more

63. Meijer, *Knowledge and Revolution,* pp. 116–17; Itenberg, *Dvizhenie revoliutsionnogo narodnichestva,* pp. 199–200.

64. Smirnov to Buturlin, 13 August 1872, typed MS in Nicolaevsky Collection, Hoover Institution Archives.

65. Smirnov to Buturlin, 4 December 1872, typed MS in Nicolaevsky Collection, Hoover Institution Archives.

impressive than the charismatic but imprecise and unpredictable Bakunin. Smirnov wholeheartedly joined the faction that formed around Lavrov in December 1872.

When the final showdown over a joint program occurred, Lavrov, Podolinskii, and Smirnov confronted Ross and El'snits, Bakunin's agents. Negotiations between Lavrov and the Bakuninists did not break down over the program as such, but rather over the editorship of the journal. Sazhin claims that Lavrov first offered him a position as coeditor, and then, after Sazhin went to Locarno to seek Bakunin's advice, withdrew the offer. Actually, neither Bakunin nor most of his followers in Zurich, other than Sazhin, were terribly interested in wresting control of the journal from Lavrov. When Sazhin returned to Zurich, instead of trying to pressure Lavrov into further programmatic changes, he directly challenged him on the problem of coeditorship. The final breakdown occurred on 16 December 1872.[66]

Ironic as it may seem, there was never a genuine confrontation between the men whose names were later to become associated with the two major revolutionary strategies of the 1870s in Russia. The split between Bakuninist and Lavrovist factions in Zurich and in Russia was primarily the creation of the younger generation, which had formed very definite conclusions about the differences between the two men on the basis of their writings and behavior. Lavrov— and in this he was mistaken—never really felt that the differences between himself and Bakunin were very great, and tended to blame Bakunin's young followers, especially Sazhin, for creating a split over secondary points.[67] In essence, the formation of the two camps reveals more about the increasing differences within the new generation of intelligenty than about the theoretical dispute between

66. See Meijer, *Knowledge and Revolution,* pp. 117–19; and Sazhin, *Vospominaniia,* pp. 39–41.

67. Lavrov recognized Bakunin's value as a revolutionary agitator but abhorred his propensity for scandal. Lavrov's necrologue over Bakunin in *Vpered!,* 1876, no. 36, said as much. In it Lavrov regretted that Bakunin had surrounded himself with disreputable types and had succumbed to their influence at times. In his numerous articles, and in his history of the revolutionary movement between 1873 and 1878, Lavrov refrained from any attack on Bakunin.

Bakunin and Lavrov. One can say with some certainty that distinct emotional and intellectual orientations existed before the ideologies themselves appeared. Bakunin appealed to the more impatient and militant types within the intelligentsia, who quickly seized the initiative in many of the developing circles in Russia, especially in the south. Lavrov himself later became convinced that Bakuninists dominated the revolutionary movement in 1873–76.[68] However, in Zurich the Lavrovists were victorious.

Sazhin's belief that Lavrov had wanted to capture leadership in the revolutionary movement is not at all convincing in view of Lavrov's attitudes both before and after the creation of *Vpered!*. Having been rejected by the raznochintsy during the 1860s, uncertain of his own qualifications for leadership in the revolutionary movement, he needed continual reassurance from the youth that they indeed wanted and needed him. He refused to lead without a mandate; but once granted the mandate, he became a zealous proponent of the revolutionary strategy which was later called "preparationism." In his own words:

I felt a moral duty to struggle with all my might in concert with people standing with me and voluntarily submitting to my personal leadership, while my past didn't provide them with the least assurance [*ruchatel'stvo*] of my competency for a political matter of this sort.[69]

He staked all on the molodezh', for the Petersburg publicists upon whom he had counted heavily as contributors to the projected journal, refused to collaborate and actively discouraged him.[70] The

68. Lavrov, *Narodniki-propagandisty,* p. 59.
69. Ibid., p. 60.
70. It must have been something of a surprise to Lavrov to find that neither Antonovich, Eliseev, or Mikhailovskii would cooperate on the journal. Their pessimism, however, did not dissuade him. Mikhailovskii's letters to Lavrov about the journal were published in *Minuvshie gody* 1908, no. 1, pp. 125–28. In view of their rather cold relationship, it seems curious that Lavrov and Mikhailovskii are so often linked together in much of the historiography of the Russian revolutionary movement. Actually they belong together only on a theoretical plane—that of a fundamentally subjectivistic and "critical" populism, to borrow Billington's phrase—and even here they were in sharp disagreement. As an editor of *Nedelia* Mikhailovskii had criticized Lavrov's *Istoricheskie pis'ma* and had wanted to suspend their serial publication, while Lavrov had criticized Mikhailovskii's formula of progress

journal was no sooner underway when objections to its program and tone further discouraged him. In 1895, more than twenty years after the founding of *Vpered!*, Lavrov wrote:

Inside, I hadn't the slightest hopes then [in the winter and spring of 1873] that it would survive for four years. If I had known the state of affairs a year earlier, as well as I knew it in the spring of 1873, I would certainly have rejected the whole business, considering it neither useful nor [even] possible to begin it.[71]

During 1873 Lavrov acquired a new public identity as a socialist leader. All of his extraordinary discipline, his hypertrophied conscience, and his sense of honor and loyalty were now poured into his conception of partiinost'. This transfer of basic values and orientations from one frame of reference to another was not completed until Lavrov's fiftieth year. A sense of depersonalization accompanied the process of transfer. Lavrov thought that the noble abstractions of socialism should be served purely—that only the best part of a man belonged to socialism and therefore to history. Any form of behavior which might injure the cause or divert energy from the struggle against exploitation and competition had to be suppressed. A man could belong to history only as a disembodied socialist conscience. One of Lavrov's letters to Shtakenschneider in April 1873 sounds very much like the self-analysis of a man who has just taken monastic vows, who has left his personal life behind him. Even in the spring of 1873, however, one finds a great deal of skepticism and bitterness in his confession to Shtakenschneider:

I am not sacrificing a thing, absolutely nothing, because I don't have anything to sacrifice.

I don't have a penny's worth of faith in people; I know that individual passions, individual egoisms, petty calculations, personal vanities play a quite important role everywhere around me, alongside sincere and half-sincere convictions. . . . I haven't any hopes. I don't believe in people.[72]

in a major article published in *Otechestvennye zapiski,* 1870, no. 2, pp. 228–55.

71. Lavrov, *Narodniki-propagandisty,* p. 60.

72. *Golos minuvshego,* 1916, no. 9, pp. 136–37.

Lavrov had always felt himself to be above the compromising St. Petersburg intelligentsia. He had learned about the foibles of the honored leaders of European socialism. He had seen the best men that European civilization had produced, yet all were the victims of vanities and passions. Hence he could only serve abstractions—the abstract ideals of socialism, his own idealization of the younger generation of socialist intellectuals, and his conception of the awakened masses.

To the younger revolutionaries Lavrov presented his concept of duty, combined with his ideas of socialist conviction, free will, and historical indeterminism. He demanded fortitude and a spirit of self-sacrifice:

But what kind of people with convictions have the *right,* the *moral right* "to relax, to forget themselves, to doze"? Who has the right to refuse the burden weighing upon him, the suffering inevitable for him, when, sustaining this burden a few paces further, enduring these sufferings a few years longer, he might move forward that which he believes in one-millionth of a stride? These infinitely small fractions comprise the entire future of humanity, and—who knows?—but for this little link, which *You,* namely *You* could place in the endless chain of events—but for this very link, the entire chain will be destroyed. It isn't fatal, but consists of will, decisiveness, and action. No, no one has the right "to relax, to forget himself, to doze" if he *believes.*[73]

Lavrov believed only in the *possible* victory of socialism, a victory that could be achieved only if all those who held socialist values disciplined themselves for the struggle and gave themselves wholly to it. In 1873 he didn't foresee a quick and decisive overthrow of the old order. Although he seemed to have had no doubts that the capitalistic state was doomed, he was fearful that the new society, which would be erected upon its ruins, would preserve the deleterious elements of the old society and that another era of misery would emerge. Only the eternal vigilance of men with socialist convictions would ensure the emergence of a better social order. Lavrov's idea of socialist discipline followed rather easily from his earlier ascetic devotion to critical thought: the embattled critically thinking minority became the embattled socialist minority. Although many important

73. Lavrov to Rosaliia Khristoforovna Idel'son (Smirnov's wife), 11 December 1873, typed MS in IISH.

features of Lavrov's socialism were later violently opposed by the Bolsheviks (most importantly his association with the Narodnaia Volia-SR stream), his ascetic, voluntaristic doctrines helped to keep alive the very tradition from which the Bolsheviks sprang. Lavrov, of course, strongly rejected the idea of a small, exclusive party. Just as he had earlier wanted the critically thinking minority to transform itself by multiplication and proselytization, he now wanted the socialist minority to carry to the masses the new ethic of science and solidarity. The socialist intelligentsia's role was to be pedagogical, not political, but in order to accomplish even its pedagogical task it had to reject the world, reject individualism, and submit to party discipline. These ideas, adumbrated in *Historical Letters,* were fully developed in *Vpered!*.

6.
The *Vpered!* Years

Immediately after the break with the Bakuninists in Zurich, Lavrov began to solicit help from leading members of the International for his journal. By mid-December 1872, he had worked out in his mind the major policies and even the format of *Vpered!*. Despite his announced intention to offer a broad program, one which would appeal to socialists of all stripes, it is quite clear that the Zurich debate had pushed him further in the direction of Bakunin's program than he himself would admit. Lavrov responded more readily to pressures from the younger generation of activists than to the attacks and criticism of his own peers, so that while claiming to stand on neutral ground between Marx and Bakunin, he actually moved closer to Bakunin's federalism and, as shall be seen shortly, even found a place for "revolutionary passion" in his strategy.

Lavrov, of course, had been scandalized by the behavior of both Marxists and Bakuninists during the crisis of the International. He therefore sought the collaboration of "neutrals" like himself. In a letter to H. Jung he wrote:

You know that your point of view was generally that with which I sympathized the most during the struggle of the parties of the International. You will do me a great service in sending me your views in general on the course of events of the International and especially in England, and it will be especially fortunate for me to count among our collaborators a man whom I particularly esteem, and with whom I share the majority of opinions. The Bakuninists . . . will set up their own publication from their point of view. It is unfortunate, but nothing to be afraid of.[1]

In February 1873 Lavrov presented Jung with a description of the journal's planned format:

1. Lavrov to H. Jung, 18 December 1872, MS in IISH. I have translated these from the original French. Boris Nicoloaevsky published the letters in Russian translation in "Pis'ma P. L. Lavrova k Germanu Iungu," *Letopisi Marksizma* 2 (1930):155–72.

The revue *Forward* will be in Russian and will appear as a volume of twenty printer's leaves, or thereabouts. It will contain in the first place . . . articles on social questions in general and on Russian social questions in particular. Collaborators will work on studies of the history of socialist theories, on the history of the International, on the history of the oppositional movements in Russia, on peasant revolts occurring in Russia in recent years, on law, on popular education, and, finally, on theoretical questions of socialism. Then will come the section devoted to the chronicle. It will contain in the first place the International workers' movement, the literary movement and its relationship to socialism, a satirical glimpse of European politics in relation to the social movement and to the disintegration of bourgeois society, and, finally, the popular, social movement in Russia and in the Slavic countries with as many details as I can get. This chronicle will be divided into general articles, grouped according to special correspondence, and these latter, the correspondence, will be of two kinds; those treating the most significant events will be published separately and in their entirety. The others (and these will constitute the most) will provide an account of the current state of affairs in different countries, and will be integral parts of the general articles.

. . . Without question it is on Russian soil and in Russian questions that our revue's most serious struggles will take place, but I do not intend to eliminate entirely general questions about universal socialism. I believe that I've written to you that I take the point of view of the international workers' movement with its general goals, independent of parties. Centralists and anarchists can find a place in the revue in which to discuss general questions, but only while avoiding quite strictly any kind of insult. Bourgeois monopoly, the bourgeois state—here are our sole enemies.[2]

It is clear from Lavrov's letter to Jung that *Vpered!* was destined to become a journal of information rather than one of inspiration. Lavrov's scholarly meticulousness and his intention to present the reading public with several points of view were disadvantages rather than assets in his new milieu. He inevitably ended by trying to convince rather than destroy his opponent. Only when he felt that his own dignity had been unnecessarily called into question, that his opponent had resorted to a "personal attack," did he rise up in righteousness and wrath. Even on these occasions he never learned how to dismiss an opponent's arguments with a sneer, or how to

2. Lavrov to Jung, 21 February 1873, MS in IISH.

heap scorn upon him. Many thought that he lacked revolutionary passion, revolutionary style.

In March 1873 Lavrov and his helpers worked feverishly to keep the Bakuninists, who were preparing to publish *Gosudarstvennost' i anarkhiia* (Statism and anarchy), from stealing a march on them. Lithographed copies of *Vpered!*'s new program were smuggled into Russia before the journal itself appeared in its initial form as a "nonperiodical."[3]

There was nothing strikingly new in Lavrov's final, narrowed program—nothing that hadn't appeared in European and Russian socialist theories during the previous two decades. The meaning of European liberalism had been clear since 1848. Bourgeois republicanism was simply the form of statism that supported monopolistic capitalism against the aspirations of the working classes. Political questions were secondary to social and, especially, economic ones.[4] Although some liberal doctrines were upheld for obvious reasons (freedom of speech and association, for example), alliances with bourgeois parties were condemned. The struggle to be joined was an international war of labor against monopolistic capitalism, but it had to be waged according to local conditions.

In Russia the zemstvo had proven to be undemocratic, and there was no reason to believe that it wouldn't remain so. The possibility of peasants being represented in a *zemskii sobor* ("national assembly") though more in keeping with the goals of Russian socialists, was thought to be remote.[5] *Vpered!*'s program had as its narrower goal the realization of Russian agrarian socialism. Central to it was a belief in the convertibility of the peasant commune into the building blocks of a socialist society.[6] Even these ideas were subordinated to Lavrov's wider vision of the struggle between science and religion, competition and solidarity. He advocated destruction of the old economic order, of the state, and of the traditional family. Society had to be completely purged of its old institutions and morals. Without this the new social order might absorb diseases and

3. See letter from Lavrov to G. N. Vyrubov, 30 March 1873, MS in IISH; *Byloe,* 1925, no. 30, p. 18.
4. "Nasha programma," *Vpered!* 1 (Zurich, 1873): 7–8.
5. Ibid., p. 20.
6. Ibid., p. 11.

poisons from the old, dooming itself from the very beginning. In short, Lavrov advocated a fresh start, based upon the only healthy institutional and moral elements within the old society in Russia—the peasant commune and the socialist intelligentsia.

To develop our commune in the sense of communal cultivation of land and communal use of its products, to convert the commune's assembly into the basic political element of the Russian social order, to absorb private property into communal, to give the peasant that education and that understanding of his social needs without which he will never be able to use his legal rights, no matter how broad, and will never escape the exploitation of the minority, even in the event of the most successful revolution—here are specifically Russian goals, which every Russian must support if he desires progress for his homeland.[7]

Lavrov clearly disassociated himself and his journal from anything that smacked of Nechaevism or intelligentsia elitism. He accepted the idea that ends justify means, but with the proviso that the means used should not undermine the ends. This stipulation, of course, was aimed at devious and highly centralized political plots.

We place at the forefront the proposition that the reconstruction of Russian society must be accomplished not only with the people's happiness as its goal, not only *for* the people, but by means of the people. The contemporary Russian revolutionary must, according to our view, abandon the obsolete opinion that one can only impose revolutionary ideas upon the people—ideas manufactured by a small group, a more highly developed minority—and that the socialist-revolutionaries, having overthrown the central government by a successful coup, can replace it and create a new order congenial to the masses by legal means. . . . We don't want to change the old coercive force for a new one, no matter what its source.[8]

He also clearly distinguished his doctrine from that of the Bakuninists by demanding that revolutionary socialists prepare themselves to teach the people socialist knowledge before a revolution. Only preparation could bring about a successful social revolution. Conscious socialist morality had to be firmly established before the destruction of the old order.[9]

7. Ibid.
8. Ibid., p. 12.
9. Ibid., pp. 14–15.

Lavrov never abandoned his idea of preparation, though later he applied it rather flexibly to the developing strategies of revolutionary populism; in fact, it became something of a fiction, just as the idea of a bourgeois phase of historical development became a kind of fiction in Bolshevik Marxist doctrine. One could not do without these ideas, because they were an essential part of historical science— of a theory of progress—but for all practical purposes they were circumvented or contradicted by revolutionary strategies. The oft-repeated idea of preparation was ultimately more significant for the further damage that it did to Lavrov's already dubious reputation as a revolutionary leader in populist circles which had, in effect, already gone through a phase of "preparation." To be sure, Lavrov's program had some appeal for individuals and groups that still believed in the tasks of enlightenment, but they themselves tended to lose credit in the revolutionary milieu after 1873.

In simplest terms, Lavrov had misjudged the mood of the new generation of the revolutionary intelligentsia. His program was designed under the influence of his experiences in Zurich in the autumn and winter of 1872, when Nechaevism and Bakuninism were strongly repudiated by the vast majority of the Russian colony.[10] The youth seemed to want something uncompromisingly revolutionary and socialistic but also solid. Lavrov felt that he could move to the left to satisfy them but simultaneously remain true to his conception of the pedagogical role of the intelligentsia. Furthermore, many of his Russian contacts, who had been part of the radical vanguard during the 1860s, had provided him with a rather pessimistic picture of Russian conditions. Hardly any of the information that he was receiving before the publication of the first volume of *Vpered!* in the summer of 1873 could have helped him to anticipate the mood of the radical vanguard in Russia or to know that Bakunin's relative decline among those in emigration was not a true indication of his appeal in Russia.

Even more important than the program itself, Lavrov's article, "Znanie i revoliutsiia" (Knowledge and revolution), which he presented as an excerpt from a letter to an unidentified correspondent,

10. Bakunin estimated that the Lavrovists outnumbered the Bakuninists several times over. See Meijer, *Knowledge and Revolution,* p. 119.

became the real focus of controversy over Lavrov's position. Copies of the first volume of *Vpered!* were smuggled into Russia in the late summer of 1873, several months after the lithographed program had been circulated. According to a prominent student of Russian revolutionary populism:

No single writing of the ideologues of populism evoked such violent quarrels among the participants of the movement as did this article. And this was not at all accidental. The youths involved [in the movement] were immediately concerned with the question about the interaction of knowledge and revolution.[11]

Many of the activists who read "Knowledge and Revolution" interpreted it to mean that the revolutionary had to undergo an extended period of self-education before he could go into the countryside to educate the peasant masses. In the introductory part of "Knowledge and Revolution" Lavrov stated that

the role of the vanguard of our youth who desire the welfare of the people, consists first of all, in drawing near to the people [*sblizit'sia s narodom*]; secondly, in preparing them for the moment when they will be able to throw off the oppressive state order, to destroy the old restrictive social forms and to establish a new society according to *their* needs, according to their goals; and last, thirdly, the role of the vanguard of our youth consists in helping the people, *with all of the strength that they* [the youth] *have acquired,* to establish, in that difficult moment when the struggle has been joined, not an ephemeral but a *solid* new state of affairs.[12]

However, although he designated "drawing near to the people" as the first part of his general strategy in this introductory statement, he devoted the remainder of the article to the proposition that a revolutionary could not possibly be effective without a rigorous scientific preparation. And here Lavrov revealed his own remoteness from the mentality of the Russian peasant masses. He believed that in order to be convincing, the revolutionary propagandist would have to be able to present his peasant interlocutors with both statistical and physiological information when explaining, for example, infant mortality rates.[13] Furthermore, how could one explain to the

11. Itenberg, *Dvizhenie revoliutsionnogo narodnichestva,* p. 213.
12. *Vpered!* 1 (1873):220.
13. Ibid., p. 227.

peasants the reasons for their economic ruin without first studying the laws of the accumulation of capital, of rent formation, of price fluctuations? One should note in passing that Lavrov cited Bakunin twice in support of his general position, without any ironic intent.[14] He actually wanted the weight of Bakunin's authority behind the argument.

The central concept in "Knowledge and Revolution" is not so much *znanie* ("knowledge") or *nauka* ("science"), as *prochnost'* ("solidity" or "firmness"). All of the phases of revolutionary preparation and consolidation described in "Knowledge and Revolution" were designed to ensure the emergence of a solidly founded socialist system. Lavrov provided the youth with several examples of revolutions that had failed for lack of critical awareness and prochnost'.[15] But from the point of view of a significant segment of the younger generation he demanded both too much and too little. Some of them came away from "Knowledge and Revolution" with the impression that Lavrov meant years of formal training in universities or technical institutes. That was simply too much. Others felt that Lavrov's program did not encourage the intelligentsia to give themselves wholly to the masses. In this respect he demanded too little.

Memoirists who compared Lavrov's *Vpered!* with Bakunin's *Statism and Anarchy,* suggest that Bakunin was closer to the mood of revolutionary youth. Peter Kropotkin, whose brother Alexander was one of Lavrov's earliest supporters, wrote:

The first number of *Vpered!* sorely disappointed us, with the exception of a very few [articles]. All of us in Petersburg—Klements, Kravchinskii, Sofie Perovskaia, Obodovskaia, Popov, Serdiukov, Tikhomirov, Charushin—conducted socialist and revolutionary propaganda among the workers in the textile factories [*fabriki*] and metal-works [*zavody*] and in the construction arteli of Petersburg. . . . In this autumn and winter the mass movement of young propagandists to the narod, to the villages and towns, was already conceived. But Lavrov's article in the

14. Ibid., pp. 223–31.
15. In fact, the only revolutions in modern history that Lavrov considered to be successful were the English revolution of 1688 and the American revolution. But these were political, not social, revolutions, according to contemporary social thought.

first number of *Vpered!* was directly contrary to these strivings. It called the youth to study in universities, instead of working at socialist and revolutionary propaganda. We were deeply disappointed with the journal *Vpered!*[16]

Actually, Kropotkin was the leader of the Bakuninist faction in the Chaikovskii circle, and he retrospectively exaggerated Bakunin's strength. The Chaikovskii circle never really committed itself clearly either to a Lavrovist or Bakuninist position, although one of the members of the circle, M. V. Kupriianov, had gone to Zurich in May 1873 and had arranged for the circle to distribute *Vpered!*[17] One would imagine that Lavrov's eclectic socialism should have appealed to the *Chaikovtsy.* Their circles read and distributed a wide variety of European and Russian socialist authors, including Marx, Lasalle, Louis Blanc, Bervi-Flerovskii, Lavrov, Chernyshevskii, and Dobroliubov. The Chaikovtsy seem to have been opposed to *Vpered!* on emotional rather than intellectual grounds. Indeed, one may say with some certainty that in 1873 Bakuninism fulfilled the emotional needs of a more significant portion of the activists from the ranks of both the raznochintsy and the "repentant nobles" than did Lavrovism. Ironically enough, Bakuninism could never be much more than an emotional attitude, since circumstances forced the *buntari* ("insurrectionists") into propagandistic activities. They never succeeded in their attempts either to fuse with the masses or to unleash their fury. However, the nature of the Bakuninists' commitment, their heroic attempt to repudiate their former identities immediately and to bring about an immediate revolution, had the effect of forcing the Lavrovists into the background. The

16. P. A. Kropotkin, "Vospominaniia o Lavrove," in *P. L. Lavrov, Stat'i, vospominaniia, materialy,* p. 438. Paul Aksel'rod described the reactions of a group of young revolutionaries in Kiev: "In general, to the revolutionary youths it seemed that Lavrovism turned them away from the true revolutionary path, that by its constant reservations it put off revolutionary activity for an indefinite time, while we wanted to give all of our strength immediately. . . . Undoubtedly, Bakunin intoxicated us, especially with his revolutionary phraseology and flowing oratory." (P. Aksel'rod, *Perezhitoe i peredumannoe* [Berlin: 1923] 1:111).

17. For a recent account see Martin A. Miller, "Ideological Conflicts in Russian Populism: The Revolutionary Manifestoes of the Chaikovsky Circle, 1869–1874," *Slavic Review* 29 (March 1970):14–15.

young revolutionaries who gravitated towards Bakuninism tended to remain in the active struggle, to develop new strategies, and to become professional revolutionaries. The relative dearth of Lavrovist memoirs suggests that Lavrovists either remained on the fringes of the movement or left it after a few years of activity. Lavrov's earlier demand that the socialist minority assess the *possibilities* for revolutionary activity and withdraw in the face of overwhelming obstacles evidently struck a responsive chord in his followers, who were less inclined than the Bakuninists either to repudiate their old identity or to unleash a great tide of destruction.

The Russian Lavrovists were concentrated mainly in St. Petersburg, but there were also Lavrovist groups in Moscow, Odessa, Kiev, Tver, and Aleksandrov.[18] The two most important Lavrovist figures in Russia were Lev Savel'evich Ginzburg (a student in the Medico-Surgical Academy in St. Petersburg) and Alexander Sergeevich Buturlin. The former was the leader of a group of about thirty Lavrovists in St. Petersburg, while Buturlin was the central figure in the smaller Moscow circle and was also the journal's major means of financial support.

The major activities of the Petersburg circle were fund-raising and smuggling. During *Vpered!*'s existence they managed to send five or six thousand rubles a year to support the journal.[19] Many of the Lavrovists (unlike Bakuninists, who thought that higher education increased the distance between them and the people and was, in any case, useless) completed their courses of studies and drifted away from the movement. Ginzburg became a zemstvo doctor, as did two other important members of the circle.[20] Furthermore, the Lavrovists refused to dress up as workers or peasants. Although some of them participated in the "drawing near to the people," most

18. The Odessa circle is described in S. L. Chudnovskii, *Iz davnikh let. Vospominaniia* (Moscow: Politkatorzhan, 1934).

19. Most of the information about the Lavrovist circles is based upon N. G. Kuliabko-Koretskii, *Iz davnikh let* (Moscow: Politkatorzhan, 1931). Kuliabko-Koretskii's estimate of the money sent by the St. Petersburg circle may be a little high, given Smirnov's estimate of the amount needed to sustain the journal and the fact that it was barely sustained financially, even with some slight support from other sources. Also see Sapir, *Vpered!*, 1:310–12.

20. Ibid., p. 172.

of the Lavrovists preferred to remain in Petersburg and to spread their propaganda in Petersburg workers' arteli. *Vpered!* was an organ of workers' socialism and was one of the first journals to spread information in Russia about the European working-class movement.[21] Stepan Khalturin, organizer of the Northern Union of Russian Workers, had had contacts with the Petersburg Lavrovists, and *Vpered!* was one of the main sources of ideas and inspiration for the Union.[22]

In no case was there a highly structured, smoothly functioning network of organizations among the Lavrovists. The usual organizational form was the *kruzhok* ("circle") in which small numbers of like-minded individuals agreed to raise funds for *Vpered!,* to smuggle it into Russia, and to distribute it.[23] Propagandist activities were evidently pursued on a highly individualistic basis. Lavrov's doctrines attracted mature, academic types who believed in socialism but did not believe that higher education should be sacrificed. The Bakuninists resented them because of their refusal to throw off the old ways at once. To the Bakuninists, their soberness and their whole demeanor suggested superciliousness, lack of enthusiasm, and compromise, just as had Lavrov's program.

In historical perspective, however, the Lavrovists seem to have had a clearer conception of Russian reality, and seem to have been less inclined than the Bakuninists to pursue mirages. Of course, in the strained emotional atmosphere of the revolutionary circles, these virtues were often seen as defects. Rarely in the literature does one find a favorable view of the preparationists like Vera Figner's description of Anton Taksis, a Petersburg Lavrovist:

21. Even G. V. Plekhanov, one of Lavrov's severest critics, admitted that *Vpered!* played an important early role in the proletarian movement, such as it was. See A. Thun, *Istoriia revoliutsionnykh dvizhenii v Rossii* (Moscow: 1923), preface, p. 15.

22. For a description of the Northern Workers' Union, see Franco Venturi, *Roots of Revolution,* pp. 551–57. E. Zaslavskii, head of the Southern Workers' Union, also had connections with *Vpered!* (ibid., p. 516). Also see Sh. M. Levin, *Obshchestvennoe dvizhenie v Rossii,* p. 439. Levin also discusses a tendency exhibited by Lavrovists in Russia to move toward the urban proletariat, as opposed to the peasants, as their main object of propaganda (ibid., pp. 379–81).

23. Difficulties of transport and smuggling are discussed in Kuliabko-Koretskii, *Iz davnikh let,* pp. 95–96, 103–16, 140–41.

He supported me in the most difficult times and provided me with some principles which have never left me. He showed me some of the reasons for the failure of the revolutionary movement. As a genuine Lavrovist he saw the evil not in an overly theoretical formulation of the cause, but in the unpreparedness, the lack of practicality, and the ignorance of those involved. He deeply believed in the future of the revolutionary cause and viewed present circumstances as an ephemeral phase, inevitable in a movement which had barely begun. Besides this, he constantly assured me that the cause did not need outbursts, but patient and painstaking work; that the results . . . might be insignificant, but that we must accept this and not give up, since every new idea embodies itself only slowly, and, in given historical circumstances, each does only what he is able to do. He even supported me in my wish to leave Moscow and to settle in the countryside to see for myself what kind of sphinx the narod was.[24]

Ironically, Lavrov himself later parted company with the Lavrovists and allied himself with the Bakuninist–Land and Freedom–People's Will stream of development—the activist current in the populist movement. G. V. Plekhanov's assessment of Lavrovists in the late 1870s probably reflects the attitude which prevailed among the activists. He described them as

a rather high-minded group of sectarians, stubbornly and monotonously condemning everything that caused the hearts of the "radicals" of those days to beat faster: student uprisings, strikes, demonstrations of sympathy for political prisoners, mass protests against the administration's arbitrariness, etc.[25]

The Lavrovists remained true to their interpretation of the *Historical Letters* and *Vpered!*'s program, continuing to spread propaganda, especially among Petersburg workers, and carefully assessing new social and economic developments. They refused to permit the heart to tyrannize over the mind.

It is the history of the Lavrovist group in Zurich and, later, in London which will be pursued here. Curious though it may seem, Lavrov's connection with Russian Lavrovism was quite tenuous, and his relations with the men who purported to represent his revolutionary strategy rather strained. Lavrov's Zurich group was establishing *Vpered!* as the dominant journalistic enterprise abroad at a

24. V. Figner, *Vospominaniia,* 2 vols. (Moscow, Mysl', 1964), 1:135–36.
25. Quoted in Levin, *Obshchestvennoe dvizhenie v Rossii,* pp. 378–79.

moment when Bakuninism was becoming the dominant tendency in the Russian movement. The victory over the Bakuninists in Zurich was a hollow one, however. After the initial excitement of getting out the program and the first volume of the nonperiodical journal, Lavrov and his dedicated group of followers suffered some severe setbacks. The first blow did not come from ideological opponents within the revolutionary movement, but rather from the Russian government. On 3 June 1873 the government issued a decree calling home the Russian woman students in Zurich, giving them until 1 January 1874 to comply with the decree. The consequences of noncompliance would be exclusion from any government-sponsored occupation and from the Russian educational system. Lavrov and Alexander Kropotkin spoke to the students on June 7, and the *Vpered!* group issued Lavrov's pamphlet, *Russkim tsiurichskim studentkam* (To the Russian woman students in Zurich), shortly thereafter.[26] In it Lavrov expressed his sense of the precariousness of the émigré's position and of his dependence upon contact with and support from Russia. Within the next few months the colony of more than 150 students (the male students left as well) melted away, and with it the communal institutions that they had created.[27] Upon their return to Russia, many of them followed Lavrov's advice to join the revolutionary movement.

During the winter of 1873–74 Lavrov also experienced the first frustrations and splits within his own group. Opposition to *Vpered!*'s general tone and to his own article, "Znanie i revoliutsiia" (Knowledge and revolution), caused him great anguish. He had evidently expected wholehearted devotion from *Vpered!*'s supporters. In an angry letter to Lopatin concerning the article "Knowledge and Revolution" and a manifesto written against it by young revolutionaries who nominally supported *Vpered!,* he wrote:

When I'm in Paris I'll read it [the manifesto] to you in its original form and . . . we'll talk about this rubbish. When I think that these are the present representatives of our *molodezh'*, and that they are not without influence, and when I compare them with the youth of the sixties, it

26. For a description of these events, see Meijer, *Knowledge and Revolution,* pp. 140–44.
27. Ibid., p. 147.

sometimes occurs to me that [there is no point in] editing a serious journal for groups who don't even know the alphabet. The only hope is that besides hypocritical and idiotic rubbish of this sort there are others. But are they numerous?[28]

Tkachev, who had joined the staff of *Vpered!* in December 1873, attempted at first to subvert the journal from within. He did this by transmitting to Lavrov the opinions of certain "radicals" who disagreed with the strategy set forth in "Knowledge and Revolution." Although Lavrov refused to alter his stand, the dissension on the journal utterly demoralized him. There was no word from his followers in Petersburg, and he had received word that *Vpered!* had been severely criticized in southern Russia.[29] One finds evidence of deep depression and fatigue in Lavrov's correspondence of this period.

Finding Zurich inhospitable after the departure of the students, Lavrov planned to transport his enterprise to London.[30] He was determined to pursue an independent course. His relationship with Marx was strained, and with Bakunin, worse still.[31] Among the members of the First International, Jung and Greulich were his closest friends and confidants. Lavrov asked Jung to help him find a house in London for *Vpered!'s* printing equipment and staff, and during March of 1874 the equipment was moved from the Forsthaus in Zurich to Tollington Park, London.[32]

The transfer of the entire enterprise to London was a healthy move. It seemed to distract Lavrov from his bitter disappointment over the reception of "Knowledge and Revolution" in Russia. However, soon after the move a new storm broke. Shortly after the group arrived in London, Tkachev deserted *Vpered!* and attacked Lavrov in a pamphlet entitled *Zadachi revoliutsionnoi propagandy v Rossii* (The aims of revolutionary propaganda in Russia). This was not an entirely deceitful move, even though Tkachev had remained on

28. Lavrov to Lopatin, 11 January 1874, MS in IISH.
29. Lavrov to Lopatin, 30 January 1874, MS in IISH.
30. Lavrov to Jung, 28 August 1873, MS in IISH.
31. "Depuis Londres je mis en froid avec Marx et pour des raisons particulières je suis plus mal encore avec Bakunine." (Ibid.)
32. Lavrov to Lopatin, 13 March 1874, MS in IISH. The printing apparatus was set up at 20 Murray Road, Tollington Park, Holloway, London.

Vpered!'s staff until the day before his pamphlet appeared. Evidently he had taken every opportunity to provoke Lavrov and other members of the staff. He teased Lavrov about his relations with Marx. Above all, he demanded an editorial role on the journal. However, despite evidence that Tkachev's views strongly contradicted *Vpered!*'s program, Lavrov did not have a clear understanding of those views.[33] Early in March 1874 Tkachev had attacked Smirnov's article—"Revoliutsionery iz privilegirovannoi sredy" (Revolutionaries from a privileged milieu), appearing in the second volume of *Vpered!*—in which Smirnov had derided the pretensions of the intelligentsia as a revolutionary force.[34] Lavrov himself dissented from Smirnov's position that revolutionaries who had grown up in a "privileged" milieu were ill-equipped for revolutionary tasks. On March 13 Lavrov wrote to Lopatin about Tkachev's anger:

It is very interesting that you've gotten together with Tkachev. They say that he is very unhappy with the article about revolutionaries from a privileged milieu, and seems to be off by himself sulking. If you should see him, try to convince him that there are no insinuations against the *molodezh'* in this article, and in general, reproach him.[35]

Tkachev's pamphlet did not appear until the end of April, and Lavrov obtained a copy on 9 May 1874.[36] At last it became clear to him that it was not simply a matter of disagreement over Smirnov's article. Tkachev had reopened the question of political struggle and had redefined the role of the intelligentsia. In "The Aims of Revolutionary Propaganda" he postulated the need for a tripartite division of labor in the revolutionary intelligentsia in which the propagandist's role was, to a significant extent, overshadowed by the roles of agitators and political conspirators. Tkachev equated Lavrov's vision of preparation for revolution through socialist propaganda

33. B. P. Koz'min, *Ot "deviatnadtsatogo fevralia" k "pervomu marta"* (Moscow: Vsesoiuznoe obshchestvo politkatorzhan i ssyl'no-poselentsev, 1933), pp. 127–28.

34. Himself a reconstructed Nechaevist, Smirnov bitterly opposed the Blanquist tradition which Tkachev had helped to inspire in Russia in the late 1860s and which he was attempting to resuscitate as an émigré.

35. Lavrov to Lopatin, 13 March 1874, MS in IISH.

36. Lavrov to Lopatin, 9 May [1874], MS in IISH.

with utopian theories of progress, and he refused to recognize it as a genuine revolutionary strategy. To add insult to injury, Tkachev accused Lavrov of unwittingly serving the Third Section by diverting revolutionary youth from more important revolutionary tasks.[37]

Lavrov's reaction to the pamphlet indicated his newness to revolutionary politics, his indelible academic streak, and (one is tempted to say) his obtuseness in such matters. Without delay he wrote to Lopatin:

I received Tkachev's brochure today and read it. It's cleverly written. It has a personal side and a general side. Of course, to answer personal attacks on my personal activity is not at all called for. But there is a theoretical part in the brochure, partially expressed, partially hidden behind a cunning mask of words. This must be clarified, perhaps in an article in the journal, perhaps in a brochure, which will have to be written and printed quickly. The latter has in its favor the advantage of a quick retort to the attack, so that my opponent's idea will not have time to sink in. Against this is the danger of giving too much significance to my opponent by calling attention to him. It would be best to know the opinions of various individuals, how far this brochure will influence young groups, and whether it is worthwhile to pick up the gauntlet. Or is it better to treat it casually? From a purely literary point of view it is better for me to reply myself, but that is not important. I would ask you to take down the reply, or would ask one of those who live at 60 Gay-Lussac to do it. (I hope it is you.)[38]

Evidently Lavrov recalled the Petersburg literary duels of the sixties, which despite their bitterness, were formal, gentlemanly affairs. He finished his reply to Tkachev on May 15 and read it publicly that evening before it went to press the next day as a pamphlet entitled *Russkoi sotsial'no-revoliutsionnoi molodezhi* (To the Russian social-revolutionary youth).[39] He was quite anxious to gain the approval of the Russians in Paris, especially Lopatin, Podolinskii, and the Fritschi group. When the Fritschi group criticized his pamphlet, Lavrov denounced them to Lopatin in the most extreme

37. For a discussion of the polemic see Koz'min, *Ot "deviatnadtsatogo fevralia" k "pervomu marta,"* pp. 129–43.

38. Lavrov to Lopatin, 9 May [1874], MS in IISH. Some members of the Fritschi group lived in Paris, having departed from Zurich, and Lavrov was no doubt referring to them.

39. Lavrov to Lopatin, 16 May 1874, MS in IISH.

Chapter Six

language, calling them empty-heads, rubbish, and—the worst of all possible insults—*baryshni* ("aristocrats"). He was evidently getting into the spirit of his new role. "He who is not with us, is against us," he wrote to Lopatin.[40] Lavrov believed that M. P. Sazhin, the Bakuninist, was exploiting Tkachev for his own purposes,[41] for Tkachev's pamphlet had been printed on Sazhin's London printing press. However, the press closed down shortly thereafter, and Tkachev found himself without resources to answer Lavrov's pamphlet. On 21 June 1874 he wrote to Lavrov and requested that the polemic be continued in the third volume of *Vpered!*, shortly to appear.[42] On June 23 Lavrov drafted a reply. He refused to devote any space in his journal to the polemic because he considered it "inappropriate" to print articles "concerned with an overly private manifestation of émigré literature."[43] Lavrov still regarded *Vpered!* as a catholic organ of socialist thought, and not as a party organ. However, he was aware that his pamphlet against Tkachev represented the views of a distinct party within the Russian socialist movement. On 27 June 1874 he wrote to Lopatin:

I sent Marx the brochure. The author of *Kapital* should have in his library the works of all parties, but his finances don't permit it. I sufficiently esteem him to ignore his hostility.[44]

Lavrov's vast sense of propriety, his pride, his meticulousness, and his sensitivity seem out of place in the cutthroat competition among revolutionary ideologues.

In July 1874, approximately two months after the outbreak of hostilities with Tkachev, Lavrov was jubilant. *Vpered!* seemed to have emerged from the struggle undamaged, and his own reputation appeared unsullied. He wrote to Lopatin:

We have support and shall continue to have it. Our channels remain intact, and, we hope, shall be multiplied and consolidated. Tkachev's

40. Lavrov to Lopatin, 7 June 1874, MS in IISH.
41. Ibid.
42. B. Nicolaevsky published this letter in *Na chuzhoi storone,* 1925, no. 10, pp. 187–93.
43. Although the draft of this letter is addressed only to "M. G." (*milostivyi gosudar'*—"dear sir"), a formal, and in this case cold, form of address, it is quite clear that it is for Tkachev. (MS in IISH.)
44. Lavrov to Lopatin, 27 June [1874], MS in IISH.

brochure made a disgusting impression. Practically no one supported him. My brochure was well received. The Bakuninists (they are called anarchists) hurled various calumnies at me, but no one listened. Tkachev's sister wrote me a sympathetic letter and even apologized for her brother. In general—life's not so bad. If only we had more correspondence and some sort of literary collaboration. As to writers, it's bad news—they're afraid. But even they generally praise us. . . . A prosecutor said to one nihilist that she could have profited from reading *Vpered!*.

There are a number of little anecdotes of this sort which I would relate, but to write them would take too long. . . . In *Russian World* there was an article against *Vpered!*.[45]

There is no question but that Lavrov enjoyed his new notoriety as the leader of a successful revolutionary journal. The debate with Tkachev had proved his strength rather than challenged it, and seemed to vindicate the strategy which Lavrov had propounded in his major articles and pamphlets written during 1873–74.

In order to counter Tkachev's Blanquism, Lavrov had attempted to make the whole argument about conspiracies and agitation seem absurd. He argued that propaganda and agitation were practically inseparable. Thus agitation was a given assumption of *Vpered!'s* program. Lavrov had always assumed that secret organizations would exist and cooperate with one another in Russia, and that they would deliver blows directly against the government, paralyzing it in the event of a revolutionary uprising.

The connection of propaganda of revolutionary ideas with agitation in their behalf and with the organization of a revolutionary party for a decisive outcome is so inevitable that it always existed for all political revolutions much earlier than ideas about the problems of a new social revolution.[46]

However, without preparation one would not achieve a genuine social revolution, but just another political revolution.

Therefore, in several later articles written in response to the attacks of critics against "Knowledge and Revolution" and to the queries of followers, Lavrov tried to clarify what he meant by preparation. Bakuninists, and apparently some of Lavrov's own followers, had interpreted this to mean an extended period of formal

45. Lavrov to Lopatin, 13 July [1874], MS in IISH.
46. *Izbrannye sochineniia*, 3:356.

education and the acquisition of encyclopedic knowledge. Although he did everything possible to erase this distorted image of "preparationism" in subsequent numbers of his journal and in separate brochures, the Bakuninists were evidently able to exploit the unfavorable impression created by the initial vagueness of *Vpered!*'s program. It seems likely that Lavrov himself was not at first certain what he meant by preparation. Eventually he outlined a pedagogical division of labor, in which young revolutionaries might master a special area of knowledge for purposes of propaganda. Furthermore, denying the value of secluded study or the acquisition of a university degree, he emphasized the need for revolutionaries from the intelligentsia to go to the people, to work and *learn* in the countryside: the young revolutionary should acquire knowledge by studying current questions and directly observing the life of the suffering masses.[47]

All of Lavrov's "clarifications" of his position carried him closer to the Bakuninist idea that the intelligentsia should go to the people, not so much as teachers but as students. However, he was still far from Bakunin's revolutionary romanticism, for he believed that social revolution also demanded the participation of newly enlightened masses. This didn't mean that the peasants should become Marxist sociologists, but it did mean that they should at least appreciate the significance of social laws and progress. Men like Nechaev and Tkachev could not inspire a true social revolution because they would not ensure the development of a genuine socialist morality. Lavrov exposed Tkachev's advocacy of dictatorship in private discussions with members of *Vpered!*'s staff and cited a section of an unpublished manuscript (rejected for publication by the staff) in which Tkachev had advocated misleading the masses with promises of a voluptuous life of idleness and self-indulgence.[48] If the masses were simply told that the successful revolution would mean more pleasures and comforts, then the old morality would not be overcome but, on the contrary, encouraged.

It is quite clear that Lavrov would not trust a social revolution to either the intelligentsia or the masses alone. It had to be a joint

47. Lavrov, "Otvet na raznye kritiki," in *Izbrannye sochineniia,* 2:90–122.
48. *Izbrannye sochineniia,* 3:362–64.

effort—not just a joint physical effort, but a joint moral effort. He wanted neither a spontaneous, undirected uprising, a *bunt,* nor a seizure of power by a disciplined minority. Much of Tkachev's appeal lay in his sense of urgency, his image of the martyred, suffering masses, and his call for decisive political action. Certainly there is no question but that Lavrov also tended to idealize the suffering of the masses. In fact, turning Tkachev's own metaphor against him, he pictured the folk as a mighty Christ crucified on Golgotha, and the members of the intelligentsia as feeble creatures standing at the foot of his cross and whispering to him:

You are God, you are omnipotent! Pull up your cross and crush your enemies. You can, you must do this! We can kill the guards, drive out the Pharisees, but we haven't the strength to uproot your mighty historical cross. You alone can do this. Those very same mighty champions, who loudly cry that *they* will tear down the cross of the people-god, with their lilliputian strength—those champions, when they reach the cross, will adorn themselves with the chasuble of a high priest, or set themselves on a proconsul's stallion . . . but the martyr will remain crucified, bleeding, as long as he is not conscious that he is God.[49]

This is simply another image of the working class similar to the one presented in Lavrov's poem "Noël," written on Christmas Eve of 1870, shortly after he had become a member of the des Ternes section of the First International:

Go! Let all of the peoples rise up! Let all of the blind see! Let the joyous news of fraternity, equality and liberty resound in all of the hidden corners of the universe! Let the worker—Lazarus—leave his tomb forever![50]

49. Ibid., pp. 345–46.
50. I have translated from a French version in Lavrov's own hand. (MS in IISH.) The Russian version is published in several collections. See V. Bonch-Bruevich, ed., *Zven'ia,* 8 vols. (Moscow: Academia, 1932–50) 8:702–11; and A. M. Bikhter, *Poety-demokraty,* pp. 76–78. James Billington's belief that this poem and some of Lavrov's articles on religion betray an attraction for millenarian sectarianism is, I believe, mistaken. See Billington, *Mikhailovsky and Russian Populism* (Oxford: Oxford University Press, 1958), pp. 126–27. M. Chernaivsky's similar position in *Tsar and People* (New Haven: Yale University Press, 1961), pp. 195–96, is no less erroneous. Although Lavrov was unquestionably a *homo religiosus* in Erikson's terms, he also was a student of various forms of religious pathology. He was fully aware of the resemblances between his position and a religious commitment, but

In the same poem we find:

The true Messiah is born, the all powerful man-god! He is incarnated in your thoughts! He is justice, fraternity and eternal peace.[51]

Both the poem of 1870 and the article of 1874 were probably written with Feuerbach's philosophy uppermost in mind; as the working classes became conscious of their strength, and as they discovered the path toward truth and justice, they would discover that they themselves were the source of godliness and would cast off their old God. Lavrov's biblical allusions are simply literary devices with which to describe the new life, the miraculous new sight and strength which had come to the masses through realism and socialism. However, it would be a great mistake to interpret this simply as worship of the power slumbering within the masses, or as deification of the folk. Although one can find in Lavrov's writings genuine sympathy for the plight of the masses and appreciation for their strength, his eulogizing is, more than anything else, an expression of his disenchantment with the intelligentsia, who by contrast with the folk were described as "microscopic midges" or else as aspirants to dictatorial power.[52] In this way he approached Bakuninism without arriving at it, since in his major theoretical articles he continued to stress

he distinguished the character of his "religion" from "unhealthy" historical religious phenomena. A student of Feuerbach, Lavrov was expressing in verse a Feuerbachian thesis about religion and alienation.

More important was Lavrov's image of the *narod,* and his belief in their growing consciousness. The need to glorify the narod, as Billington points out, was an extremely important emotional component of Russian populism. Lavrov had exhibited this tendency in some of his earlier verse, but had simultaneously shown awareness of the narod's weaknesses. In a recent study, Richard Wortman has examined the agonizing emotional problems of the *narodniki,* in which he traces changes in the conception and image of the narod in individuals and in the narodnik movement as a whole. See R. Wortman, *The Crisis of Russian Populism* (Cambridge: At the University Press, 1967). I do not believe that Lavrov ever felt a deep need to glorify the masses. His deepest needs were related to his image of the intelligentsia, and his glorification of the folk is probably a symptom of a mood of relative self-disdain issuing from a sense of weakness, dependency, or ineffectiveness.

51. "Noël," MS in IISH.
52. *Izbrannye sochineniia,* 3:346.

the need for science and the role of the intelligentsia. He still prof-
fered his readers the image of the heroic, dedicated intellectual, a
purely Russian figure struggling with uniquely Russian problems;
but this image was an idealization based upon the men of the sixties
rather than upon Lavrov's real life encounters in the émigré milieu.
From his letters to Lopatin it is quite clear that the flesh and blood
intelligenty of the seventies did not at all measure up to his idealized
picture of the men of the sixties. However, as a revolutionary leader
he had to praise and exhort the intelligenty as well as to blame them
for their failings. Lavrov's obviously overdrawn image of the powerful, stirring masses groping towards consciousness and freedom is
a mixture of compensation for the failings of the intelligentsia and
publicistic dramatization of theoretical conclusions, as well as a
reflection of the impact of the Paris Commune upon him.

Of the numerous articles which Lavrov wrote for the first three
volumes of *Vpered!* (published in August 1873, March 1874, and
December 1874), "Komu prenadlezhit budushchee?" (To whom
does the future belong?) is the most interesting from the point of
view of dramatic presentation. He had conceived this piece late in
1871 and had sent it to Blagosvetlov for publication in *Delo* in
1872, but it had been rejected by the censor.[53] The original title,
"Posledovatel'nye liudi" (Logical people), reveals a great deal about
Lavrov's approach to radicalism. Though somewhat fleshed out for
dramatic effect, the "logical people" in "To Whom Does the Future
Belong?" are in fact embodiments of a typology drawn from late
nineteenth-century European and Russian society. Thinking like a
true radical, Lavrov reduced his types to their "truest" form: the
master-mind Prussian bureaucrat; the amoral, detached, positivistic
scientist; the artist, equally withdrawn and absorbed in aesthetics;
the ruthless, but rational, bourgeois entrepreneur; the cleric, waiting confidently for men to relapse into their old religious ways; the
European socialist; and finally, the Russian socialist-revolutionary
intellectual, who is easily recognized as a realist of the sixties transformed into a narodnik activist—an agrarian socialist and an uncompromising enemy of the modern state. Lavrov's "logical people"
engage in a colloquium dramatically set in a tavern near Clerken-

53. See "Posledovatel'nye liudi," *Zven'ia*, 1:413–58.

well. Each of them in turn presents his peculiar vision of the future, whether demonic or healthy from Lavrov's viewpoint.

The Prussian bureaucrat in "To Whom Does the Future Belong?" is obsessed with statecraft, with the idea of an ordered polity. Science, art, and religion are valued only insofar as they serve the state. All areas of life are to be regulated. Eugenics is to be employed for the production of useful types of people, in accordance with the plans of the state. All public gatherings are to be under strict state supervision. Every speech will be monitored by an ingenious electrical system of receivers and transmitters, and recorded on special strips of paper in the section for the recording of public speeches in the office of the Ministry of Police. The Postal Section of the Ministry of Police is conceived and planned with equally diabolical ingenuity. Papers, pens, and ink will be a state monopoly and supplied without cost. Citizens will be able to go to the postal division in any town and write letters, but all the pens will be tied to long cords—electrical conduits—which will transmit every word to the Postal Section of the Ministry of Police, where it will be recorded in abbreviated, microscopic form. The Library Section of this ministry will be organized on the same principle. Tied electrically to every printing press in the land, it will receive a microscopic facsimile of every book printed. A complicated system of automatic classification, combined with the brevity of the symbols and their microscopic dimensions, will make possible the storage of a vast amount of materials. Finally, there will be a section which will monitor private conversations by means of sensitive tiles and paving stones laid in all streets and fields.[54]

Lavrov's vision of modern capitalists was equally interesting. His modern capitalist was a true Social Darwinist—confident in his role as the prime mover in modern society. He was lean, hard, and astute. He had nothing but contempt for the slack, liberal-minded members of his own class, who were doomed to disappear in the struggle for supremacy. Lavrov saw the great financiers and industrialists as a breed apart. They were tough-minded, willing and able to employ the discoveries of science for their own ends. Furthermore, their interests and the interests of the bureaucrats who controlled the mod-

54. *Vpered!* 2 (Zurich, 1874), pp. 12–13.

ern state did not always coincide. The state taxed them and fought wars which were contrary to their interests. In order to protect themselves, the great capitalists sometimes had to struggle against the state and the church. Eventually they would have to crush these forces.[55]

The dramatic unwinding of Lavrov's sociological drama occurs when an unknown young man enters the debate:

He was tall. Thick blond hair fell in disarray from beneath the soft, threadbare cap framing his handsome face. Lively blue-grey eyes full of thought and energy looked outward through steel-rimmed spectacles. His suit was quite threadbare, but evidently he paid not the slightest attention to his clothing. He was built like an athlete. He entered the tavern accidentally soon after the beginning of the meeting of "the logical people," asked for a mug of beer and some cold mutton—a request which surprised the waitress, given the time of day—devoured the mutton and some bread to the last crumb, and listened extremely attentively to the speeches of the interlocutors. His eyes alternately flared up and died down. He exercised considerable self-restraint in order to keep from interfering in the conversation. Suddenly, he decisively walked over to the group and began to speak in broken English, inserting a few German and French words when his English failed him, although he spoke all these languages incorrectly and with extremely poor pronunciation. Suspiciously and rigidly, the professor [the amoral positivist] directed his cold stare at the youth. The gambler [the modern capitalist] examined his rather unseemly costume from head to foot with a disdainful look. The inquisitor [the religious thinker] looked at him maliciously, sensing a foe. Only Babeuf [the European socialist] from his first words felt sympathy for the speaker's open gaze, his brave and sincere speech—and a wide grin displayed both rows of the Provençal's white teeth.[56]

At great length, the young Russian presents all of Lavrov's basic ideas about human evolution, historical indeterminism, ethical science, and the revolutionary struggle. Lavrov's historical indeterminism appears in either/or form: either labor will win in its struggle against capital or the ongoing historical-anthropological differentiation between exploiters and exploited will lead to the extinction of the latter. The victory of labor will lead to the disappearance of the deficient human types which have developed historically, and re-

55. Ibid., pp. 14–21.
56. Ibid., p. 52.

place them by a superior universal type—a new "race" of intelligent workers *(intelligentnyi rabotnik)*.[57]

One by one the "logical people" leave the tavern where the drama is set—first the inquisitor, then the gambler. The professor, who waited until the young man pronounced the last word of his harangue, "quickly slipped a card into his hand and said: 'I haven't any time now; drop by to see me; here are my hours; we'll talk about this.' "[58] Only Babeuf remained, symbolizing the unity of the European and Russian socialist cause.

"To Whom Does the Future Belong?" is Lavrov's contribution to the literary genre of which Herzen's *From the Other Shore* and Dostoevsky's "Grand Inquisitor" in *Brothers Karamazov* are examples. But Lavrov could never get beyond merciless logic to the agonizing ultimate questions and the possibility of absurdity—or if he could, he would not. For him, *posledovatel'nost'* ("logical consecutiveness") inevitably led to a merciless struggle between irreconcilable opponents, but not to absurdity. As for the idealized picture of Russian revolutionary youth—that, of course, was a pedagogical device, a model to guide the new radical generation. The picture of Russian youth drawn by Lavrov in his private correspondence is quite different. One may speculate that Lavrov's insecure position as an aging, lonely, impecunious scholar, whose career had somehow meshed with the lives of revolutionary youths half his age, deterred him from expressing his disappointment with them publicly.

All things considered, the period 1874–75 was the high point of Lavrov's career as a revolutionary publicist. Although the more established populist writers had refused to collaborate on the journal, Lavrov had attracted a number of dedicated young students, who labored heroically over the substantial articles that went into the journal's thick volumes. They published Chernyshevskii's *Pis'ma bez adresa* (Letters without an address), procured for the journal by Lopatin. The journal contained a vast amount of information about the vigorous European workers' movement, counterposing to it articles about the corruption of Europe's bourgeois civilization and Russia's autocracy. Both in the pages of *Vpered!* and in separate

57. Ibid., p. 71.
58. Ibid., p. 73.

pamphlets Lavrov presented the history of the peasant movement in Russia and vivid exposés of the brutal condition of contemporary Russian workers, both rural and urban. Correspondents supplied information about the student movement and censorship. In addition, the *vperedovtsy* printed some of the new literature that the populist propagandists were carrying into the countryside for the peasants, and they hopefully followed developments in the villages. Finally, *Vpered!* contained revolutionary poems and songs, some of which achieved considerable popularity.[59]

Thus, despite all of the problems which had plagued it in its first few months, *Vpered!* flourished. Lavrov lacked Herzen's literary genius—indeed, he completely lacked the instincts of a publicist—but he guided the journal capably, and some of his theoretical articles demonstrated extraordinary intellectual breadth. During the course of 1874 *Vpered!*'s reputation grew. N. A. Morozov's memoirs reveal this quite clearly. Although he himself belonged to the editorial staff of the nascent *Rabotnik,* he wrote:

But our *Rabotnik* seemed to me to be something quite different from *Vpered!,* about which the entire Russian intellectual world knows. . . . I defended myself from the reproaches of my friends by saying that . . . I placed it [an article about propaganda activities in Danilovskii district] in *Vpered!* only because there was no other revolutionary journal for the intelligentsia, and besides, I wanted to acquaint the Russian youth with all of the details of the arrests and searches in Danilovskii district, since everyone in Russia read *Vpered!*[60]

The circulation of the journal, initally 1000 copies, more than doubled during 1874.[61] A group of accomplices in Prussia, Lithuania, and Bessarabia managed to smuggle thousands of copies into European Russia.[62] Lavrov began to show some signs of overweening pride. Even Engels' condescending and sarcastic assessment of *Vpered!* in *Volksstaat* (October 1874), in which he referred to Lavrov as "freund Peter" and derided his eclectic and conciliatory approach to the internecine struggles of European socialism, did

---

59. For a complete listing of publications see Sapir, *Vpered!,* 1:175–79.
60. Morozov, *Povesti moei zhizni,* 1:342–43, 344.
61. Lavrov to Vyrubov, 24 April 1874, printed in *Byloe,* 1925, no. 2, p. 27.
62. Sapir, *Vpered!,* 1:314–21.

not upset Lavrov very much. Perhaps this was because Engels' article was more of a renewed assault on Bakunin and Nechaev than a direct attack on *Vpered!*, and his acrimonious reply to Tkachev in the same series of articles was far more devastating than anything that he had launched against Lavrov. Lavrov could now feel secure in his righteousness and in the relative solidity of his enterprise. To be sure, much of the solidity of *Vpered!* was illusory. Lavrov himself knew that an émigré organ could not really lead the Russian movement and, as events bore out, could not exist without the movement's moral and financial support. His journal was not destined to become another *Kolokol*.[63] Nonetheless, *Vpered!*, first as a series of volumes and then in its biweekly form (1875–76), was the most reliable, sound, and dignified Russian émigré journal to appear since the demise of Herzen's *Kolokol* in 1867. It may be true that although the journal had many readers, few followed its program, and that more than anything else it fulfilled the demand for information. This in itself was a significant role during the period 1873–76, before the revolutionary underground in Russia had coalesced into real parties with their own organs. So it was that even those who sympathized with the Bakuninist orientation supported *Vpered!*

The decision to convert *Vpered!* into a biweekly journal was based upon the assumption that the Lavrovists in Russia would continue to supply both funds and correspondence. By the autumn of 1875, however, it was clear to the London organization that their supporters in Russia were wholly unreliable. During the course of 1875 they received only 2,850 rubles from Russia, almost all of it supplied by Buturlin.[64] According to Smirnov's estimate, it took a minimum of about 400 rubles a month to sustain the enterprise.[65] Evidently, the money which the London group received was channeled through the St. Petersburg circle, and both Smirnov's and Lavrov's letters in the autumn and winter of 1875 reveal that there was increasing tension and mistrust between the circle and the

63. Lavrov, at the very outset, apologized to his readers for lacking Herzen's talent. See *Vpered!* 1(1873):1.

64. Smirnov to Idel'son, 24 November 1875, typed MS in Nicolaevsky Collection, Hoover Institution Archives.

65. Smirnov to Idel'son, 9 December 1875, typed MS in Nicolaevsky Collection, Hoover Institution Archives.

émigrés. Beginning in November 1875, Smirnov and Lavrov began to bombard the Petersburg Lavrovists with pleas for money.

Meanwhile, Lavrov was negotiating with Charles Dilke for a cheaper publishing rate. They concluded an agreement, and in November the journal switched from N. Trubner (who had also published *Kolokol*) to Dilke.[66] Despite this new economy, the financial position of the London group was so desperate that the type-setters joked about printing an announcement in one of the December issues: "Young men, fully competent, for a moderate compensation offer their services to maidens sixty-five to ninety-five years old."[67] On December 15, Smirnov sent a letter to the Petersburg circle:

Send money quickly by telegram. If we don't get the money by December 27, then on December 28 we will announce closure. Our debts alone are more than eighty pounds.[68]

Almost the same letter was sent to Moscow as well. The receipt of 500 rubles from Geneva on the very day that they had written to St. Petersburg and Moscow averted disaster. The threat of closure had not been a mere tactic to squeeze money out of the Russian circles, however. Lavrov had been deadly serious about printing an announcement of closure in the twenty-fourth issue of the bi-weekly. He had also planned to print a plea for financial aid, so that they could revive the journal within three months.[69] The money that they received from Geneva was only enough to guarantee survival for a few more issues.

At approximately the same time, developments in the Russian revolutionary underground began to affect the journal directly. Through their agents, the vperedovtsy began to receive rumors about a revolutionary "union" which would unite in one organization the most significant groups in the revolutionary underground. Mark Natanson, who had been one of the founders of the Chaikovskii circle, was the prime mover in the new impulse towards the organi-

66. Ibid.
67. Smirnov to Idel'son, 14 December 1875, typed MS in Nicolaevsky Collection, Hoover Institution Archives.
68. Typed MS in Nicolaevsky Collection.
69. Lavrov to Lopatin, 15 December [1875], MS in IISH.

zation of the group, which in a year's time yielded the first effective party of professional revolutionaries in the history of the Russian movement: Zemlia i Volia (Land and Freedom). In late 1875 some of the groups which had formed after the disintegration of the Chaikovskii circle and the Zurich diaspora began to lay the groundwork for the new party.[70] Natanson arrived in London on 24 December 1875 to negotiate with the vperedovtsy. He was not happy with the journal's tone. It was not sufficiently involved with "burning questions" and practical problems.[71] His presentation displeased Smirnov, who had become a doctrinaire antiBakuninist since his conversion to Lavrovism, and who detected a Bakuninist taint in Natanson's references to "instinct" and "passion."[72] Lavrov had been under attack precisely for his lack of revolutionary instinct and passion. In October 1875 he had received a crushing indictment along these lines in two lengthy letters from Sergei Kravchinskii, at that time a dedicated Bakuninist *buntarist* ("insurrectionist").[73] However, Lavrov himself was attracted to the idea of a union of revolutionary groups.

A sudden and ultimately fatal disagreement over editorial policy now came to the surface. While Lavrov was increasingly inclined to make concessions to the Bakuninist strategists, Smirnov—and the Lavrovists in Russia as well held to Lavrov's position of 1873–74. The new Bakuninist strategy called for "propaganda by deed"— agitation for strikes, *bunty* ("insurrections") and agrarian violence. The agitators were to direct their efforts at selected points. Lavrov was impressed by the fact that there would be a central fund and

70. Among those involved were Chaikovtsy, Lavrovists, and the remnants of the alliance between a group of Caucasian students and the Fritschi women, the latter two groups having formed the "Pan-Russian Social-Revolutionary Organization" in 1874–75 in Moscow, only to have their numbers decimated by arrests. See Itenberg, *Dvizhenie revoliutsionnogo narodnichestva,* pp. 363–73; G. M. Lifshits, "K istorii moskovskogo s'ezda narodnikov 1875 g.," *Istoriia SSSR,* 1965, no. 4; Sapir, *Vpered!,* 1:337–46.

71. Smirnov to Idel'son, 25 December 1875, typed MS in Nicolaevsky Collection.

72. Ibid.

73. See *Na chuzhoi storone,* 1925, no. 10, pp. 200–204; also see V. Bogucharskii, *Aktivnoe narodnichestvo semidesiatikh godov* (Moscow, 1912), pp. 126–30; Sapir, *Vpered!,* 2:357–74.

central "institutions," and that there was also provision for autonomous action by independent groups—a kind of federalism.[74]

Natanson was prepared to back *Vpered!* if Lavrov and Smirnov would agree to his editorial suggestions and to the following conditions: they were to publish twenty-four issues annually, plus fifty printers' leaves of literature for the intelligentsia and an equal amount for the narod; for this they would receive 500 rubles monthly and a guarantee that they would be supplied with correspondence from Russia; Lavrov would keep the revolutionary organization's funds in a bank account in his name.[75] Smirnov was evidently adamant in his opposition to a change in editorial policy, while Lavrov announced that he was prepared to withdraw from the editorship in order to pursue an independent policy under his own name. However, Natanson was not empowered to commission Lavrov to write anything for the "union."[76] Had Natanson and the union been prepared, Lavrov might have transferred his allegiance to them immediately.

74. Smirnov to Idel'son, 25 December 1875, typed MS in Nicolaevsky Collection.

75. Smirnov to Idel'son, 29 December 1875, typed MS in Nicolaevsky Collection.

76. Lavrov described the situation in two letters to Lopatin. In the first, dated 28 December [1875], he wrote: "I had intended to write at length today, but I can't, my nerves are so shaken. I'll only transmit the information that affects you as well. In September and October there were daily (in October) conferences of a union of two circles who put together a general program and organization and arrived at several decisions about *Vpered!*. They decided to support it, but there was general dissatisfaction with its direction for various reasons, and they found it impossible to recognize it as the organ of the union. I refused the editorship [in order to facilitate matters], but because of an unexpected turn in the deliberations and actions [at the meetings] which irked me all the more, I was forced to stay on temporarily. The details vex me so that I can't even write about them, and in any case, they're not important now." On 31 December 1875 he wrote: "I refused the editorship and argued that I would be more useful if I were to devote myself to separate works, for which I alone would answer. But since N[atanson] was not empowered to arrange this and it was impossible to do it quickly, then I will temporarily [—] . . . everything in my name, saying from *me* and not from *we*." (MSS in IISH.)

According to information given to Lavrov by Natanson, the meetings held in the autumn of 1875 were attended by twenty-five delegates, and a future meeting of even more groups was planned for August 1876. Lavrov was quite impressed by Natanson's description of the planned union.

In fact, however, all of the evidence points to the union's lack of confidence in Lavrov's capacity to pursue their line. On 21 January 1876 Lavrov received a written statement from the union which presented a somewhat different picture of the editorial policy to be pursued under its sponsorship than that conveyed by Natanson in conversation. Lavrov had been led to believe that he would be obligated to publish only articles sent by the union as a *collective* entity, but that he would have editorial powers over articles sent by *individual* members of the union. He would only have to submit to the collective as an act of party discipline and would reserve the right to pursue his own policy with regard to matters which did not have the weight of the full party behind it. However, the clear intentions of Natanson and the union, as expressed in a document written in December 1875, were to reduce Lavrov's function to that of a collaborator rather than a formulator of policy.[77] Thus there may have been more than a small element of self-deception in Lavrov's perception of his relationship with the union. Given the precariousness of his journal's position, his disappointment with the Lavrovists, and the sense of crisis communicated to him by the Bakuninists, Lavrov must have found the prospects of joining a more vigorous revolutionary tendency rather enticing. In any case, Lavrov's attempts to establish a modus vivendi with the union were first complicated by the document described above, and then were terminated by the union's own failure to consolidate itself in the winter and spring of 1875–76.

Meanwhile, Smirnov and the typesetters, especially A. L. Linev, who evidently broke into tears over Lavrov's announcement that he intended to leave the editorship, exerted pressure on him to stay.[78] The period of crisis, which began on December 28, extended into the new year. Smirnov refused to take full responsibility for the editorship. Lavrov, unable to extricate himself from the journal, was constantly depressed and thought about leaving London for Paris.[79]

77. Sapir, *Vpered!*, 2:199–200.
78. Smirnov to Idel'son, 28 December 1875, typed MS in Nicolaevsky Collection.
79. Smirnov to Idel'son, 21 and 26 January 1876, typed MSS in Nicolaevsky Collection.

All the while the journal limped along, still waiting for word from the union, and still suffering from lack of funds and correspondence from the Lavrovists in Russia. By mid-February they were again contemplating closure, this time after the twenty-eighth issue; but the deadline was extended for two more issues.[80] On 19 February 1876 they received 200 rubles from Turgenev through Lopatin, with a promise of 300 more, and on February 21 the receipt of 500 rubles from St. Petersburg once again saved them.[81]

Recurring financial crises were an important factor contributing to the breakdown of Lavrov's enterprise but were only one symptom of the artificiality of the tie between the vperedovtsy and their constituency. The active members of the circle hardly ever made a pilgrimage to London. In a letter to Lopatin written during the summer of 1875, Lavrov wrote:

I don't know *even one member of the Petersburg circle closely*, and besides two or three others [Russian Lavrovists], I don't know any at all.[82]

On 27 October 1875 he had written to Rosaliia Idel'son, Smirnov's wife: "Yesterday I saw a mythical being—a *vperedovets* from Russia."[83] Throughout 1874 and 1875 the journal was run mainly by the little commune which had begun editing and printing the journal in Zurich and which in the Spring of 1875 had moved into a house at 3 Evershot Road, London. The history of the disintegration of the journal is also the history of the breakdown of the commune. It was an extraordinary group of men, of diverse background and temperament, bound together only by their allegiance to the journal and, to a lesser extent, to Lavrov or Smirnov.

Lavrov was the editorial mainstay of the journal. He rose earlier than the others, donned his dressing gown and black velvet slippers, and went to work on his voluminous articles. At 8:00 A.M. the German housekeeper, Gertrude, served breakfast to the entire staff,

80. Smirnov to Idel'son, 16 February 1876, typed MS in Nicolaevsky Collection.
81. Smirnov to Idel'son, 19 and 21 February 1876, typed MSS in Nicolaevsky Collection.
82. Lavrov to Lopatin [August or September 1875], MS in IISH.
83. Lavrov to Idel'son, 27 October [1875], MS in IISH.

including Smirnov and the typesetters. At 12:00 they had tea, and 5:00 P.M. dinner.[84] The typesetting apparatus was in the house on Evershot Road. It was a communal enterprise, very much like the arteli that Russian populists believed would flourish under socialism. There were no salaries, and everyone shared both menial and intellectual work—although Lavrov exhibited such incompetency in the former area that his colleagues were always quick to relieve him of any manual task. Smirnov, for example, sometimes went to Lavrov's room to make a fire for him. Lavrov was the most ascetic of the group—so much so that Smirnov was always complaining to Idel'son that "the old fellow ought to get himself ventilated."

Smirnov was a student of medicine and fancied himself a psychologist. He had two fundamental prescriptions for whatever ailed his colleagues—chloral hydrate and sex. He himself seems to have been addicted to chloral hydrate, while the typesetters preferred sex. As a student of Kraft-Ebbing, Smirnov clinically observed and recounted to his wife the sexual escapades of the typesetters. Gertrude, the unmarried housekeeper, was the object of some attention, and Smirnov took upon himself the salvation of her body, as well as her soul, for socialism. He failed in both respects. Gertrude was pregnant most of the time, but proved utterly impenetrable when it came to socialist theory.[85] Smirnov liked to picture himself as the manipulator in the enterprise, forever saving the others from their own excesses and guiding them toward healthy equilibrium. His initial reverence for Lavrov turned into condescension as time went on. To Smirnov, Lavrov was a product of an entirely different cultural generation, a petulant and irrational old fellow with a weakness for little treats like two-penny pies, pears, and coffee.

The typesetters were a rather earthy bunch, with nicknames like "Bear" (Linev) and "Lobster" (Liberman). Linev, the head compositor, was the most emotional member of the commune, bursting into tears at every moment of crisis. He was devoted to Lavrov. Lazar Gol'denberg, who became a member of the commune in January 1876, had been a typesetter for the Chaikovskii circle in Zurich.

84. Kuliabko-Koretskii, *Iz davnikh let,* p. 193.
85. In his letters to Idel'son, Smirnov jokingly referred to the ongoing story of Gertrude's trials as the "Gertrudiade."

Gol'denberg found Lavrov "a cold aristocrat"—a typical reaction by the younger generation to Lavrov.[86] Aaron Liberman joined the commune in 1875. He had been involved in the Jewish socialist movement in Vilno, Lithuania, and had fled in order to escape arrest. One of Liberman's colleagues in Vilno, Aaron Zundelevich, became *Vpered!*'s main smuggler in the northern route through Prussia and Lithuania. Liberman was an orator and publicist in his own right, and founded the first Jewish workers' union in London in 1876. Mikhail Iantsin, nicknamed "Captain" because of his former career as an army officer, was one of Smirnov's closest allies on the journal. One of the most devoted typesetters was Iakov Voshchakin. The men mentioned above were the major figures in the years 1874–76, but there were others as well.[87] For example, Nikolai Kuliabko-Koretskii, a St. Petersburg Lavrovist, joined the printing crew in August 1876. He followed in the footsteps of his brother Alexander, who had been a part-time typesetter during the spring of 1873, when the journal was launched in Zurich. Nikolai Kuliabko-Koretskii's memoirs are one of the few sources for the history of the St. Petersburg group, and his observations about the London group during its decline in 1876–77 confirm the impression one gathers from Lavrov's and Smirnov's correspondence of the period. He himself became Smirnov's agent in the latter's machinations to keep the St. Petersburg group in control of the journal toward the end of 1876. Eventually Kuliabko-Koretskii, Smirnov, and Gustav Brocher—an Alsatian Russophile—ran the journal in 1877, after Lavrov's departure for Paris and the other typesetters' abandonment of the enterprise.[88]

Smugglers and agents, like Zundelevich, were also quite important for the journal's existence. Dmitrii Rikhter (nicknamed "Dunechka") had been the central figure in the Lavrovist group in Tver, but had emigrated, and now served as the journal's agent in both London and Leipzig. Rikhter was suspected of being a Russian spy in Leip-

86. L. Gol'denberg, "Vospominaniia," *Katorga i ssylka,* 1924, no. 5, p. 112.

87. For more extended treatment of these and other figures, see Sapir, *Vpered!,* 1:264–309.

88. See *G. P. Brocher, et al.* (Paris, 1924), pp. 6–8; Kuliabko-Koretskii, *Iz davnikh let,* pp. 210 ff.

zig, and in June 1876 Lavrov had to convince Marx and Liebknecht that Rikhter was a loyal member of his group.[89] It was one of the low points in the relationship between Russian and German socialists.

It is clear from all accounts that Lavrov never really lived with his men, although he worked with them. He rarely accompanied them on their outings. Sometimes on Saturday nights the group visited Whitechapel to observe the working class at leisure. After the completion of each biweekly issue, they had a little holiday—an evening at the theater, a stroll, or a boat trip down the Thames.[90] According to Smirnov, Lavrov had almost no personal life. So long as things were going well with the journal, he did not seem to suffer from the absence of one. However, when the open break between him and Smirnov occurred in December 1875, and as the situation worsened in 1876, he began to exhibit more self-concern. Smirnov mistakenly believed that "the old fellow" would collapse if the journal failed. Actually, Lavrov had continued his "serious" scholarly articles, now mainly in the area of anthropology and the history of thought, and derived considerable satisfaction from their publication. This was an important safety valve for him—an alternative role to which he would return periodically. Throughout the *Vpered!* period Lavrov's scholarly work appeared in Russian periodicals (mainly *Znanie*), and he even had a book, *Opyt istorii mysli* (Toward a history of thought), published in St. Petersburg in 1875.

Lavrov also tried to revive his personal life. During the course of 1876 he began to correspond with Alexandra Vasil'evna Weber, a young woman whom he had known and influenced during her nihilist adolescence in Russia during the mid-1860s. She was now in Switzer-

89. Some of the correspondence over Rikhter has been published in A. K. Vorob'eva, *K. Marks, F. Engel's i revoliutsionnaia Rossiia,* pp. 327–29. Smirnov's hearty detestation of leading German socialists was another point of disagreement between him and Lavrov. While the former tended to carry on a Russian émigré tradition of provoking the Germans, Lavrov did everything possible to conciliate them and to present the most respectable side of the Russian movement. Lavrov's Germanophilia remained intact. For example, in a letter to Idel'son Lavrov criticized Smirnov's lack of courtesy to Tussy Marx at a chance meeting on a London street.

90. Kuliabko-Koretskii, *Iz davnikh let,* p. 196; Gol'denberg, "Vospominaniia," p. 112.

land for therapeutic reasons, but could not resist the temptation to become involved in émigré circles. In Lugano she met Bakunin and devoted herself to him during the last months of his life.[91] It hardly seems accidental that Lavrov began courting her—for that is what he was evidently doing in his letters to her—during the second half of 1876, the last few months of his participation on the journal. In a letter written on 24 August 1876, Lavrov proposed a secret rendezvous with her in a northern Swiss town for two or three days.[92] In another letter, written two days later, he expressed the hope of seeing her before Christmas.[93] He began closing his letters with "I embrace you my dear one." Lavrov commissioned Lopatin to bring Alexandra Vasil'evna a photograph of him in October 1876.[94] She visited him at least once in London, in April 1877, and it is likely that they met in Paris after Lavrov moved there.[95] Some of his letters to her are not only of considerable personal interest—revealing Lavrov's tendency to present himself in the most dramatic light to women—but also of wider historical interest. In them he expresses his ideas about the prospects for socialism frankly and succinctly. In several letters, Lavrov tried to convince Weber that the anarchist movement that had grown up under Bakunin's influence in Italy had no secure future, however much it appealed to her love for the spectacular and heroic.

All of the illusions and former revolutions in the name of *freedom, patriotism, free thought,* must be regarded as childish and not worthy of the present task. The economic question of the building of the worker's cause must become the major content of *justice;* if justice is to be more than an empty word, a tool of intriguers, it must be a justice of material welfare, the realization of egotistic goals in the general

91. Carr, *Michael Bakunin,* pp. 503–6. Alexandra Weber was married to a judicial investigator at the time of her correspondence and, possibly, affair with Lavrov. She wrote her own reminiscences, in which there is scant reference to Lavrov, for *Byloe,* July 1907.

92. Lavrov to A. V. Weber, 24 August 1876, typed MS in Columbia University Russian Archives.

93. Typed MS in Columbia Russian Archives.

94. Lavrov to A. V. Weber, 11 October 1876, typed MS in Columbia University Russian Archives.

95. This is mentioned in Smirnov's letters to Idel'son. Smirnov described Weber as "puny."

good, not the denial of personal interests, but the passionate desire to realize them only in the form of *general* welfare.

The old revolutionary traditions must be thrown off, the old idols of hero-revolutionaries destroyed before the new paths can be traveled.

From this shall issue the conditions by which the victory of a socialist revolution is probable and possible, or, at least, there will be possible a defeat of such a nature that it will leave behind a lesson for the fighters of the new generation. There is a socialist future for that nation which alongside of several conditions beneficial to socialism, has the psychological bent, not toward the dualism of the renunciation of material comforts in a moment of religious, national, or political enthusiasm, but to the keeping in mind of its material interests, to the "self-centeredness" [*"sebia na ume"*] activity. This is the first point. In that people, which has in its past the *least* tradition to which to bow, the least heroes to set up as idols. This is the second point.

Therefore, it is my opinion that in the Russian people there is a mighty socialist future. Several conditions beneficial to socialism are contained in the agricultural commune [*obshchina*] and in the artisan commune [*artel'*] . . . , but this is only the point of departure—much more important is precisely that absence of tradition and idols. Stenka Razin and Pugachev are almost forgotten and this is all to the good, because it is worthless to remember heroes of the past. Surely neither Razin in the seventeenth century nor Pugachev in the eighteenth century could realize or possess the socialistic ideas of our time. They are precious to us because they demonstrate not the fervor of ascetics, following a great idea, but immediate *material, economic* questions about land, about salt, about the worker and the landowner. It is just as well that the old cannot repeat itself.

Illiteracy, backwardness, coarseness of family morals . . . are quite inelegant, but in them there is something better, for they haven't bound the Russian people to the bourgeoisie, or to that good humane old society: the Russian peasant can either remain what he is, under the yoke of duties and extortions, or he must turn away from the past. Russia can, in the near future, go to pieces and fall prey to Germans, Jews, Armenians, English, Chinese, or it can develop a socialist order —but to become a self-satisfied, stagnant bourgeois ant hill, itself not cognizant of its moral degeneration, it cannot, because it did not bow to such an order in the past or in the present.

Hence, all symptoms of a lack of ascetic enthusiasm in her past are dear to me—and lack of service to an idea, and lack of all traditions calling forth idol worship, that healthy "self-centeredness" which never forgets that one must stand for material interests and that one must never bow to the past. You ask me: Are there countries in the world which can be victorious in Socialism? Yes, I say, there are, and a few that depend upon geography purely. I know *three* such countries, which can be victorious [*mozhet*], but are not *certain* to prevail. These are the United States, Great Britain, and Russia. The geographic position of each of these is such that interference in their internal affairs by neighbors by way of invasion is quite difficult, and therefore in each of these countries victory could be achieved despite the existence of bourgeois countries on their boundaries. And each of these countries has a few conditions favorable to Socialism: in England, a mighty organization of the workers; in America, the habit of huge public gatherings and independent decision, in Russia—as I said—the obshchina and artel' tradition. And, further, each of them doesn't have an idol-worship tradition of revolution, although all of them had in the past strong revolutionary explosions. Now your Italy.

I will not speak of the word *anarchism*. I consider it devoid of an exact meaning and do not consider that either during or after a revolutionary outburst it is applicable. Let them write it on the banners. It is like the French word *Liberté*. It is harmful only in that it encourages idol-worship of words that are not understood. The Italians idol-worship before people who, because of [historical] conditions, died and were sacrificed for ideas which had nothing in common with the great question of the reconstruction of the economic life of the people.

The Italians suffer because of their tradition of hero-worship.

I do not see victory anywhere in the near future.

For me the Russian seminarist or the Russian midwife who would attempt to organize a group of socialists in four villages and who would for a year succeed in their work, would be more instructive than [Italian] revolutionaries, because the former would have taken a step forward; but the socialists in Italy only write new words on their banners, and act exactly as the Carbonari acted.[96]

In his letters to Alexandra Weber, Lavrov could reveal his truest views about the character of European socialist movements, which he would never bring out totally in his articles for fear of increasing the split within the socialist camp. However, his articles of 1876 are more adventurous and interesting, and to some extent less guarded, than his earlier publicistic ventures.

During the course of 1875–76 Lavrov developed and refined his conception of the role of the intelligentsia and the role of the people. Pressure from the Bakuninists on one side, and the Blanquists on the other, forced him to present a detailed picture of the process of social

96. Lavrov to A. V. Weber, 17 April 1877, typed MS in Columbia University Russian Archives.

revolution. His sympathy lay with the Bakuninists—their moral zeal and their commitment to the summary destruction of the old order were very attractive—but his description of the organized network of amalgamated revolutionary groups (the intelligentsia and the narod) is within the "political" tradition in a limited sense. There is no need to assume that he had incorporated elements of Tkachev's program into his own, since the idea of an organized, disciplined party had appeared quite early in the *Historical Letters*. His preferences for federalism and a wide party clearly distinguished him from the Jacobin and Blanquist traditions. He was against a seizure of power by a revolutionary vanguard. If anything, Lavrov made a more serious attempt to incorporate Bakuninist ideas into his program. During the polemic with Tkachev he had glossed over the distinction between agitation and propaganda. Now he attempted to distinguish them and to find an appropriate place for agitation in his conception of the social revolution. Under the pressure of young Bakuninists like Kravchinskii, he began to stress the need for revolutionary ardor, for passion. Although he feared "blind passion" in the revolutionary movement, he now began to praise and proclaim the necessity for a "passionate desire" to bring about revolution quickly and to shorten the suffering of society.[97] He suggested a division of labor. The thinkers, possessing full socialist knowledge, would carry propaganda to the people, while the passionate fighters would agitate them. Propaganda would bring knowledge, agitation would inspire hate.[98]

Despite this clear attempt to conciliate the impatient young Bakuninists, Lavrov found it impossible to entrust the social revolution to the peasants' socialist "instincts." Although he dramatized the strength and suffering of the narod, he had no illusions about its moral condition. He believed that the commune could serve as the basis for a future society of small, cooperative associations, but he presumed that it was infected with the moral diseases of the old order. The commune's greatest virtues were its size, its organization, and its solidarity. Within its framework a truly whole and human individual could develop. However, in its present condition it had

97. *Vpered!,* 1876, no. 26, p. 41.
98. Ibid., p. 42.

many defects—the ignorance and moral diseases of the old order infected it "to the very marrow of its bones." Furthermore, Lavrov
had committed himself to the notion that the same forces which had
created large-scale industrial capitalism in Europe were at work in
Russia.[99] The liberation of the serfs, their subsequent impoverish-
ment, and the creation of a landless proletariat signaled the onset
of this process. However, Lavrov clung to the agrarian socialism
that he had inherited from Herzen. His hopes for progress, based as
they were on conceptions of human solidarity and human development within relatively small groups, did not issue from a developed
theory of the progressive character of the bourgeois system of production. Unlike Marx, he didn't really distinguish between the "progressive" organization of productive forces in bourgeois society and
the exploitation that it entailed.[100] Thus, industrial capitalism for
Lavrov was simply another form of exploitation, another aspect of
the ruinous competition which prevented human progress, and
which might extend even further the period of suffering of the
masses. Using the same kind of reasoning that had appeared in the
Historical Letters, Lavrov simply calculated the quantity of suffering, assessed the possibilities of a real social revolution, and decided
that it was best to opt for agrarian socialism and a quick revolution.
In summary, his two major assumptions were: (a) the quantity of
suffering had to be minimized and (b) the possibilities of success
had to be maximized.

99. See, for example, his lead articles in *Vpered!,* 1875, no. 16; and
Vpered!, 1876, nos. 27 and 34. Although he accepted Marx's basic economic
doctrine, there is little evidence that he studied it attentively. As noted earlier,
Lavrov was not really interested in economics, and though he could not admit
it, he probably had a strong aversion to economic literature. As a mathematician, Lavrov was better equipped than most socialists to handle the more
advanced economic thought of his day, yet he showed no inclination to come
to grips with theoretical economics. One Soviet historian, V. Zamiatin, argues
that Lavrov did not really understand Marx's theory of surplus value
("Ekonomicheskie vzgliady P. L. Lavrova," *Ekonomicheskie nauki,* 1961,
no. 3).
100. Lavrov evinced little interest in the technical achievements of modern capitalism. In the article "Vsemirnoe bankrotstvo" (*Vpered!,* 1876, no.
25), he expressed skepticism about any further great strides in industrial
technology comparable to the invention of the steam engine. (This may seem
curious in view of his imaginativeness about the uses of technology in statecraft in "To Whom Does the Future Belong?")

Following Marx's economic analysis in one respect, Lavrov assumed that capitalism in Russia, as elsewhere, was inevitably doomed. But this in itself was only the fatalistic aspect of history. The important thing was the appearance of socialist morality and its spread throughout *all* oppressed groups. The right kind of morality would produce a progressive society. Although Lavrov distinguished workers' socialism or scientific socialism from other varieties of socialism, he viewed Marx's scheme of progress and Marx's socialism as only one species of the genus scientific socialism. It must be stressed that Lavrov did not evince a deep or total committment to any one path of development, and that he was not unduly alarmed over the appearance of capitalism in Russia. In the last analysis, Lavrov was not a Marxist. He was a socialist with anarchist leanings who, with all of the intellectual passion of the Romantic nobility of the 1840s, despised the pettiness and corruption of the bureaucratized commercial-industrial state, and who attacked it with slogans and methods learned from the "realists" of the 1860s.[101] Lavrov established his own categories of Russian socialists. These were legalists, Jacobin-socialists, narodnik-experimentalists and narodnik-preparationists. He didn't see any possibility of cooperation between his group—the narodnik-preparationists—and the former two categories. However, he always regretted the inability of the only two genuine socialist-revolutionary narodnik groups to unite.[102]

If there is any dominant note in Lavrov's major theoretical articles of 1876 (his last year of active participation in *Vpered!*) it is his increasing awareness of the spiritual diseases of the intelligentsia. He had witnessed the collapse of individuals and groups, reversals of affiliation, suicide and mental illness. One feels that he understood the intelligentsia's excruciating position—its alienation from official

101. Even when Lavrov did turn to hard statistics, it was to expose the human suffering—the hunger and misery—implicit in them. Ethics was always uppermost in his mind. Lavrov's economic views are also examined in Alexander Gerschenkron, *Economic Backwardness in Historical Perspective* (Cambridge, Mass.: Harvard University Press, 1962), pp. 177–78; and N. K. Karataev, ed. *Narodnicheskaia ekonomicheskaia literatura* (Moscow: Sotsekgiz, 1958).

102. *Vpered!*, 1876, no. 34, pp. 315–16. The term *narodnik-experimentalists,* of course, applies to the Bakuninists.

society—which permitted it to reach out for the newest, highest
ideals, but which also separated it from the masses. The individualism of its members permitted the formation of only transitory
kruzhki ("groups," or "circles"), which centered upon one or two
extraordinary men, but which disintegrated with the demise or defection of such leaders. The only cure for the intelligentsia's pathology was the renunciation of its isolation and its individualism. Once
again, these ideas had been adumbrated in the *Historical Letters*.
In order to cure itself, the intelligentsia first had to submit to party
discipline and, secondly, had to overcome its separation from the
masses. It had to destroy its own essence. Lavrov's attitude toward
himself and toward the revolutionary intelligentsia was a mixture of
admiration, contempt, and pity. His long existence in the same
milieu with the intelligentsia at last convinced him that:

The entire history of the Russian intelligentsia placed personal problems in the forefront, gave even the public activity [*obshchestvennaia
deiatel'nost'*] of its members a personal character; and personal questions
will almost inevitably remain the predominant influence in any kind of
revolutionary activity depending primarily upon the forces and shapes
[*na sily i na formy zhizni*] of the intelligentsia's way of life in Russia.[103]

Depersonalization was the only answer to the intellectual's dilemma.
He had to surrender his conscience, his will, and his intellect to the
revolutionary struggle, and suppress the remainder of his personality. Lavrov's rejection of individualism, and his total commitment
to the regimen of a professional revolutionary, are briefly summar-
ized in a letter to V. N. Smirnov:

The socialist-revolutionary party is now an army, and it must have
military discipline, not only as a whole, but in its parts. No matter how
talented and full of initiative the individual soldier, in the face of the
struggle he is not so much an individual entity as an element of a
battalion or squadron. Therefore, one cannot permit behavior which
tends to bring about defeat, nor actions which, given the general intellectual and emotional condition of the army, would call forth dissatisfaction and disrupt unity. As long as he is in the ranks before a
battle, he must submit, even though he understands better [what to do],
or else he must be removed from the army. He belongs entirely to the
battle which is going to occur.[104]

103. *Vpered!*, 1876, no. 28, p. 99.
104. Lavrov to Smirnov, 5 August [year unknown], MS in IISH.

Throughout the *Vpered!* period and afterwards, Lavrov carefully watched changes in the composition and mood of the revolutionary "army," always identifying himself with what appeared to him to be the unifying force in the movement, the force most likely to succeed. His sense of separation from the struggle and his insecure position as an émigré leader lowered his defenses to the criticism of the passionate young *aktivisty* who attacked him and *Vpered!*. In later years he transferred his allegiance to the terrorists of Narodnaia Volia, not because he believed in terror, but because he believed that Narodnaia Volia was a unifying force, a potent socialist army, without whose activity the spread of socialist ideas would be impossible.

Some of Lavrov's theoretical articles of 1876 about the revolutionary movement in Russia, and about revolutions in general, were brilliant. In his article, "The Historical Moment," he presented an extremely modern-sounding description of the process of revolution. He believed that the moment of revolution comes when there is a coincidence of three conditions: 1. An increase in the suffering of the masses, and the impossibility of mitigating that suffering within the framework of the old order. 2. The intellectual and moral paralysis of the ruling groups of society, and their inability to attract to themselves the best talents of their time. 3. The existence within the old order of a more or less significant number of "developed" individuals, hostile to the old order, who agree generally upon a program which can serve to establish a new order to replace the old one, who are sufficiently vigorous to risk everything for the realization of that program, and finally, who are sufficiently adroit to link the formulas of their program with the interests of the suffering majority, so that the latter may hope to improve their position by realizing that program.[105] Lenin probably would have found little to object to here, although he might have replaced "formulas" with "slogans."

The articles, "The Historical Moment," written in July 1876, and "A Difficult Moment," written in October 1876, reflect sudden reversals of mood about the possibilities of revolution in Russia. These and other articles written in 1875 and 1876 reveal Lavrov's susceptibility to the pressures of the Russian activists. Since he himself could

---

105. The above paraphrase adheres basically to the text; the divisions, however, are mine. See *Vpered!,* 1876, no. 37, pp. 431–32.

not assess the possibilities for revolution in Russia, he had to rely upon their information. Furthermore, he had to demonstrate to them that he did not lack revolutionary zeal and optimism. His dependency upon them, his need to be accepted by them, largely determined *Vpered!*'s increasing militancy during this period. Whenever disasters occurred, Lavrov simply fell back upon his basic position: preparationism.

Lavrov was always aware of the painful ambiguity of his position. He was never quite certain whether he was guiding history or whether history was controlling him. Psychologically, the passive element dominated. He was more concerned with understanding events than shaping them. He never believed that his activities or his journal led the revolutionary movement; rather, they were a manifestation of it called forth by the historical moment. In the final issue of *Vpered!* as a periodical, he said as much:

Undertaking *Vpered!*, the participants of the journal were only unconsciously obeying the general current of the age, which demanded social-revolutionary literature and a definite guiding [*rukovodiashchii*] program, all of whose elements were already evident.[106]

Men acted as if they were free, as if they directed their own wills, but all the while they obeyed larger historical forces of development. Like other theoreticians in the Russian revolutionary movement, Lavrov stressed the importance of discipline and will in the revolutionary movement, but like most of them, he was a thinker and not a man of action. He was Hamlet playing Don Quixote.[107]

Vpered!'s final issue of 1876 is a strange document, almost a confession on Lavrov's part that the journal had been thrust upon him by fate, that his publicistic activities were only an interim employment.[108] Now that the journal was on the verge of collapse, he indulged his penchant for writing history in mid-stream by presenting a brief description and assessment of *Vpered!*'s role in the

106. *Vpered!*, 1876, no. 48, p. 784.
107. Lavrov had been present at Turgenev's reading of his piece, "Hamlet and Don Quixote," for the Literary Fund in January 1860, and later wrote an article about Turgenev in which he both praised Turgenev and critically examined his portrayals of the Russian intelligentsia (*Vestnik Narodnoi Voli*, 1884, no. 2).
108. *Vpered!*, 1876, no. 48, p. 786.

revolutionary movement. It is indeed an excellent summary and convincing assessment. Lavrov believed that despite censorship, the Russian legal press had more direct control and influence over the revolutionary movement than did the émigré journals. Just as *Sovremennik* had had a wider audience and more influence than *Kolokol, Otechestvennye zapiski* had greater influence than *Vpered!* and other émigré journals.[109] The illegal press could treat in detail subjects and questions which could only be hinted at in Russia; and this was its primary function, although distance from local conditions limited the value of its pronouncements about practical revolutionary activity. Above all, an émigré journal could establish programs and formulate plans of action. It could also publish the views of revolutionaries active in Russia, thus acting as a kind of information agency.[110]

During its four-year existence, this is exactly what *Vpered!* had done. Driven to some extent by the competition of the Bakuninists and Blanquists, Lavrov had created a thoroughly socialist revolutionary program with provision for both propaganda and agitation, and had plotted in some detail the growth of a vast federation of social-revolutionary organizations. He had arrived at a curious solution to the problem of the role of the intelligentsia. The socialist-revolutionaries, he declared, would comprise only the first cadre of the revolutionary organization. In 1876 Lavrov predicted that at the end of six years of propaganda among workers and peasants the intelligenty would represent only a tiny percentage of the revolutionary force.[111] In his farewell article, Lavrov reiterated these and other major positions which the journal had taken during its existence as both a nonperiodical and periodical organ: The work of the socialist-revolutionary organizations was to be conducted secretly. The intelligenty would settle in the villages, attracting to themselves by skillful propaganda the best material from the peasants: the peasants in turn would propagandize their brethren. But Lavrov feared that the "diseases" of the intelligentsia might corrupt some

109. Ibid., p. 784.
110. Ibid.
111. Lavrov calculated that a handful of propagandists could create an organization of 36,050 at the end of six years (*Vpered!,* 1876, no. 34, p. 308).

of the peasant youths, causing their communal, solidary instincts to disintegrate in the milieu of the intelligentsia. Therefore, he demanded that the revolutionary work take place in the villages, in communes and artels where the habits of peasant solidarity would be strong enough to prevent the appearance of a corrupted peasant intelligentsia.[112] This aspect of Lavrov's teaching has been completely forgotten, but it is true that by 1876 he was almost as anxious to guard the narod against the intelligentsia as he was to induce the intelligentsia to go to the narod.

According to Lavrov's prognosis, there would come a time when the initiators, the intelligentsia, would be absorbed into a vast, organically linked socialist-revolutionary federation. All the while, inexorable historical forces would be at work, leading to a massive revolutionary outburst. The law of increasing misery would prepare the soil for propaganda and agitation. Revolutionaries would infiltrate the army, the universities, even the government itself. The Russian Empire, a tottering structure, would collapse in the moment of crisis, and, unless outside forces came to its aid, the old regime would be swept aside.[113] The lessons of the French Revolution were not wasted on Lavrov. He foresaw and forewarned against the seizure of power by a small, disciplined group of revolutionaries, who would rule by decree and eventually split into warring factions. On the other hand, he did not feel that the fate of the emerging society could be entrusted to the instincts of the narod, either.[114] In the last analysis, Lavrov's strategy of preparationism demanded that society undergo a radical transformation *before* a revolutionary outburst. The difficulties of this position are obvious: The process of increasing misery had to occur simultaneously with the process of socialist education. If a revolutionary seizure of power occurred before the new socialist morality had taken root, then the new society would simply perpetuate the diseases of the old. The suicidal competition, the mutual depredation which threatened to destroy civili-

112. *Vpered!*, 1876, no. 28, p. 106 ff.
113. *Vpered!*, 1876, no. 29, p. 128 ff. Lavrov presumed that the growth of the German Social Democracy would prevent Bismarck's intervention. Also see *Vpered!*, 1876, no. 48, where he summarizes his views on revolutionary strategy.
114. *Vpered!*, 1876, no. 28, pp. 99–105.

zation, would then continue in somewhat altered form. Nothing solid
would be achieved.

In numerous articles written throughout the *Vpered!* years, but
especially in 1876, Lavrov had elaborated his vision of a healthy
revolutionary process in Russia, but from the beginning he had also
wanted to contribute a major treatise to socialist thought. This
treatise, entitled *Gosudarstvennyi element v budushchem obshchestve* (The state element in the society of the future), was completed on 19 June 1876, several days after Lavrov's birthday.[115] Its
completion and publication were quite important both for his morale
and for the élan of the commune. He had labored over it for fourteen months and, according to a custom often followed by theorists
among the intelligentsia in those days, read installments of it to his
appreciative coworkers. However, though published as a separate
brochure, it seems to have attracted little attention. It was extremely
long, abstract, and academic—a "serious work," according to Lavrov's way of thinking. If anything, by clarifying his position he
alienated some of his former supporters. Its thesis amounted to a
gradualistic anarchism based upon the gradual growth of social solidarity, the "state element" forever diminishing towards zero as the
socialist order, with its new morality and new social forms, rendered
the old instruments of coercion obsolete. Lavrov pictured this as a
lengthy process, which would begin before the socialist revolution
and continue after it.

There is no question but that *The State Element in the Society of
the Future* is Lavrov's most elaborate statement of his vision of the
socialist future. In it he replied to "semi-socialists" like E. Dühring,
who believed in evolutionary socialism, and to colleagues like
Ceasar de Paepe, who believed that some forms of state administration would exist in a socialist society. It is one of those utopian works
which, through excessive detail, becomes increasingly quaint as the
years pass. Lavrov's vision of the revolution itself, as noted above,
was quite prophetic, and portions of *State Element* restate positions
developed in Lavrov's lead articles for *Vpered!* in 1876. The original
part of his treatise resides in its translation of the slogan, "From each

115. Smirnov to Idel'son, 19 June 1876, typed MS in Nicolaevsky Collection.

according to his ability, to each according to his need!" into a rather complete sketch of the socioeconomic system of the future. It corresponds to numerous articles, written both before and after *State Element,* in which Lavrov presented a historical-anthropological analysis of human needs, which he classified as natural, pathological, and temporary. The major problems in the treatise issue from Lavrov's openmindedness about the environment-versus-heredity problem. He noted that since human behavior had only been observed in harmful environments, one could only speculate about human behavior in a benign environment.

Lavrov assumed that after several generations, the values associated with workers' socialism would be as deeply internalized and as reflexive as the old bourgeois morality had been. In this new kind of society, crimes against property would disappear within two or three generations. In the presence of universal labor, social property, material abundance, and the development of the individual to the limits set by his own physiological and psychological peculiarities, any individual who would want to appropriate social goods would be exceptional, perverse—even psychopathic.

In the new social order, egoistic passions would be replaced by feelings and passions of an altruistic character. There would be no antagonism between reason and feeling. However, Lavrov was not certain about feelings and passion, even in the new social order. One had to take into account the possibility of ungovernable passions leading to crimes against individuals. Lavrov believed that normal passions could be restrained more effectively by public opinion than by fear of the law or religious beliefs. His anthropological investigations and, no doubt, John Stuart Mill's *On Liberty* as well, had convinced Lavrov of the enormous power of the individual's need for approval and recognition by his peers. Indeed, he recognized that the pressure of public opinion could become a form of tyranny, and even developed a concept which, freely translated can mean "surplus repression" (*izbytok podchineniia*). Herein lay the central problem of *State Element:* Lavrov wanted individuals to develop their inclinations freely and undistortedly, yet the kind of education and group pressure described throughout the treatise are, to all appearances, overwhelming. To his credit, Lavrov refused to ignore the problem, which was not really the one which he had originally posed. He had been intent upon proving that in the society of the future, all coercive organs could be abolished without endangering the security of its members. In the course of demonstrating the force of public approval or disapproval, however, he realized that he had uncovered a new problem, and possibly one calling for the most astute social engineering.

Lavrov's solution to both problems—ungovernable passions and surplus repression—is extraordinarily facile. Given the existence of ungovernable passions and atavisms, there had to be some form of coercion in the socialist society of the future. But since criminal acts would be exceptional, law enforcement would be left to individual action. Therefore, each individual in the new society would have to assume responsibility for acting decisively and energetically in the face of crime. Herein lies Lavrov's solution to both problems for the society of the future:

> Thus, together with the growing influence of public opinion—the major substitute for the various existing forms of state power—there must, precisely because of the absence of this power, develop in both individuals and free groups the habit of acting with one's own powers with full responsibility for one's actions, and consequently, the habit of self-help in both the individual and the group; a habit which must to some extent counteract the danger of the stifling of the independent individual and the small group by a monolithic public opinion. In the working out of the proper balance between these two social forces—the leveling force of public opinion and the individualizing force of the habit of independent and energetic decision-making in the individual and free, small group—there will reside, in all probability, one of the most important and most difficult problems of the community in the future edifice of workers' socialism.[116]

Always a great believer in the forces of custom and habit, Lavrov put them to work in his society of the future. He was confident that in the new society they would not freeze into routines.

Again and again one finds in Lavrov an aversion to physical coercion or violent, retributive actions. Thus, although he assumed that immediately after the revolution there would be a sizable number of social parasites unfit for physical labor, he chose the humane

116. *Izbrannye sochineniia*, 4:286.

solution of caring for them as one cares for children, invalids, and decrepit old people, rather than forcing them to work or demanding that they choose between physical labor and starvation.

However, if there is a utopian side to *State Element,* it most clearly appears in Lavrov's vision of freely cooperating communes (*obshchiny*). He believed that population would no longer be concentrated in great industrial centers, but in modestly proportioned communes, which would cooperate in clusters of about one hundred. For example, one such cluster of communes might pool their resources in an attempt to exploit the best coal resources in a given area. The project would be publicized and discussed in each commune. A free union of commune members interested in the problem would elect a temporary committee for the purpose of planning the enterprise. Once the needs of the communes had been established, the best sites for mines found, and the best techniques of extraction, processing, and distribution determined, the committee would issue a general invitation to the commune members to join the society for fuel production. Everything would be done on a voluntary basis, and only when a sufficient number of volunteers had appeared would the work proceed. Lavrov assumed that the nature of civic spirit in the new society would be such that no project would lack for volunteers, and that even unpleasant tasks, such as garbage disposal, would not repel the men and women of the future.

Lavrov also sketched out the work day of a typical member of a commune in the society of the future. Specialists would determine the correct proportions of manual and intellectual work for various age groups, types, and individuals. Everyone except young children, invalids, and senile adults would have work norms. For example, one man's norms might be five hours of physical labor and seven hours of intellectual labor each day. Thus, a volunteer for the society for fuel production might have the following work day: two hours in the coal mines; two hours maintaining and repairing dams and canals; one hour working on optical instruments; one hour cleaning streets; seven hours working in the bureau of statistics, in the society of translators, and at problems in higher mathematics. The same individual therefore might be a simple coal miner, the director of an enterprise for the manufacture of optical instruments, and the president of a union of mathematicians. Thus, each individual's position in a given enterprise would vary according to his degree of development in any given area. The only rewards for his work, whether as a shoe repairer or as the chairman of the committee for fuel production, would be approval, respect, and, possibly, wide recognition. Under such a system there would be no rewards for competition and no strivings for monopoly. Individuals would seek to satisfy only their "natural" needs. The expected disappearance of competition, monopoly, and exploitation permitted Lavrov to conclude:

At the moment when the society of the future is infused with the principles of workers' socialism, the state element in that society cannot only be reduced to a given minimum, it can completely disappear.[117]

Much of *State Element* is devoted to blueprinting the formation of a secret socialist-revolutionary organization to be organized mainly on federalist principles but also containing central coordinating organs, and describing the activities of the organization in the revolutionary period. Lavrov was responding to the growing demand for precise organizational thinking in the Russian movement, a demand which was being fulfilled by *praktiki* ("practical revolutionaries") like Mark Natanson and Alexander Mikhailov in Russia. Indeed, some of the men and women who participated in the powerful drive toward party organization in 1876 perpetuated the party tradition long after the collapse of Zemlia i Volia, Narodnaia Volia, and Chernyi Peredel ("Black Repartition"). While the leaders of the generation of the 1860s—Chernyshevskii, Dobroliubov, and Pisarev—lived on as inspirational figures through their writings, many of the leaders of the movement of the 1870s actually survived to witness the revolutionary era and to play significant roles in the formation and development of new parties. Lavrov's sense of the historical moment was quite sound, and even though he may not have had a direct influence upon the formation of Zemlia i Volia, he was an important contributor to the climate of opinion which led to the formation of underground parties.

During the winter and spring of 1876, while Lavrov was concentrating his final major efforts on the journal on *State Element*

117. Ibid., p. 281.

in the Society of the Future, the *Vpered!* commune began to disintegrate into warring factions. The split between Lavrov and Smirnov was now open and unresolvable. Lavrov remained editor only because Smirnov had made it quite clear to him that he too would also leave; and Lavrov knew that the journal would not survive for more than a week or two if they both left. Smirnov's position was a rather strange one. He apparently had no feelings of friendship for Lavrov, but regarded him as the only suitable editor for the journal and refused to see it fall into the hands of less competent thinkers and writers. Smirnov seems to have been more concerned with guarding the integrity and dignity of the journal than anything else. He did not want Lavrov to yield to pressures from the activists. Although he was somewhat vain about his clinical vision and his powers of manipulation, he never claimed to have Lavrov's capacities, which he genuinely admired. Smirnov even described himself as a "neuropath." He suffered from frequent attacks of neuralgia, and later discovered that he had tuberculosis. In fact, he collapsed for a time during July 1876, leaving most of the editorial burden to Lavrov. Lavrov, on the other hand, had abandoned all duties pertaining to money matters and to transport and distribution of the journal in January 1876, mainly because he had no confidence in these aspects of the journal's life.[118] He quickly disassociated himself from anything that could involve him in a scandal or threaten his reputation. For Smirnov, then, it was a matter of preserving *Vpered!*'s dignity, and for Lavrov it was a matter of protecting his own.

Another major crisis occurred in May 1876, when Lopatin arrived with word from the "union." They wanted the vperedovtsy to return to the old format that the journal had had in 1873–74 and, in addition, to publish separate commissioned histories—one on the period 1830–48 and the other about Stenka Razin. They would send 1000 rubles shortly. Lavrov and Lopatin continued to try to convince Smirnov that he should assume editorship of the journal, thus permitting Lavrov to write theoretical works, which would be issued as separate brochures; Smirnov need only be responsible for the journal's chronicles of the workers' movements in Europe and

118. Smirnov to Idel'son, 21 January 1876, typed MS in Nicolaevsky Collection.

Russia. However, Smirnov refused to yield under the renewed pressure, and the journal and commune limped on as before.[119]

In May a dispute also arose between Smirnov and the typesetters, who demanded a more democratic arrangement in the house on Evershot Road. They wanted control over the domestic duties and treasury, matters which Smirnov had previously handled. They also wanted free access to *Vpered!*'s collection of journals, and the creation of a common reading room.[120] In a word, they wanted to remove the crude hierarchy of the editorial board and compositors that had existed for several years, and to create a genuinely democratic artel'. When Smirnov refused to grant these conditions, the artel' set itself up as a distinct body, and Smirnov found the situation intolerable; he even feared that he would be beaten up. Lavrov went along with the idea of a democratic reorganization of the commune. This situation was at least partly resolved when, in June 1876, at their landlord's request, the typesetting equipment was moved to another house.[121]

In June, however, several factors temporarily raised the morale of the vperedovtsy. On June 19 Lavrov finished *State Element in the Society of the Future,* and everyone in the commune was quite impressed with it. At precisely this time, Bismarck excluded *Vpered!* from Germany, which delighted the vperedovtsy because the story was carried in Russian journals and served as free advertisement for *Vpered!*. Lavrov always exhibited delight at any sign that the authorities feared his journal. Finally, the flow of money from Russia had increased, so that in late June 1876 they had sufficient money on hand for seven biweekly issues.[122]

Meanwhile, the question of reorganizing the commune was still

119. Smirnov to Idel'son, 8 and 10 May 1876, typed MSS in Nicolaevsky Collection.

120. Smirnov to Idel'son, 19 May 1876, typed MS in IISH.

121. Smirnov to Idel'son, 20 June 1876, typed MS in Nicolaevsky Collection.

122. Smirnov to Idel'son, 22 June 1876, typed MS in Nicolaevsky Collection. On 30 June 1876 Engels wrote to Lavrov, "In regard to Mister Bismarck's exclusion of *Vpered!* from Germany, I can comfort you with the knowledge that not more than six days ago I saw it [the journal] in Heidelberg openly displayed in the windows of bookstores. Mister Bismarck hasn't found a way to teach all of his policemen to read Russian." *(K. Marks, F. Engels i revoliutsionnaia Rossiia,* p. 329.)

causing tension among the vperedovtsy. Part of the problem concerned the relation between the commune and the St. Petersburg
circle. Herein lay the essential ideological problem, for Lavrov was
trying to separate *Vpered!* from the ideological influence of the St.
Petersburg Lavrovists, even though they were still financing the
journal. Smirnov, on the other hand, did not feel that any important
questions—such as the reorganization of the commune—could be
resolved without the participation of the Peterburgtsy. It seems
that Smirnov and the St. Petersburg circle, still led by Ginzburg,
were afraid of a Bakuninist takeover of the journal, and although
they never directly accused Lavrov of plotting anything, they seemed
to feel that his actions were leading in that direction. It was a curious situation. Lavrov wanted Smirnov to edit a journal guided by
an ideological tendency which Smirnov violently opposed, while
Smirnov wanted to tie Lavrov and the journal to a group which
Lavrov heartily detested. The maneuverings to reorganize the journal in late June 1876 were seen by Smirnov as an attempt by Lavrov
to avoid having to deal with the delegates from St. Petersburg who
were expected to arrive within a few days. The commune split in two
over the issue: Gol'denberg, Linev, and Prince Levan Cherkezov,
who had joined the commune a few weeks earlier, sided with Lavrov; Iantsin, Voshchakin, and Liberman sided with Smirnov.[123]
Smirnov was reinforced by the arrival of Kuliabko-Koretskii later
that summer.

It is difficult to determine what political maneuverings might have
been behind the formation of the "Society of the Publications of
the Journal *Vpered!*" in August 1876. Smirnov may very well
have attributed more guile to Lavrov than he actually possessed.
The growing spirit of collectivism among the typesetters accorded
very well with the message of Lavrov's *State Element,* and, to all
appearances, Lavrov approved this impulse toward collectivism
and a democratic restructuring of the commune as heartily as
Smirnov contemned it. The new Society confirmed Lavrov in his
editorship on 23 August 1876.[124] Apparently, he believed that this

123. Smirnov to Idel'son, 24 June 1876, typed MS in Nicolaevsky Collection.
124. Sapir, *Vpered!,* 1:353 and 2:215–19.

made him the agent of a free collective, further clarifying his position
that he was not a hired editor responsible to an outside group—
namely the St. Petersburg Lavrovists. Through the Society Lavrov
intended to work for the continuation of *Vpered!* as a bi-weekly
rather than a bimonthly journal. The bimonthly arrangement was
being pressed upon him by Ginzburg, whose St. Petersburg group
found it increasingly difficult to support the bi-weekly journal.

Ginzburg and the London group had agreed in July that a
conference should be held to determine the fate of the journal. Discussions began in London early in November but quickly dete-
riorated; this led to a full-scale congress in Paris consisting of the
groups which supported and distributed *Vpered!* in Russia.[125] There
were seven official delegates and an undetermined (though not
large) number of unofficial delegates to the Paris congress of December 1876. A quarrel immediately broke out over Smirnov's
right to be an official member of the St. Petersburg delegation, led
by Ginzburg. Lavrov lost this battle, and both Smirnov and another
member of the London group, possibly Kuliabko-Koretskii, acted
as delegates for the St. Petersburg circle. Lavrov and Linev represented the journal. There were in addition two official delegates
from Kiev and one from Odessa. Lavrov immediately saw that
the delegates were against him, and resigned his editorship. After
having resigned, Lavrov presented an eight point program whose
major goal was the formation and extension of a secret revolutionary
organization.[126] Although he opposed the Bakuninist idea that local
bunty ("insurrections") should be a goal of the revolutionary organization, he took the position that once an insurrection burst out,
the members of the secret organization were duty-bound to join it,
to fight with the masses, and to share their fate. In this way he remained true to the credo which he had first expressed after the
Paris Commune. Ginzburg, backed by the three Russian circles,
presented his own program. This program differed from Lavrov's
mainly in spirit. While Lavrov's major concern was the moral problem of self-sacrifice and the sacrifice of the peasants in spontaneous
and hopeless local bunty, the Russian delegates' major concerns

125. On the Paris conference see Sapir, *Vpered!,* 1:347–63, and 2:213–46.
126. Sapir, *Vpered!,* 2: 236–39.

were of a different sort. They were far more interested in the immediate problems of propaganda and agitation, settlement, concrete forms of organization and activity, and the transition from "circle" activity to the organization of a party. It is apparent from the protocols of the congress that the Russian delegates were skeptical about the possibility of the intelligentsia's achieving a great deal by settling in the countryside and mingling with the narod. The Kievan delegates in particular appeared to be the most conservative, presenting ideas about preparing the new generation of the intelligentsia which harked back to the period 1873–74.

To sum up, Lavrov's program reflected the tension between his knowledge that isolated insurrections (as opposed to a general outburst) would only waste the people's strength, and his sense of the Bakuninists' moral fervor and his own belief that it was immoral to stand outside the fray. Once again, as in similar dilemmas earlier in his career, he chose morality over knowledge, presumably willing to sacrifice the intelligentsia in a hopeless cause. The St. Petersburg Lavrovists professed to share this position in that they too had a clause in their program in which they pledged to fight with the narod even in the event of a premature uprising. But they planned to do this in order to present their program more effectively, and not merely to "share the fate of the narod." To all appearances, the major substantive theoretical difference between Bakuninists and Lavrovists in 1876 lay in their attitude towards evoking popular outbursts: Lavrov used the word *vzryv* ("explosion") as opposed to *vspyshka* ("flash"), and the idea of a general, widespread insurrection as opposed to local or partial uprisings. A general insurrection could only occur at the moment when the revolutionary organization would be strong enough to unify the separate flashes into a major explosion. The Bakuninists simply did not believe that one could consciously prepare for such a moment. In practice the Lavrovists were unwilling to sacrifice themselves in a hopeless bunt, while the Bakuninists, ironically, in the absence of an insurrection were forced into the kinds of propaganda, agitation, and organization that the Lavrovists advocated. Both Lavrovists and Bakuninists were aware of this situation, and each side hoped to recruit from the other. Lavrov, in effect, had himself drawn closer to professed

Bakuninists whose moral fervor impressed him, and had by 1876 rejected his own followers, whom he believed were "morally bankrupt," whatever their professed position. Finally, the impulse toward organization, ironically enough, was greater among the Bakuninists who had emerged from the Chaikovskii circle, than among Lavrov's own followers. For these reasons, Lavrov repudiated the Lavrovist circles which had supported his journal.

At the end of 1876 a spirit of mutual disenchantment ended the relationship between him and his former followers. According to Lavrov:

The first overseas congress of the propagandist-preparationists was not only its last, but, evidently, pronounced a death sentence over the political significance of the factions. . . . In 1878 the "propagandist-preparationists" barely existed as a faction. Their banner was laid low, but hardly one of them joined any of the new Russian revolutionary parties.[127]

All that remained was the final severing of the attenuated connection between Lavrov and the journal. In January 1877 Lavrov moved from 57 Fonthill Road, where the typesetting equipment had been moved, to an apartment at 21 Alfred Place, Tottenham Court Road. In order to pay for his new apartment, Lavrov had to pawn a fur coat, some silver, and a bracelet which Alexandra Weber gave him for that purpose.[128] It was a bitter moment. Lavrov wrote to Idel'son:

There isn't any kind of communalism. There is a "management," *appointed* according to a constitution, which none of the members has discussed, and there is an editor, who is "commissioned," and so on. Executive bureaucrats and an expert invited to run things—that is, purely bourgeois elements—this is what our commune has come to. . . .

127. Lavrov, *Narodniki-propagandisty,* pp. 296–97.
128. Kuliabko-Koretskii to Smirnov, January 1877, MSS in Nicolaevsky Collection. In several letters to Weber, Lavrov asked for loans; a letter dated January 27 to Weber mentions the sale of the bracelet (typed MS in Columbia University Russian Archives). Weber's last real contact with Lavrov was in 1877, and that was probably mainly epistolary. There are indications in Lavrov's last letters to her that she was having an affair with Lopatin (the mysterious "G." of the letters probably stood for "German") against Lavrov's advice. His last letter to her, very cold and correct, was written in 1882.

I impatiently await the moment when the curtain will fall to end this farce.[129]

The crises which accompanied the collapse of the journal severely affected Lavrov's health. He was so nervous that he found it un-endurable to stay by himself. He told Lopatin that he felt very much the way he had while in prison after his arrest in 1866. He suffered from "hallucinations."[130] The only thing that seemed to calm him was the atmosphere of the British Museum, where he spent a great deal of time in early 1877. To Idel'son he wrote:

I am beginning a new period of my life. What will it be like? We'll see. It can't be a good one, but one can ask in what measure it will be en-durable and in what measure it will be repugnant.[131]

He slipped into a grey routine, which he described in another letter:

Every day at nine in the morning I leave my house and go to the Museum, stopping off along the way to drink a large cup of coffee; at one o'clock I go to a cafe nearby and dine on English meat and vege-tables and immediately return to the Museum, where I remain until four o'clock, or a little earlier since it gets dark earlier now. In the evening I eat again. What more? I have a bed, a room, I have enough to eat, once I even asked to have heat.[132]

Even during these lonely months in London, Lavrov did not se-clude himself entirely from the revolutionary movement. He in-quired into the background and consequences of the Kazan Cathedral demonstration of December 1876, and wrote an article about the trial of those involved. He followed the Trial of the Fifty in March 1877 with mixed emotions, since the Fritschi group was involved. Heroism and flamboyance impressed him negatively, if at all. Exposure to the "heroes" of the revolutionary movement had convinced him that they only served as idols and were quite fre-quently morally repulsive and intellectually muddled individuals. Lavrov also followed with interest the developments in the émigré movement, comparing the merits of *Vpered!, Nabat,* and *Rabotnik* with considerable detachment. He viewed with some alarm indica-tions that Tkachev had gained influence. In general, Lavrov re-

129. Lavrov to Idel'son, [January or February 1877], MS in IISH.
130. Lavrov to Lopatin, 24 February [1877], MS in IISH.
131. Lavrov to Idel'son, 12 January 1877, typed MS in IISH.
132. Lavrov to Idel'son, 17 January 1877, typed MS in IISH.

turned to his earlier belief that only a long, drab period of preparation could bring about a revolution. The more flamboyant the movement (he had southern European anarchism in mind) the less likely its chances of success. Lavrov's relations with Marx improved somewhat during this period, but they were still far from cordial. They quarreled over the attitude of the German socialist journal *Vorwärts* towards Russian socialists.

The London period ended on 1 May 1877, when Lavrov moved to Paris. In a letter to Lopatin, written in October 1877, he cast a bitter, retrospective glance at his life in London:

I say that I hadn't any "friends" in either the London circle or among my comrades on the editorial staff. We had more or less amicable relations, but nothing more than that. I never fully trusted any one of them. To count on any "solid" organizational ties, given the situation, would have been simply ludicrous on my side. This [the journal] was a temporary weapon, which, under favorable circumstances and the introduction of the right people, might have assumed significant proportions, but, by itself, remained insignificant. It was a good touchstone for finding out the moral bankruptcy of the Petersburg circle, and led me to break with them. That was a service. . . . People are riddles to an unbelievable extent, and the longer one lives, the more one feels contempt and loathing for *almost all of them*. They are necessary ingredients of life, because man is a social animal. The very greatest miracle in the universe is that this human rubbish creates history, and therefore one must get involved with them. . . . But the bitterest thing of all—if you believe in them or get attached to them, the chances are only one in a million that you'll make the right choice.[133]

Smirnov, no less bitter than Lavrov, accused the man whom he had revered in Zurich of senile egoism and maliciousness. Although Smirnov and his helpers managed to produce one more volume of the journal, for all practical purposes *Vpered!* died in May 1877, when Lavrov moved to Paris.[134]

133. Lavrov to Lopatin, 12 October 1877, MS in IISH.
134. A great deal of unpleasant quarreling ensued over questions about the rights to correspondence in the hands of the editorial board. More importantly, M. A. Antonovich, A. N. Pypin, and Lavrov were trying to prevent Smirnov and Kuliabko-Koretskii from publishing Chernyshevskii's novel, *Prolog prologa* (Prologue of a prologue), which had been smuggled out of Siberia. Eventually, Lavrov and Smirnov settled their differences and maintained friendly correspondence with each other.

7.
The Last Steps

In May 1877 Lavrov returned to Paris, where he had begun his life as an émigré in 1870. He moved into a small apartment in the building at 328 Rue St. Jacques, near the intersection of that street with the Boulevard Port Royal. During the last twenty-three years of his life he lived almost continuously in the same second-floor apartment. The apartment consisted of a sitting room, a study, a bedroom, and a kitchen. The first two rooms contained most of Lavrov's library—the walls were not visible for the books—but there were bookshelves and piles of books and journals in the bedroom and kitchen as well. Lavrov's friends had free access to his library and would sometimes work alongside him in the apartment. With so many books, a sofa, an armchair, a desk, and several tables and chairs, there was very little open space in the apartment. Yet, on occasion, Lavrov managed to squeeze more than fifty guests into it on his Thursday evening gatherings.

Lavrov followed a Spartan regime in Paris, as he had in London. He arose early, received his breakfast—café au lait and two croissants—in his lodgings at 8:00 A.M. from a local *crémerie*, ate quickly, and set to work in his study. At noon he received a modest lunch consisting of one course and some bread—once again from a nearby cafe. After lunch he would rest for a while. Between 2:00 and 4:00 P.M. Lavrov opened his door to any and all visitors. At 4:00 P.M. he went to eat supper in a cheap restaurant—the only meal which he ate outside the apartment. After supper he returned to the apartment for some light reading and received more guests, usually close friends, but frequently "legals" from Russia,[1] who avoided the apartment during daylight hours because of the open and somewhat casual police surveillance. Needless to say, this regime was interrupted frequently by special occasions, but Lavrov

1. "Legals" were Russian citizens in good standing, without a record of arrests for political activities.

was never away from his apartment for very long. He never stayed
out later than 11:00 P.M., and on those occasions had to be es-
corted home because of his night blindness. Generally speaking, the
socialist émigré world came to him.

Thus Lavrov withdrew from the center of the stage in 1877, disappointed and disillusioned, but not disaffected. He engaged in a
variety of activities—publicistic, scholarly, and organizational—
which eventually brought him into contact with the new leaders of
the Russian revolutionary movement. At first he remained relatively
isolated from the Russian émigré movement, although he continued
to write articles for Russian legal journals—*Otechestvennye zapiski*
and *Delo*—and collaborated on the French socialist journal *Egalité*.[2]
He also wrote for other French and German socialist journals.[3] In
addition, Lavrov maintained his contact with the younger generation of Russian students in Paris, reading a series of lectures in his
own little apartment at 328 Rue St. Jacques.[4]

For one such series in 1879 he read the manuscript of his study
of the Paris Commune.[5] It was first published in 1880 under the
title, *18 Marta 1871 goda* (The Eighteenth of March, 1871), and

2. Lavrov's relations with *Delo* were quite strained for a short while after
it published an article by Tkachev attacking his *Opyt istorii mysli*. In a letter
to Alexandra Weber he wrote, "The journal itself is insignificant. Something
in the nature of a doss-house. . . . The editor himself is trash but no worse
than Nekrasov and many others." (Lavrov to Weber, 26 March 1877, typed
MS in Columbia University Russian Archives.) Nevertheless, Lavrov continued to collaborate on the journal.
3. For a brief description of his activities during this period, see *Izbrannye
sochineniia*, 1:84–85. Marx wanted to establish ties with the *Fortnightly
Review* for Lavrov. Through Charles Dilke, Lavrov already had ties with
Athenaeum, for which he wrote a review of Turgenev's *Virgin Soil* (*Athenaeum*, no. 2573 [17 February 1877]). At Marx's urging he wrote an article on the trial of those involved in the demonstration on Kazan Square in St.
Petersburg. It appeared in *Vanity Fair*, 14 April 1877, under the title "La
justice en Russie." Lavrov's immediate response to the Kazan demonstration
of 6 December 1876 was negative. In a letter to Idel'son he wrote, "Do you
know about the mindless demonstration in front of the Kazan Cathedral on 6
(18) December? . . . What mindlessness, and this will affect all socialists. . . .
Could the Bakuninists have enough strength to organize this? Or the
Jacobins?" (Lavrov to Idel'son, 4 August [1877], typed MS in IISH.)
4. See N. Kareev, "Iz vospominanii o P. L. Lavrove," *Byloe*, 1918, no. 3,
pp. 12–13.
5. Izbrannye sochineniia, 1:85.

later as *Parizhskaia Kommuna* (The Paris Commune). In it, Lavrov once again emphasized the need for decisive actions at the moment of revolution. His prescriptions could have served well as a handbook by Lenin in 1917.

At the moment when a combination of historical events permits the workers of any country, even though temporarily, to throw over their opponents and to take control of the flow of events, they must by any expedient means, *no matter what these means are,* complete the economic revolution and ensure its firm establishment, insofar as that is possible.[6]

Lavrov also pointed out that a revolutionary party had to have its own political program. Both the party organization and the program had to be prepared before the moment of insurrection, so that the wavering masses would have firm leadership.

Whether their programs are complete or incomplete—in the absence of better ones they must decisively realize theirs, leaving it to the future to correct their mistakes. . . . At decisive historical moments, the masses always follow that banner on which the most definite programs, and simplest, clearest, and most definite goals are written; the masses follow those who are ready and do not waver.[7]

In this later study of the Commune and its lessons, Lavrov paid more attention to the need for technical military knowledge and planning, and showed considerable concern about party discipline. It is therefore not surprising that an anonymous Bolshevik found good Leninist principles in *Parizhskaia Kommuna* and praised Lavrov in an article written several years after the October Revolution.[8] Furthermore, Vladimir Bonch-Bruevich wrote that Lenin prized Lavrov's work on the Paris Commune, and thought it second only to Marx's.[9]

In 1879 Lavrov wrote an article for the first volume of the *Jahrbucher für Sozialwissenschaft und Sozialpolitik.*[10] He displayed un-

6. P. L. Lavrov, *Parizhskaia Kommuna 18 marta 1871 goda* (Petrograd, 1919), p. 212.
7. Ibid., p. 215.
8. N. L—r, "P. Lavrov o roli partii v proletarskoi revoliutsii," *Molodaia gvardiia,* 1923, no. 4-5.
9. Itenberg, *Rossiia i parizhskaia kommuna,* p. 130.
10. See "Russland," *Jahrbucher für Sozialwissenschaft und Sozialpolitik* no. 1 (1879). Lavrov did not write well in German, so he wrote the article in Russian and it was translated into German for him by Morris Wintchevskii. The article was published in Russian in *Katorga i ssylka,* 1925, no. 1.

usual detachment in his analysis of the development of the Russian revolutionary movement, especially in his description of the split that had occurred between Bakuninists and Lavrovists in the early and mid-1870s. He felt obliged to explain and defend the activities of Russian revolutionaries, and to try to inspire sympathy for them among Western European socialists. However, in 1879 he was reluctant to affiliate himself with any of the factions. When, in the autumn of 1879, A. I. Zundelevich asked him to write articles on behalf of Narodnaia Volia, Lavrov refused on the grounds that he did not agree with the party's program.[11] If anything, he tended to support the program which Paul Aksel'rod had outlined in *Obshchina*. He opposed the political struggle and the use of terror advocated by Narodnaia Volia.[12]

Between 1880 and 1882 Lavrov was exposed to the arguments of both *chernoperedeltsy* ("black repartitionists") and *narodovoltsy* ("followers of Narodnaia Volia") who had emigrated from Russia. He had to reorient himself, to adapt his principles to the latest historical phase of the revolutionary movement. At first gravitating towards the chernoperedeltsy,[13] Lavrov made his first contact with Lev Deutsch and Vera Zasulich (chernoperedeltsy who later helped Plekhanov form the Gruppa Osvobozhdenie Truda) during their involvement in the Gartman affair. L. Gartman was a narodovolets who had fled Russia after the unsuccessful attempt to blow up Alexander II's train on the Moscow-Kursk railway in November 1879.

11. B. Nicolaevsky, ed., "Pis'ma Lavrova k Tikhomirovu," *Na chuzhoi storone,* 1925, no. 12, pp. 186–87.

12. See L. G. Deutsch, *Russkaia revoliutsionnaia emigratsiia* (St. Petersburg: Gosudarstvennoe izdatel'stvo, 1920), p. 50. In a conversation with Deutsch around 1880, Lavrov said, "You and your comrades did the right thing in leaving Russia. The fascination with terror is a temporary mood, and one could foresee its appearance long ago. But this will soon pass, and once again one will have to return to the only true method—to propaganda. I haven't ceased to believe in it. But I am not a "Lavrovist," and have long since ceased to have anything to do with people who carry that title. They have compromised themselves and me by their behavior." That Lavrov bore a powerful grudge against the St. Petersburg group is evident in his correspondence. He called them "morally repulsive."

13. See L. G. Deutsch, ed., *Gruppa Osvobozhdenie Truda,* collection 1 (Moscow, 1924), p. 72; also see Deutsch, *Russkaia revoliutsionnaia emigratsiia.*

When the Paris police arrested Gartman, socialist émigrés feared
that he would be turned over to the Tsarist agents. Despite their
disagreements with Narodnaia Volia's strategy, émigrés of all stripes
rushed to support the party, especially in view of the opportunities
provided for antitsarist propaganda abroad. Lavrov and other émigrés asked Léon Gambetta (president of the French Chamber of
Deputies) for his release. Gartman was released on condition that
he leave France immediately.[14]

Lavrov's next step in the direction of active involvement in the
new phase of the revolutionary movement came in the autumn of
1881, when he accepted an invitation to become an overseas agent
of the Red Cross of the People's Will.[15] Together with Vera Zasulich,
he placed an announcement of the society's purposes in several
European journals. The announcements appeared at the end of
December 1881. The Red Cross of the People's Will performed
charitable and publicistic functions on behalf of Russian political
criminals. Since one of the society's primary purposes was to incite
public opinion against the Russian government, the French government used this as a pretext to expel Lavrov from France, and on
10 February 1882 he was told to leave immediately.[16] In all likeli-
hood, the expulsion provided him with a great psychological lift,
and influenced him in his decision to increase his role in the revolutionary movement once again. News of the expulsion provoked a
demonstration. A long procession of well-wishers flooded Rue St.
Jacques for two days before his departure on 13 February 1882.
Students, soldiers, working-class men and women, intelligenty with
bouquets—all came to wish him bon voyage as he prepared to leave
for London. According to one observer:

Looking like an old boyar . . . tall and bearded, with a good-natured,
round physiognomy framed by a luxurious growth of grey hair, Lav-

14. For accounts of this episode, see Vyrubov, "Revoliutsionnye vospominaniia," pp. 68–69; and Deutsch, *Russkaia revoliutsionnaia emigratsiia*, p. 57.
Also see Lavrov's letter to Idel'son, 10 March 1880, written shortly after
the affair was settled. (Typed MS in IISH.)
15. See *Izbrannye sochineniia*, 1:86; B. Nicolaevsky, "Iz literaturnogo
nasledstva V.I. Zasulicha," *Katorga i ssylka*, 1929, no. 6; and "Dokumenty
dlia istorii Obshchestva Krasnogo Kresta Partii Narodnoi Voli," *Byloe*, 1906,
no. 3.
16. *Izbrannye sochineniia*, 1:86.

rov's aspect, emotional yet solemnly rapt, somewhat resembled that of a believer getting ready to receive the eucharist. . . . He stood, his head inclined, and with a pensive smile absent-mindedly accepted the salutes.[17]

He no longer felt deserted, as he had between 1877 and 1880.

Lavrov was absent from Paris for only three months. While in London he decided to switch his support from the chernoperedeltsy to the narodovoltsy. Even after forming ties with Deutsch, Plekhanov, and Aksel'rod in 1880, Lavrov had maintained contact with Narodnaia Volia. In a letter written in May 1880, N. Morozov had tried to explain the role of terror in the party's program, in the hope that Lavrov would permit Narodnaia Volia to participate in the Russian Socialist-Revolutionary Library.[18] Plekhanov, one of the organizers of the library, opposed the inclusion of articles supporting terrorism,[19] and Lavrov evidently acceded to his wishes. The library's five publications were all highly theoretical, anyway, and did not deal directly with the Russian revolutionary movement. To all appearances Lavrov had allied himself with Chernyi Peredel, for in the winter of 1881 he wrote "Neskol'ko slov ob organizatsii partii" (A few words on party organization) for the third issue of the party's journal. In this article, however, he refused to condemn the terrorists outright.

Terrorists, men who have set for themselves the immediate goal of a political revolution in Russia, organizers of the masses, propagandists of socialist ideas in the narod and in the intelligentsia—all are inevitable products of Russian history in recent years. Each faction, each dedicated socialist-revolutionary has the same right to act according to their convictions, to defend them against other factions. . . . Only he who does not act to further his convictions is guilty in these present, difficult years. But since all of the factions have a common theoretical and practical soil, they can be transformed into organs of a unified organism, whose goal is—the struggle with the existing economic and political order, the preparation and erection of a new, socialist order.[20]

        17. Vinitskaia, "Iz prikliuchenii v Parizhe," p. 133.
        18. Morozov to Lavrov, 27 May 1880, MS in AOR, fond 1762, opis' 4, ed. khr. 317.
        19. "Pis'ma G. V. Plekhanova k P. L. Lavrovu," in *Dela i dni,* vol. 2 (St. Petersburg: Gosudarstvennoe izdatel'stvo, 1921), pp. 78–79.
        20. P. L. Lavrov, "Neskol'ko slov ob organizatsii partii," *Chernyi peredel* (Moscow: Gosudarstvennoe izdatel'stvo, 1923), pp. 256–57.

Just as he had earlier managed to find a place for "revolutionary passion" during the *Vpered!* years, Lavrov now incorporated provision for terrorism into his program.[21] Once again he advocated a division of labor—this time among propagandists (preparationists), agitators (Bakuninists), organizers (chernoperedeltsy), and terrorists (narodovoltsy). In "A Few Words on Party Organization" he described in detail a coordinated network of specialized revolutionary groups, each contributing to the general cause.[22] Several months later, he wrote another programmatic essay in which a new sense of urgency appeared. All of the evidence coming from informants in Russia and appearing in the foreign press indicated that the Russian government was experiencing a profound crisis. The assassination of Alexander II, and the willingness of prominent government functionaries to dicker with revolutionaries in order to insure the safety of the new Tsar, led Lavrov to believe that a full-scale revolution might occur at any moment. He wrote:

Our homeland is in serious condition, since the government is evidently completely confused and without any real plan of action, while peasant uprisings, quite independently of any kind of socialist propaganda, grow irrepressibly. A change in the existing order has to occur.[23]

Under these circumstances he ascribed a great deal of importance to the political struggle. While continuing his demands for more propaganda and agitation among the narod, and clarification of theoretical questions from the intelligentsia, he described the political struggle as the "urgent question of the moment."[24] Furthermore, he supported the idea of a highly disciplined, highly organized party with a strong central committee which would include elected members from three separate branches of the party—the combat group

21. In August 1880 Lavrov conveyed to L. Gartman the impression that he sympathized with the terrorists. See: V. I. Iokhel'son, "Iz perepiski s P. L. Lavrovym," *Byloe,* 1923, no. 21, pp. 148–49.
22. *Chernyi peredel,* pp. 252–65.
23. B. S. Itenberg and S. S. Volk, eds., *Revoliutsionnoe narodnichestvo 70-kh godov XIX veka* 2 vols. (Moscow; Nauka, 1965), 2:308. According to memoirists, Lavrov was quite shaken by the assassination of Alexander II. See Kareev, "Iz vospominanii," pp. 21–22.
24. Itenberg and Volk, *Revoliutsionnoe narodnichestvo,* 2:309.

(terrorists), the Narodnik group (propagandists and agitators), and the theoreticians.[25]

At the end of 1881, shortly after Lavrov's second plea for unity, the Executive Committee of Narodnaia Volia sent their own plea to Lavrov, the chernoperedeltsy, Kropotkin, and Kravchinskii.[26] In a separate letter Lavrov and Kravchinskii were invited to become co-editors of *Vestnik Narodnoi Voli,* the prospective overseas organ of Narodnaia Volia. Lavrov's own response to the two letters reveals how far he had repudiated the apolitical approach which he had taken in *Vpered!*'s program in 1873.

I was never an anarchist, and had always assumed that for a long time the state element, the element of power, would be completely essential both in the organization of a social-revolutionary party, and in the organization of a future society.[27]

Although he warned against the misuse of centralized power by a minority in party organization, and still held to his former view that under normal social development after a social revolution the "state element" would dwindle to insignificant dimensions, he did not protest against the Executive Committee's plans to assume "guardianship" over the masses.

For some reason or other, Lavrov's first letter, written on 15 March 1882, did not reach the Executive Committee, and his collaboration on the proposed journal remained an open question.[28] However, by April 1882, he had become an active supporter of the party. In a letter to Aksel'rod he wrote that, despite the mistakes of its leaders, "history had placed Narodnaia Volia at the head of the revolutionary movement."[29] In the course of 1882 and 1883 Lavrov fell under the influence of M. N. Oshanina and L. Tikhomirov, members of the Executive Committee, and gradually alienated the cher-

25. Ibid., pp. 309–11.
26. Ibid., pp. 315–22.
27. Ibid., 329.
28. This is revealed in a document in the IISH, dated 21 February 1883. Lavrov refers to his earlier letter of 15 March 1882, presumably the one cited above. He even quotes it at length. The second letter is simply another draft of his conditions for collaboration on *Vestnik Narodnoi Voli.*
29. *Iz arkhiva P. B. Aksel'roda* (Berlin, 1924), p. 30.

noperedeltsy.[30] Lavrov and Tikhomirov became coeditors of *Vestnik Narodnoi Voli*.[31]

Lavrov's eventual, though reluctant, affiliation with Narodnaia Volia is still further evidence of his conscious effort to keep pace with the developing revolutionary movement. In his first major article in support of Narodnaia Volia—a historical survey of the Russian revolutionary movement—he attempted to legitimize the present political struggle. None of the old strategies of the period 1873–78 sufficed in the new phase of the struggle against the old order, he wrote. Five years of experience had proven that propaganda reached only a few individuals in the masses, that the work in Petersburg and the southern industrial towns was insignificant, and that the autocracy had placed insurmountable obstacles in the path of the revolutionaries.

Therefore, the element of the struggle with the government—a direct inheritance from the Decembrists and the only task of the Russian Jacobins—from this moment moves more and more to the forefront, and attracts more and more of the most energetic individuals.[32]

Questions about federalism or centralism, about knowledge or immediate revolutionary activity, were replaced by new questions. Lavrov believed that the major split between Chernyi Peredel and Narodnaia Volia had occurred over a practical question—whether

30. This process was observed and analyzed by Deutsch. See his *Gruppa Osvobozhdenie Truda,* collection 2 (Moscow, 1925), pp. 140–41; "O sblizhenii i razryve s narodovoltsami," *Proletarskaia revoliutsiia,* 1923, no. 8; and "Pervye shagi gruppy," in *Gruppa Osvobozhdenie Truda,* collection 1, p. 72. Also see B. Nicolaevsky, ed., "Pis'ma Lavrova k Tikhomirovu," *Na chuzhoi storone,* 1925, no. 12, pp. 186–87.

31. There are a number of interesting aspects to Lavrov's career between 1880 and 1883 that are not examined in detail here—for example, his role in the discussions with the "Consecrated Guard," and his relationship with Plekhanov. The former is discussed in Deutsch, *Gruppa Osvobozhdenie Truda,* collection 2, p. 140; M. Kovalevskii, "Stranichki iz vospominanii," *Vozrozhdenie,* 1951, no. 15 (Paris), pp. 78–79; A. Yarmolinsky, *Road to Revolution* (New York: Collier Books, 1962), pp. 303–5; and V. Ia. Bogucharskii, *Iz istorii politicheskoi bor'by v 70-kh i 80-kh godakh XIX veka* (Moscow: Russkaia mysl', 1912), pp. 268–385. Lavrov's relationship with Plekhanov is more important for Plekhanov's biography than for Lavrov's.

32. First published in *Kalendar Narodnoi Voli* in 1883. I have used the 1906 edition, P. L. Lavrov, *Vzgliad na proshedshee i nastoiashee russkogo sotsiali tma* (St. Petersburg: Severnaia Rus', 1906), p. 27.

or not the masses could be organized under present conditions or whether a political revolution had to occur before the people could be organized and educated. He was careful to point out that Narodnaia Volia had not repudiated propaganda, but had carried on propagandist activities simultaneously with terror. Lavrov became convinced that Narodnaia Volia was the only faction that could unify Russian socialists and create an effective, militant party.

Under the banner of the Executive Committee stood almost all of the most energetic groups of the younger generation. One after the other the best elements of Chernyi Peredel went over to this camp.[33]

Lavrov was also aware of the development of a new group, one "strictly believing in Marx's dogmas (perhaps too literally understood), believing that . . . Russia had to pass through the phase of capitalist society, and therefore seeing a Constituent Assembly in the future."[34]

The idea of waiting for the development of capitalism repelled Lavrov as immoral. The class struggle had emerged from all preceding history and had inevitably brought with it revolutionary socialism. However, the victory of the socialists and the principle of solidarity were not inevitable.

History all too often has demonstrated that the outcome of a severe social struggle is not always the victory of the progressive party, but is sometimes simply the destruction of the society in which the struggle developed, and the disappearance of the civilizational form which had led to the social struggle. In history, right is by no means always victorious.[35]

Lavrov therefore demanded eternal vigilance from all genuine socialists. Any withdrawal from the ranks threatened the outcome. Since Narodnaia Volia had demonstrated its ability to organize socialist forces and to conduct the struggle, he felt that any group which attacked the party endangered the socialist movement and, therefore, progress itself. Even as late as 1883 Lavrov did not realize that Narodnaia Volia was moribund.

33. Ibid., p. 29.
34. Ibid., p. 34.
35. P. L. Lavrov, "Zadachi sotsializma," *Vestnik Narodnoi Voli,* 1883, no. 1, p. 13.

The turning point in Lavrov's career as a socialist came in the summer of 1883 when he sided with L. Tikhomirov and M. N. Oshanina against Plekhanov in the struggle to decide the policy of *Vestnik Narodnoi Voli*. Since the two camps could not agree upon either a common title or a common policy for the journal, Plekhanov and his followers withdrew and formed the Gruppa Osvobozhdenie Truda (Emancipation of Labor group). L. Deutsch regarded Lavrov as a victim of the duplicity of Tikhomirov and Oshanina. Lavrov, however, did not permit his younger colleagues to control the journal completely, and he opposed the anti-Marxist tone which Tikhomirov tried to give the journal.[36] In the summer of 1884 Lavrov drafted a letter to the Executive Committee of Narodnaia Volia in which he resigned as coeditor of *Vestnik Narodnoi Voli*.[37] He proposed that the enterprise be converted into a pamphlet series called *Biblioteka Narodnoi Voli*. However, the difficulties with Tikhomirov were evidently resolved, for Lavrov continued to play an important role in the journal as a member of the editorial board, as a contributor of major articles, and as a reviewer of socialist literature.

Vestnik Narodnoi Voli endured for three years—from the autumn of 1883 until the winter of 1886. Like most émigré journalistic ventures, it led a precarious existence, and by July 1884 Tikhomirov was forced to write Lopatin that the journal could not continue without more funds.[38] As usual, Lopatin managed to secure funds, and the journal survived. However, Lopatin himself was arrested in Russia in October 1884 in an extraordinarily embarrassing manner—with the names and addresses of his Russian contacts on his person. Thus ended the career of one of the most effective and reliable revolutionary actors during the period of revolutionary populism. Not only was Lopatin's arrest a personal blow to Lavrov, his negligence also dealt the *coup de grace* to any attempt to revive the

36. See *Na chuzhoi storone,* 1925, no. 12, pp. 186–89; Rusanov, *V imigratsii* (Moscow, 1929), pp. 145–46; and E. A. Serebriakov, "P. L. Lavrov," in *P. L. Lavrov, stat'i, vospominaniia, materialy,* pp. 461–62.
37. Letter from Lavrov, headed, "Pis'mo Narodnoi Vole," dated Paris, 4 August 1884, MS in IISH. Also see Serebriakov, "P. L. Lavrov," pp. 461–62.
38. L. Tikhomirov, *Vospominaniia* (Moscow: Gosudarstvennoe izdatel'stvo, 1927), p. 175.

Executive Committee of Narodnaia Volia. *Vestnik Narodnoi Voli* became the overseas organ of a nonexistent party. Nonetheless, the editors managed to issue five numbers of the periodical. They had planned to issue four numbers annually. During the last eighteen months of the journal's existence only one issue appeared; this fifth and last number of *Vestnik Narodnoi Voli* was almost sabotaged when the journal's printing press in Geneva was vandalized in November 1886 by agents of the Okhrana (secret police) under the direction of P. Rachkovskii.

In the pages of *Vestnik Narodnoi Voli,* Lavrov clarified and brought up to date his ideas about socialism in general and about the strategies of Russian revolutionary socialism in particular. It may seem strange that the man who had opposed Nechaevism so vigorously in the 1870s should support a highly centralized party devoted to terrorist activities. Yet in the article "Sotsial'naia revo-liutsiia i zadachi nravstvennosti" (The social revolution and moral aims), appearing serially in the journal in 1884–85, Lavrov tried to demonstrate to his readers that a bloody struggle was inevitable. Not only was it inevitable, but it had to occur under the banner of a party. Following his usual ruthless logic, Lavrov concluded:

Just as soon as the socialist nucleus creates itself and places itself in the historical struggle for existence, its strengthening is the direct moral duty of every faithful socialist. Whatever the mistakes and deficiencies of this nucleus of the party, if it supports the socialist program, it has an incomparably greater chance to move toward the victory of social-ism, than all of the socialist groups which have not yet won a place for themselves in history.[39]

Thus, Lavrov justified his commitment to Narodnaia Volia, first of all by saying simply that it was *there* and had already demonstrated its strength, and second by saying that even if the party made mis-takes in the struggle, it had to be supported. This was one justifica-tion for suspending criticism of its choice of the means to conduct the struggle—or at least it was a way of remaining committed to the party even if the means that it employed appeared to be mis-taken. Finally, Lavrov returned repeatedly to the idea that obsta-cles to socialist propaganda and to the formation of a workers' party

39. *Vestnik Narodnoi Voli,* 1885, no. 4, p. 39.

in Russia had to be removed. Political questions—including that of
the use of terror against existing political obstacles to socialist development—could not be avoided. A socialist had to adapt his strategies to the political forms in his own historical environment. In
Russia, this meant striking blows directly against the autocracy and
its administration.

By Lavrov's own definition, he never really changed his party
affiliation. He had long ago committed himself to the "party" of
socialist solidarity. He was simply allying himself with a special form
of the party, a nucleus around which the party could gather its
forces. Any movement away from Narodnaia Volia, in Lavrov's
eyes, could only be retrograde. This approach made him a determined opponent of Gruppa Osvobozhdenie Truda, the new Marxist
group headed by Plekhanov. He viewed them as a renegade faction but refused to attack them severely, because he saw them as
members of the same general party who could return to the fold—
a typical approach for Lavrov.

Lavrov's attitude towards Marxism was shaped by the same peculiar mixture of universal and particular considerations. He considered Marx's theory to be too important a weapon in the revolutionary struggle for socialists to permit any elements of the theory
to be attacked.[40] Lavrov agreed with Plekhanov that, no less than
Darwin's theory, Marx's theory had to be developed further. He
wrote:

I am firmly convinced that this teaching, worked out by its author
primarily by using the data provided by the contemporary economic
position of Western Europe and by virtue of its being the firmest scientific basis for the Western European workers' social-revolutionary movement, can by rational extension of its essential points become just as
sound a scientific basis for other progressive historical processes as
well.[41]

Lavrov worked out his own version of Trotsky's law of combined
development (having earlier done something similar in the area of
critical thought in the 1860s). He began by assuming as fundamentally correct Marx's idea that all social "products" had to emerge

40. *Vestnik Narodnoi Voli*, 1884, no. 3, p. 38.
41. Ibid., p. 41

from economic bases. However, once these "products" were shaped, they had an autonomous existence and could act as forces influencing and transforming economic processes. This was Lavrov's resolution of the old problem of the relationship between "infrastructure" and "superstructure." Lavrov also believed that a society in a relatively backward stage of economic development could learn from the example of neighboring societies which were relatively advanced economically. Backward societies could shorten the process of transition through intermediary stages of development. Lavrov compared this to pedagogy, by means of which some kinds of knowledge and skill could be transmitted in a few years, although their acquisition by mankind might have taken a century. Ultimately, this meant that one had to examine Marx very closely, to see if all societies, past, present or future, did indeed exhibit Marx's basic laws of economic and social evolution, and to see whether or not *apparent* differences in evolutionary phases could eventually be described in the terms that Marx had developed in his examination of Western European economics and society.[42]

Had Lavrov chosen to associate himself with Plekhanov's Marxist group instead of with Narodnaia Volia, he would perhaps have ensured kinder treatment for himself at the hands of Soviet historians. For as it turned out, Plekhanov's group proved to be the historical nucleus of Russia's victorious socialist party. However, in 1882–83 he had chosen the party which seemed to be the most promising of all revolutionary groups, not only to him, but to the leaders of European socialism. Ironically, Marx himself had been impressed by the achievements of Narodnaia Volia and shortly before his death had supported them. Marx, like Lavrov, had believed that Russia might abbreviate the phase of capitalism, but only in the event of a general European revolution. By adding his prestige and authority to Narodnaia Volia, Lavrov made life very difficult for Plekhanov and the Gruppa Osvobozhdenie Truda in the first years of its existence, and even in the early 1890s.

Lavrov's association with *Vestnik Narodnoi Voli* ended painfully when Tikhomirov returned the Geneva typesetting apparatus to Kaspar Turskii, the Tkachevist, thus delaying the publication of an

42. Ibid., p. 42.

émigré edition of Lavrov's introduction to a history of thought.[43] Tikhomirov had even more unpleasant surprises in store for his former colleagues than his dubious handling of the liquidation of the journal. In June 1888 his pamphlet *Pochemu ia perestal byt' revoliutsionerom* (Why I ceased to be a revolutionary) appeared. This followed the serious rupture between Tikhomirov and the central figures in the group that had published *Vestnik Narodnoi Voli*— Lavrov, Oshanina, and Rusanov—over the new preface to the second edition of his book, *La Russie politique et sociale,* which had appeared in March 1888.[44] Tikhomirov did not merely become a legalist, he also repudiated the entire revolutionary tradition in favor of monarchism and, after returning to Russia, became the most influential renegade from the intelligentsia since Mikhail Katkov.

Despite the termination of *Vestnik Narodnoi Voli* in 1886 and Tikhomirov's defection from the party in 1888, Lavrov committed himself all the more strongly to Narodnaia Volia. At the Paris Congress of the Second International in 1889, as representative of several Russian and Polish émigré groups, he called for a revival of the Executive Committee and the party.[45] At the same congress, Plekhanov presented the position of the Gruppa Osvobozhdenie Truda: that the peasant commune was in a state of decline, and that the urban proletariat was the new revolutionary force.

Even after the split, in the spring of 1889 Lavrov and Plekhanov attempted to establish a modus vivendi for a new journal. Lavrov typically demanded that polemics should be forbidden, and that those positions which could lead to disunity should be put aside in favor of "general principles." (Evidently, Plekhanov had even wanted to try to bring the London émigrés—the liberal Free Russia group—into the enterprise, but Lavrov was irreconcilably opposed to any kind of alliance with liberals at that time.) One issue of the journal *Sotsialist* appeared in June 1889. The program of the journal was clearly Marxist rather than populist. Although the editors

43. Tikhomirov, *Vospominaniia,* p. 205.
44. See Abbott Gleason, "The Emigration and Apostasy of Leo Tikhomirov," *Slavic Review* 26, no. 3 (1968):414–29.
45. Excerpts of the speech are published in *Katorga i ssylka* 10 (1924): 123–26.

affirmed the continuity of the revolutionary movement and did not
denounce Narodnaia Volia, they relegated the peasants to a secondary role in the revolutionary movement. Lavrov, on the other
hand, suggested in his article a critical approach to Western experience, and the selection of those elements which were relevant to
Russia's historical development. The single issue of *Sotsialist* rep-
resents the last real collaboration between Lavrov and Plekhanov.
When Plekhanov characterized the narodovoltsy as Blanquists at
the Brussels Congress of the Second International in 1891, Lavrov unsuccessfully demanded a public retraction of the statement.[46]
Even at this time Lavrov enjoyed higher status as a representative
of Russian socialism than the Marxist émigrés, as evidenced by the
fact that in 1891 he, rather than Plekhanov, was invited by *Vorwärts*
to contribute articles on the Russian revolutionary movement.

Lavrov reacted very strongly in the early 1890s to the revival of
Russian liberalism, when veteran Russian socialists tried to further
the socialist movement by liberal methods. He strongly attacked the
Free Russia group in London. Ironically, he found himself attacking Kravchinskii for not being sufficiently radical. This is simply
another example of the implacable logic of Lavrov's radicalism.
While men like Kravchinskii were willing to retreat to secondary
positions, and were beginning to think in terms of two phases of
development in Russia—the liberal-constitutionalist and then the
socialist—Lavrov refused to hide his socialist banner. In this respect he seemed dogmatic and sectarian to other socialists who tried
to form cooperative ventures. Consequently, in December 1891,
Lavrov was reluctant to join Kravchinskii, Vladimir Burtsev, Plekhanov, and Aksel'rod in an organizational and propagandistic effort for the Committee of the Society for the Struggle with Hunger,
which hoped to use the widespread famine of 1891 to press for
constitutional reforms in Russia.[47]

Besides feeling some antipathy for the leaders of the other émigré
factions—Vladimir Burtsev in particular was one of his bêtes noirs

46. *Iz arkhiva Aksel'roda*, p. 129.
47. Ibid., pp. 117–31. Also see Lavrov's letters to the *Obshchestvo Bor'by
s Golodom* (28 December 1891 and 25 February 1892, MSS in the Nicolaevsky Collection).

—Lavrov also refused to join any campaign in which he felt so-cialists would be diverted from their true goals. He stated his views publicly in 1892 in a preface to Rusanov's pamphlet, "Hunger in Russia," in which he described philanthropic activity as a private and not a party matter.

However, Lavrov responded enthusiastically to every sign that Narodnaia Volia might be reviving in Russia. This happened toward the end of 1892, when he received word from Russian contacts about the appearance of new groups of narodovoltsy. The émigrés received the first issue of a new narodovolets journal. Lavrov be-came involved in discussions about new émigré journals and about fund raising. All of the major émigré groups in London, Paris, and Geneva were involved in unification plans. However, the émigrés received an unexpected setback when, on 9 December 1893, the French anarchist Auguste Vaillant hurled a bomb into the midst of the French Chamber of Deputies. This led to much stricter surveil-lance of terrorist groups on the continent. According to the report of an Okhrana agent in Paris, Lavrov was thoroughly frightened by the episode, and began sending panicky warnings to his colleagues to quiet down until the "storm passed over."[48]

Nonetheless, Lavrov continued to try to resurrect the party. In the early 1890s (the founding date of the group is difficult to es-tablish exactly) Lavrov, E. A. Serebriakov, I. A. Rubanovitch, M. N. Oshanina, N. S. Rusanov, and M. Pokhitonova formed the Gruppa Starykh Narodovoltsev (Group of old narodovoltsy), which with the Free Russia group in London and the Gruppa Osvobo-zhdenie Truda comprised the three centers of émigré leadership during the mid 1890s. Lavrov's major efforts during the early and mid 1890s were devoted to historical works—his *Narodniki-propa-gandisty 1873–1878 godov* (Narodnik propagandists 1873–1878) for a series published by the Gruppa Starykh Narodovoltsev, and his own never-ending major work, which he was not destined to finish.

In the period from 1894 to 1900, the last years of his career as a revolutionary publicist, Lavrov showed no signs of losing his sec-tarian devotion to Narodnaia Volia. For example, in a letter to the

48. Report of Okhrana agent in Paris, XVIb–1–(4), Hoover Institution Archives.

editor of *Russkii rabochii* (The Russian worker), published in its
first issue in 1894, Lavrov emphasized the propagandistic activities
of the narodovoltsy, and tried to show that they were no less active
in this respect than the chernoperedeltsy or the Russian Marxists
who grew out of the latter party.[49] In "O programmnykh voprosakh"
(On programmatic questions), his programmatic statement in a
narodovolets publication,[50] Lavrov tried to show that there were no
essential differences between the narodovoltsy and Russian Marxists. The question of the disappearance of the commune and the
development of capitalism did not trouble Lavrov as much as the
question of the revolutionary nature of the Russian peasants. He
had long ago agreed with the Marxists on the question of developing capitalism, but he refused to admit that the peasants were poorer
revolutionary material than the urban proletariat. Perhaps the most
important difference between Lavrov and the Russian Marxists lay
in his refusal to regard the development of capitalism as a progressive and necessary phase in historical development. He resembled
the Bolsheviks (or rather, they resembled him) in his detestation
of liberalism and his contempt for alliances with liberal parties. He
had inherited this attitude from the men of the sixties. It had been
reinforced during the days of the Paris Commune and had remained
one of the axioms of his revolutionary strategy in the 1870s, 1880s,
and early 1890s. There are indications that by the mid 1890s Lavrov had begun to yield in the direction of accepting limited contact
with liberals, at least in order to inspire them to organize themselves
into an effective oppositional group.[51] However, throughout the
1890s he reaffirmed his belief that the liberals would be the weak
partner in any liberal-socialist alliance. He was grasping for com-
binations and alliances which could overthrow the autocracy, the

49. *Russkii rabochii,* 1894, no. 1, p. 8.

50. *Letuchii listok,* no. 4 (9 December 1895).

51. See P. Kudelli, *Narodovoltsy na pereput'i* (Leningrad, 1925), p. 157;
and Richard Pipes, "Russian Marxism and the Populist Background," *Russian
Review* 19 (October 1960.) In "Zadachi russkikh sotsial-demokratov" [The
tasks of Russian social-democratics] (1902), one of his first programmatic
articles, Lenin attacked Lavrov's position of 1895. It seems clear, though,
that Lenin's own ideas were not too far from Lavrov's, especially in his *Chto
delat'?* [What is to be done?], in which he refers to his polemic against Lavrov.
He had to work rather hard to distinguish his position from that of an old
narodovolets.

first point in his program. Ultimately, he believed that only a disciplined, militant party, with the centralized organization of the old
Executive Committee of Narodnaia Volia, could lead the struggle.
If the Russian Marxists could organize a workers' party in spite of
absolutism, then the methods of political struggle used by Narodnaia
Volia would be superfluous. But Lavrov did not believe that this
was possible.

Lavrov, therefore, spent the last years of his life trying to resurrect Narodnaia Volia, or to create a party built along similar lines.
He struggled against Narodnaia Volia's critics, answering their attacks in articles and letters to European socialist leaders, explaining the use of terror and the party's philosophy and goals. Yet he
never regarded himself as a real leader of Narodnaia Volia. On 3
January 1897, he wrote:

I never stood at the head of any kind of "revolutionary party," much
less Narodnaia Volia, never participating in any kind of committees nor
even in the negotiations of Narodnaia Volia with the Polish Party
Proletariat during the publication of *Vestnik Narodnoi Voli*. I was
only a socialist writer, the editor of a journal in one instance, a member
of the editorial board in two others. In the last two instances I was a
literary ally of the party—not more.[52]

He still tended to think of himself as an outsider, someone living
on the fringes of the revolutionary movement.

During the 1890s Lavrov's writings and speeches became increasingly censorious. He attacked fin de siècle aestheticism, meta-
physics, and mysticism, and careerism in the new generation of
students. He felt that the students were less political and more
compromising than they had been in the 1880s. The ascetic, self-
sacrificing spirit of earlier generations seemed to him to have dis-
appeared. After a New Year's Day sermon to the Russian students
in Paris in 1897, Lavrov evidently had little to do with the younger
generation. His last years were further embittered by the Franco-
Russian alliance, and the inability (or unwillingness) of French
socialists to do anything about it.

52. A reply to criticisms of his New Year's speech to the younger generation, delivered in Paris on 31 December 1897; MS (not in Lavrov's hand)
in IISH.

Lavrov's personal life had always reflected the strange contradiction between his logical commitment to a radical variety of revolutionary socialism and his cultural and personal qualities. Ironically, his liberal and amorally positivistic friends and acquaintances —Maxim Kovalevskii and I. I. Mechnikov—were quite important to him during his last years in Paris. Kovalevskii, the liberal sociologist, jurist, historian, and friend of Marx, had first met Lavrov at Marx's home, probably in 1876 or 1877.[53] Also, for a time in 1880 Lavrov joined a group of Russian scholars who held discussions at the Cafe Voltaire every Tuesday.[54]

It was Kovalevskii in particular, however, who later assisted Lavrov in financial matters. By 1883 the reaction in Russia, and stricter censorship, had stopped the steady stream of articles to legal journals which had been Lavrov's major source of income. He had spent almost all of his limited funds on books and journals, acquiring a vast library, the volumes of which he willingly lent to friends and acquaintances. He also freely lent money to socialist comrades, when he had it. In 1885 or 1886 Lavrov told Tikhomirov that he had only enough money to maintain himself for two months.[55] To N. A. Rusanov, who after June 1885 became one of his closest friends, Lavrov revealed that he planned to commit suicide if no relief came before the two months ended.[56] He had even written a suicide letter and put aside sufficient money for a common burial. It was at this point that Kovalevskii came to his aid. Through Kovalevskii, Lavrov obtained a post as London correspondent for *Russkie vedomosti* in 1886.[57] Between 1886 and 1897 the topical articles that he wrote for *Russkie vedomosti* were a major source of income. Kovalevskii

53. Kovalevskii, "Stranichki iz vospominanii," p. 77.
54. Kareev, "Iz vospominanii o P. L. Lavrove," p. 15.
55. Tikhomirov, *Vospominaniia,* p. 312.
56. Rusanov, *V imigratsii,* pp. 138–39.
57. "Pamiati M. M. Kovalevskogo," *Russkie zapiski,* 1916, no. 3, p. 308; "Pis'mo Lavrova," *Russkoe bogatstvo,* 1914, no. 1, pp. 193–98. Lavrov's contributions to the journal dropped off sharply after 1892, but the editors continued to pay him as their London correspondent. Eventually the journal sent a real correspondent to London, and Lavrov's pride was hurt. He didn't want to accept charity that openly, and proposed a scheme for mortgaging his history of thought. Lavrov also offered them a planned fantasy about the distant future of humanity—"The Unusual Adventures of John Fidget." I have not seen the manuscript, which presumably survives.

also arranged for the publication of Lavrov's *Zadachi ponimaniia istorii* (The problems of understanding history) and *Vazhneishie momenty v istorii mysli* (Paramount moments in the history of thought).

According to Kovalevskii, Lavrov never seemed happier than when they were discussing the latest word in scientific research. During his last years, Lavrov also used to dine with Il'ia Mechnikov, the prominent Russian émigré chemist, whose apartment was located across the street from the Pasteur Institute where Mechnikov worked. Thanks largely to Mechnikov, Lavrov received medical care of the first order during his final illness.[58]

As the years passed, Lavrov's advanced age and unwavering commitment to socialism gave him a certain grandeur in the émigré socialist community. By the late 1880s he was a socialist patriarch, a central figure in the Russian and Polish émigré movements. On 14 June 1885 revolutionary groups abroad arranged a banquet celebrating both his birthday and the silver anniversary of his activity as a publicist.[59] Congratulatory telegrams from Russian activists and from European socialist leaders renewed his confidence in the rectitude of the course that he had taken.

Lavrov seemed to be the focus of a great deal of admiration and affection. Memoirists note that he always seemed to be surrounded by a coterie of Russian female students. He was generous with his ideas and books, and set many young scholars and publicists on their feet. Because of his wide contacts with European and Russian socialists, he became almost a central communications agency for Russian socialist émigrés in Paris. Lavrov's recommendation could open many doors to aspiring young socialists.[60]

58. Semen Rappaport, Lavrov's secretary and constant companion during his last years, described the eagerness with which Lavrov anticipated his meetings with Kovalevskii and Mechnikov. Through Mechnikov, Lavrov was introduced to Dr. Charcot, who treated what was probably a cardiac condition. Lavrov complained of acute asthma (just as Bakunin had), but the symptoms are as easily read as heart disease.

59. *Izbrannye sochineniia*, 1:87.

60. Serebriakov's memoirs (see n. 31) constitute one of the best descriptions of Lavrov's wide activities from the mid-1880s to the mid-1890s. Charles Rappaport (not to be confused with Lavrov's secretary, Semen Rappaport) is another excellent source. Much of the above description is

On Saturday evenings Lavrov frequently attended meetings of the Russian Workers' Association, sometimes reading speeches to the workers. He had close ties with the Jewish workers' groups in Paris. In addition, he read lectures to gatherings of Russian and Polish students. During the late 1880s Lavrov led an extremely active life, and was probably the unofficial head of the large colony of Russian and Polish émigrés who lived in the Latin Quarter during this period.

Lavrov's Thursday soirees were a well-known aspect of his orderly existence. They were usually attended by fifteen to twenty persons, primarily Russian and Polish émigré socialists and students. Petits fours and tea were served by Lavrov, while often a bearded escapee from Siberia presided over a decrepit samovar, which, despite its appearance, was regarded with affection by the émigrés.[61] (The French maid-servant wouldn't touch the infernal "tea machine.")[62] Even some of Lavrov's old enemies, like Sokolov, attended these soirees, although when Sokolov, who brought his own refreshment, became drunk and abusive, Lavrov would have to show him the door.[63]

Precisely because of his rather ordered and secure way of life after the crisis of the mid-1880s, Lavrov was forever troubled by the nature of his position. He suffered agonies of doubt and guilt for sending young revolutionary fighters to death or exile, sometimes to madness or suicide, while he himself remained safe. Once he even entertained ideas of smuggling himself into Russia disguised as a monk.[64] One feels that he longed to prove himself by some supreme sacrifice, but that it remained beyond him. It is probable that he secretly accused himself the way Tikhomirov later accused him in his memoirs:

---

based upon his "Memoirs" (typed MS in the Manuscript Collection of the Bibliothèque Nationale, Paris).

61. Charles Rappaport, "Memoirs," p. 33.
62. Gintovt-Dzebaltovskii, "Parizhskie vstrechi," *Sibirskie ogni,* 1927, p. 80.
63. Charles Rappaport, "Memoirs," p. 33.
64. Kovalevskii, "Stranichki iz vospominanii," p. 79.

He personally did not suffer, he didn't endure trials, didn't make serious sacrifices for the cause; he never wore himself out, never overtaxed his strength. . . .

Tkachev couldn't bear the failure of *his* cause and lost his mind. Sokolov became a drunk. Herzen sank into dismal disappointment. Kropotkin isolated himself from other Russians. All of them believed in a *living,* concrete cause and therefore suffered, grew, and wore themselves out with it. Lavrov's cause was not living, not real, but a bookish, abstract formula, which, of course, remained the same, no matter how the real world changed. *That* kind of cause could not inspire, could not bring joys, nor could it lead to despair, because it possessed no life—it didn't grow, didn't decline, didn't suffer dangers, just as a mathematical formula suffers no danger when the building around it collapses. The building collapsed. For a living man this is terrible. What is the use of a formula when everything around you is in ruins? The building itself did not interest Lavrov, and he didn't even have any conception of its beauty or ugliness, its strong points and its weaknesses. Only his own *thought* interested him, his formula, and it always remained whole. A more vital man asks himself: is this formula really true? If life isn't so, then surely the formula is nonsense, fantasy. Such questions couldn't enter Lavrov's mind.[65]

Although the questions did indeed enter Lavrov's mind, they always fell before his merciless logic.

Lavrov had enjoyed reasonably good health until 1895, although during the last thirty years of his life he constantly complained about eye trouble and had even lost the sight in one eye temporarily in 1885. His health began to fail in the late 1880s, but he was still quite strong until he suffered a stroke in the spring of 1895, this time losing his sight altogether for two months. His eyes never completely recovered. Shortly thereafter, a carriage ran over his foot and injured one of his toes. Someone—either his secretary or his daughter, who lived with him during his last years, or one of his friends—had to accompany him on his walks after that incident; but he began to have difficulty breathing, and in the last one and a half years of life he hardly left his apartment. Fearing that the end was near, he began to work feverishly on his history of thought.

Shortly before his death Lavrov entered a new phase of his career as a revolutionary socialist. He approved the program of the League

65. Tikhomirov, *Vospominaniia,* pp. 308–9.

of Agrarian Socialism and promised to support it.[66] He became acquainted with Michael Gotz and Victor Chernov, two of the organizers of the nascent Socialist Revolutionary Party.[67] Lavrov's conscious effort to side with the progressive revolutionary vanguard in Russia thus carried him one step further—the last step in a long and complex evolution.

On 18 January 1900 his daughter found him unconscious in his room. He recovered, but three days later suffered a stroke, which paralyzed the left side of his body and affected his speech. During his last days he refused any medicine except bromine.[68] Semen Rappaport, Lavrov's secretary between 1894 and 1900, noted that even in a drugged sleep, the dying scholar moved his hands as if writing in the air. On 6 February 1900, shortly before noon, Lavrov died.[69]

Lavrov's will is extremely characteristic of the man. In the fifth paragraph he stated:

Je ne fais aucune disposition concernant mes funerailles parce qu'une fois mort je ne saurais m'intéresser à ce qui arrivera a mon cadavre C'est l'affaire de mes amis. . . . Si mes coreligionnaires croyaient pouvoir utiliser ma mort pour la cause que nous avions servi ensemble, je leur laisse pleine liberté de le faire; s'ils croyaient, au contraire, qu'à ce moment toute démonstration serait inopportune, je demande qu'ils s'abstiennent complètement.[70]

His friends chose to demonstrate. The funeral cortege comprised 6,000 or more marchers carrying floral tributes. Among them were representatives of Russian and European socialist parties, students, workers, French socialist deputies, and local officials. At the corner of the Boulevard Port Royal and the Boulevard St. Michel, a group of Guesdists unfurled a red banner and

66. Semen Rappaport, "Pierre Lavroff," *Le mouvement socialiste,* 1900, no. 29, p. 284.

67. Charles Rappaport, "Memoirs," p. 81.

68. Semen Rappaport, "Poslednie dni P. L. Lavrova," in *Pamiati P. L. Lavrova* (Geneva: Tipografiia Gruppy Starykh Narodovolstev, 1900), pp. 15–22.

69. Ibid., pp. 22–23. Also, see O. Shreider, "Poslednie minuty Petra Lavrovicha Lavrova," in *P. L. Lavrov, stat'i, vospominaniia, materialy,* pp. 513–14.

70. Lavrov's last will and testament is preserved in the Nicolaevsky Collection. It is dated 20 September 1899.

tried to join the cortege, when they were assaulted by police agents. This was the first incident of the day. A young man was arrested for striking one of the police agents with a flower pot. The next incident occurred when the cortege reached its destination, the cemetery of Montparnasse, and two red banners were unfurled just before the graveside eulogies were to begin. There was another clash with the police. When things quieted down, Elie Rubanovitch gave the first speech, and was followed by twenty-three more speakers, among them several prominent French radical deputies, and the singing of revolutionary songs.[71] It was a fitting burial for a man who had devoted almost three decades of his life to the socialist cause. His friends placed a rough pyramid of red granite over his grave, which is close to an obelisk commemorating those who died in the Paris Commune.

What has been attempted in this biography is the exploration of the dynamics of personality as well as of the ideas, events, and generations which helped to make Lavrov a unique—and in some ways uniquely lonely—figure in the revolutionary movement. The historian who deals only with ideas and who does not consider these other aspects is possibly the poorest guide to a deeper understanding of Lavrov's complex evolution. He is likely to link Lavrov together with Mikhailovskii as one of the systematic libertarians in the Russian movement. Although this label fits Mikhailovskii well, it does not accurately describe Lavrov. Lavrov's life and the entire corpus of his writings must be examined together for examples of his ideas in action. Consonance of thought and deed is central to the intelligentsia's creed, and Lavrov was one of the most conscious formulators of that creed. Of course, any biographer encounters severe problems when he attempts to match a man's deeds and their apparent consequences against his expressed ideas and intentions. Perspective is itself a problem, for from one perspective great ideas dwarf the activities of those who try to implement them, and from

71. This account is pieced together from several newspaper accounts, mainly French. Several of the graveside speeches were published in *Pamiati P. L. Lavrova.*

another viewpoint, men who try to act in behalf of great causes acquire some of the largeness of the cause, whatever their personal dimensions. Actors in great causes are subject to the retrospective judgments of those who believe that they served the cause poorly in comparison with others. (The latter type of judgment appears in mild form alongside positive evaluations in the most recent Soviet statements about Lavrov's contribution to the revolutionary movement.) Finally, historical actors are open to the imprecations of retrospective judges (such as crude Stalinist historians, or conservative historians), who believe the cause itself to be a harmful one, as well as to the "clinical" judgments of the psychopathologists of rebellion. Although it is almost impossible to avoid one or another of these perspectives or types of judgment, one can still try to resolve certain paradoxes or ambiguities in a man's career. This at least is true for the problems of Lavrov's libertarianism and his revolutionism, problems which recur in the literature about him.

In order to place Lavrov in the libertarian tradition, liberal historians must ignore some of Lavrov's writings and activities before 1870, and most of them after that date. Lavrov's ideas of freedom in history and individual liberty in society were always being strongly modified at different moments in his career by a theory of limited possibilities, Marx's "scientific" economic theory, the idea of scientific ethics, and the idea of a unified, disciplined, scientific party. One should add to the above intellectual constructions Lavrov's personal fatalism, loyalty, and sense of civic duty, all of which were combined in his psychological propensity to feel that he was fated to act in the service of great social and cultural causes. Lavrov's fatalistic and often guilt-ridden sense of duty evidently contradicted his belief in the psychological theory that men inevitably act as if they are free. In his own mind he tended to equate the realm of personal freedom with self-indulgence or with delinquency from service to the cause. Many of Lavrov's writings and actions, then, lead to the conclusion that he was not a true libertarian. Whatever his theory of historical indeterminism and individual liberty, he often acted as if men were instruments of historical forces, never left much free play for the individual in practice, and felt considerable guilt for his own moments of self-indulgence.

On the other hand, for many years the critical, historical perspective which made Lavrov an early neo-Kantian blunted any impulse in him toward rash, absolute, or final commitments. Throughout the 1860s and early 1870s he appeared to be something less than a dedicated revolutionary socialist. In the mid 1870s, after he had clarified his position, he remained suspect. One might argue that he appeared in this light at a moment when a rather uncritical, emotional anarchism dominated the Russian revolutionary movement. But there were several things about Lavrov's personality that struck a wide range of contemporary observers: critical thoroughness; personal gentleness; love of decorum and order; meticulousness; patience; willingness to discuss and respect other points of view; and a deep aversion for violence and violent retributive acts—all impressed many of his associates as nonrevolutionary traits. By temperament and employment Lavrov had been and continued to be fundamentally a thinker and a teacher, as the traits mentioned would seem to suggest.

Lavrov began his revolutionary career quite late—so late, in fact, that he had little or no capacity to change deeply implanted habits of mind and style of expression. Yet he could be quite stubborn as well, and the irenic qualities exhibited by him in theoretical discourse were more than counterbalanced by another tendency: once convinced that he had found the most advanced theory and the correct strategy with which to implement it, Lavrov defended them as if they were absolutely right. Thus, despite his stated aversion to dogmatism and rigid authority, he submitted to "scientific" authorities like Marx, especially in economic and social matters. The historical, relativistic aspect of his neo-Kantianism tended to recede in importance before the deontological ethics which dominated Lavrov's actions and before his deep commitment to scientific authority. But Lavrov did not exhibit his radical commitment in a personal style that other radicals could easily identify. Thus the personal qualities noted above surprised many who equated revolutionism with acrimoniousness and furious activity. Both colleagues and outsiders associated his personal qualities less with radical revolutionism than with a cosmopolitan and genteel (though philosophically radical) variety of liberalism. Add to this the social and cultural

differences between Lavrov and the younger revolutionary generation and it is hardly surprising that he stood out from his corevolu-
tionaries.

These ambiguities and incongruities complicated Lavrov's life
without depriving it of integrity. It is not uncommon for personality
and theory, or temperament and ideology, to conflict in an individual. Lavrov's merciless logic ultimately guided his life. It was the
logic of duty and loyalty to a cause, rather than any kind of abstract or pure logic. In Lavrov's logic the end tended to justify the
means, ethics tended to guide knowledge, and the ideal, to dominate
the reality. The same mercilessly logical approach to social and
political problems that had impressed Lavrov's friends in Shtakenschneider's salon during the 1860s later appalled his revolutionary
colleague, Lev Tikhomirov, who had lost his taste for immediate
suffering and untimely death. Lavrov's personal gentleness yielded
to a historical vision in which the cost of delaying revolution far into
the future enormously exceeded the price in human suffering to be
paid for a revolutionary struggle in the present and near future. He
was certain that the cure was less painful than the disease. This certainty, along with his unflagging devotion to the idea of a unified
party, and his flexibility about the means to be employed by the
party, places him well within the historical tradition of the professional revolutionary during the period 1873–1900. However,
Lavrov's personal qualities did not permit him convincingly to play
a role which demanded simultaneously the qualities of teacher and
executioner. And that, finally, is to his credit.

Bibliography

This bibliography mainly includes works which are directly related to the areas of Lavrov's life treated in this biography. However, I have also included books and articles which are concerned primarily with Lavrov's wider influence. Since it would be impractical to list separately all of Lavrov's hundreds of books, articles, reviews, sundry writings, and published speeches, I will instead indicate under "Bibliography and Reference" those books which contain the best bibliographies of Lavrov's works.

Primary Sources

Unpublished Materials

Moscow. Tsentral'nyi Gosudarstvennyi Arkhiv Oktiabr'skoi Revoliutsii. Fondy 1762, 109, and 95, primarily.

Moscow. Tsentral'nyi Gosudarstvennyi Arkhiv Literatury i Iskusstva. Fondy 923 and 285, primarily.

Amsterdam, Netherlands. The International Institute for Social History. The *Vpered!* archives, primarily, and Lavrov's correspondence with European socialists.

Stanford, California. The Hoover Institution Archives. The Nicolaevsky Collection: correspondence of Lavrov's children and grandchildren; Lavrov's will; V. N. Smirnov's papers (copies of MSS in the International Institute for Social History). The Okhrana overseas files, primarily XVI a and b.

New York. Columbia University Russian Archives. Lavrov's letters to A. V. Weber.

Paris. Manuscript Collection of the Bibliothèque Nationale. "Memoirs" by Charles Rappaport. Typed MS.

Collections of Lavrov's Published Works

Lavrov, P. L. *Sobranie sochineniia.* Edited by N. Rusanov, P. Vitiazev, and A. Gizetti. Series 1–6. Petrograd, 1917–20.
———. *Izbrannye sochineniia na sotsial'no-politicheskie temy.* Edited by I. A. Teodorovich. 4 vols. Moscow, 1934.

————. *Filosofiia i sotsiologiia.* Edited by A. F. Okulov. 2 vols. Moscow: Akademiia nauk, izdatel'stvo sotsial'no-ekonomicheskoi literatury, Mysl', 1965.
————. *Etiudy o zapadnoi literature.* Edited by A. Gizetti and P. Vitiazev. Petrograd, 1923.

Lavrov's Major Published Works Not Included in the Above Collections

Lavrov, P. L. *Istoriia, sotsializm, i russkoe dvizhenie.* Vol. 1: *Materialy dlia istorii russkogo sotsial'no-revoliutsionnogo dvizheniia.* Geneva, 1893.
————. *Iz rukopisei 90-kh godov.* Geneva, 1899.
————. *Narodniki-propagandisty 1873–1878 godov.* St. Petersburg, 1907.
————. *Opyt istorii mysli.* St. Petersburg, 1875.
————. *Opyt istorii mysli novogo vremeni.* 2 vols. Geneva, 1894.
————. *Parizhskaia Kommuna 18 marta 1871 goda.* Petrograd, 1919.
————. *Sovremennye ucheniia o nravstvennosti i ee istoriia.* St. Petersburg, 1903–4.
————. *Tsivilizatsiia i dikie plemena.* St. Petersburg, 1903.
————. *Vazhneishie momenty v istorii mysli.* Moscow, 1903.
————. *Vzgliad na proshedshee i nastoiashee russkogo sotsializma.* St. Petersburg, 1906.
————. *Zadachi ponimaniia istorii: proekt vvedeniia v izuchenie evoliutsii chelovecheskoi mysli.* Moscow, 1898.

Bibliography and Reference

Deiateli revoliutsionnogo dvizheniia v Rossii: Bio-bibliograficheskii slovar'. Edited by B. P. Koz'min, F. Ia. Kon, V. I. Nevskii, I. A. Teodorovich, and Ia. B. Shumianskii. 5 vols. Moscow, 1927–34.
Knizhnik-Vetrov, I. S. "Bibliografiia sochinenii P. L. Lavrova i o nem." In *Izbrannye sochineniia,* 1:492–510; 3:403–12; 4:420–25.
Masanov, I. F. *Slovar' psevdonymov russkikh pisatelei, uchenykh, i obshchestvennykh deiateli.* 4 vols. Moscow: Izdatel'stvo vsesoiuznoi knizhnoi palaty, 1956–60.
Istoriia russkoi literatury XIX veka: Bibliograficheskii ukazatel'. Edited by K. D. Muratova. Moscow: Akademiia nauk SSSR, 1962, pp. 401–5. This contains a listing of many of Lavrov's published letters.
Ocherki istorii Leningrada. Edited by M. P. Viatkin, B. M. Kochakov, S. S. Volk, N. V. Kireev, and Sh. M. Levin. 6 vols. Moscow: Izdatel'stvo akademii nauk, 1955–70.

Pamiati P. L. Lavrova. Geneva: Tipografiia gruppy starykh narodovolt-sev, 1900, pp. 80–87. This is an excellent bibliography of Lavrov's books, articles, reviews, and published speeches between 1857 and 1900; it also lists his unpublished manuscripts.

Vitiazev, P. "Literaturnyi skandal s Lavrovym." *Literaturnaia gazeta,* 10 December 1934. This is an exposé of the bibliographical errors made by Knizhnik-Vetrov in the first volume of the 1934 collection cited above, and of L. A. Chizhikov's "monstrous and illiterate bibliography," not listed here.

Zaleski, Eugene. *Mouvements ouvriers et socialistes, chronologie et bibliografie: La Russie.* 2 vols. Paris: L'Institut Français d'Histoire Sociale, 1956.

Books by Other Authors

Aksel'rod, P. B. *Perezhitoe i peredummanoe.* Vol. 1. Berlin, 1923.

Antonovich, M. A. *Izbrannye stat'i.* Leningrad, 1938.

Aptekman, O. V. *Obshchestvo "Zemlia i Volia."* Petrograd, 1924.

Boborykin, P. D. *Za polveka.* Moscow, 1929.

Charushin, N. A. *O dalekom proshlom.* Moscow, 1931.

Chernyi peredel. Moscow, 1923. This is a single-volume reissue of the journal.

Chudnovskii, S. L. *Iz davnikh let: Vospominaniia.* Moscow, 1934.

Chernyshevskii, N. G. *Selected Philosophical Essays.* Moscow: Foreign Languages Publishing House, 1953.

———. *What Is to Be Done?* Translated by B. R. Tucker. New York: Vintage Books, 1961.

Debogorii-Mokrievich, V. K. *Ot buntarstva k terrorizmu.* Moscow, 1930.

Deutsch, L. G. *Russkaia revoliutsionnaia emigratsiia.* St. Petersburg, 1920.

Dnevnik P. A. Valueva. Edited by P. A. Zaionchkovskii. 2 vols. Moscow: Izdatel'stvo akademii nauk SSSR, 1961.

Figner, V. *Vospominaniia.* 2 vols. Moscow: Mysl', 1964.

Gruppa osvobozhdenie truda. Edited by L. G. Deutsch. Collections 1, 2, and 3. Moscow, 1924–25.

Herzen, A. I. *Polnoe sobranie sochinenii i pisem.* Edited by M. K. Lemke. 22 vols. Petrograd, 1919–25.

Iz arkhiva P. B. Aksel'roda. Berlin, 1924.

Ivanchin-Pisarev, A. I. *Khozhdenie v narod.* Moscow, 1929.

K. Marks, F. Engel's i revoliutsionnaia Rossiia. Edited by A. K. Vorob'-eva. Moscow: Institut Marksizma-Leninizma pri TsKKPSS, Izdatel'-stvo politicheskoi literatury, 1967.

Kuliabko-Koretskii, N. G. *Iz davnikh let.* Moscow, 1931.

M. M. Stasiulevich i ego sovremenniki v ikh perepiske. Edited by M. K. Lemke. Vol. 2. St. Petersburg, 1912.

Literaturnoe nasledie G. V. Plekhanova. Edited by A. V. Lunacharskii. Collection 1. Moscow, 1934.

Morozov, N. A. *Povesti moei zhizni.* 2 vols. Moscow: Izdatel'stvo akademii nauk SSSR, 1962.

Nikitenko, A. V. *Dnevnik.* 3 vols. Moscow: Gosudarstvennoe izdatel'stvo khudozhestvennoi literatury, 1955–56.

Ovsianiko-Kulikovskii, D. N. *Vospominaniia.* St. Petersburg, 1923.

Pamiati P. L. Lavrova. Geneva, 1900.

Panteleev, L. F. *Iz vospominanii proshlogo.* Moscow-Leningrad, 1934.

Perepiski K. Marksa i F. Engel'sa s russkimi politicheskimi deiateliami. 2nd ed. Moscow: Gospolitizdat, 1951.

Pisarev, D. I. *Selected Philosophical, Social and Political Essays.* Moscow: Foreign Languages Publishing House, 1958.

Revoliutsionnoe narodnichestvo 70-kh godov XIX veka. Edited by B. S. Itenberg and S. S. Volk. 2 vols. Moscow: Nauka, 1965.

Sazhin, M. P. *Vospominaniia.* Moscow, 1925.

Sochineniia N. V. Shelgunova. Third edition. 3 vols. St. Petersburg, 1904.

Shelgunov, N. V. *Vospominaniia.* Moscow, 1923.

Shtakenschneider, E. A. *Dnevnik i zapiski.* Moscow, 1934.

Tikhomirov, L. A. *Vospominaniia.* Moscow, 1927.

Arkhiv Zemli i Voli i Narodnoi Voli. Edited by S. N. Valk. Moscow, 1930.

Vodovozova, E. *Na zare zhizni.* St. Petersburg, 1911.

Vpered! 1873–1877. Edited by Boris Sapir. 2 vols. Dordrecht, Netherlands: D. Reidel Publishing Company, for the International Institute for Social History, 1970.

Wintchevskii, M. *Memoirs.* Moscow, 1926.

Secondary Sources

Books

Baron, S. H. *Plekhanov: The Father of Russian Marxism.* Stanford: Stanford University Press, 1963.

Billington, James H. *Mikhailovskii and Russian Populism.* Oxford: Clarendon Press, 1958.

Bogucharskii, V. Ia. [Iakovlev] *Aktivnoe narodnichestvo semidesiatikh godov.* Moscow, 1912.

———. *Iz istorii politicheskoi bor'by v 70-kh i 80-kh godakh XIX veka.* Moscow, 1912.

Cherniavsky, M. *Tsar and People.* New Haven: Yale University Press, 1961.

Dan, F. *Origins of Bolshevism.* Translated by Joel Carmichael. New York: Harper and Row, 1964.

Hecker, J. F. *Russian Sociology.* New York, 1915.

Istoriia parizhskoi kommuny 1871 goda. Edited by E. A. Zhelubovskaia, A. E. Manfred, M. N. Mashkin, et al. Moscow: Nauka, 1971.

Itenberg, B. S. *Dvizhenie revoliutsionnogo narodnichestva.* Moscow: Nauka, 1965.

—————. *Rossiia i parizhskaia kommuna.* Moscow: Nauka, 1971.

Ivanov-Razumnik, R. V. *Istoriia russkoi obshchestvennoi mysli.* 2 vols. St. Petersburg, 1907.

Kazakov, A. P. *Teoriia progressa v russkoi sotsiologii kontsa XIX veka.* Leningrad, Izdatel'stvo leningradskogo universiteta, 1969.

Kimball, R. A. "The Early Political Career of Peter Lavrovich Lavrov, 1823–1873." Ph.D. dissertation, University of Washington, 1967.

Knizhnik-Vetrov, I. S. *P. L. Lavrov.* Moscow, 1930.

—————. *P. L. Lavrov: Ego zhizn' i trudy.* Leningrad, 1925.

—————. *Russkie deiatel'nitsy pervogo internatsionala i parizhskoi kommuny.* Moscow: Nauka, 1964.

Kornilov, A. A. *Obshchestvennoe dvizhenie pri Aleksandre II.* Moscow: 1909.

Koz'min, B. P. *Iz istorii revoliutsionnoi mysli.* Moscow: Izdatel'stvo akademii nauk SSSR, 1961.

—————. *Ot "deviatnatsatogo fevralia" k "pervomu martu."* Moscow, 1933.

—————. *Russkaia sektsiia pervogo internatsionala.* Moscow: Izdatel'stvo akademii nauk SSSR, 1957.

Kudelli, P. *Narodovoltsy na pereput'i.* Leningrad, 1925.

Lampert, E. *Sons against Fathers.* Oxford: Clarendon Press, 1965.

Levin, Sh. M. *Obshchestvennoe dvizhenie v Rossii v 60-70-e gody XIX veka.* Moscow: Institut istorii akademii nauk, Sotsekgiz, 1958.

Malia, M. *Alexander Herzen and the Birth of Russian Socialism.* New York: Grosset and Dunlap, Universal Library, 1965.

Masaryk, T. G. *The Spirit of Russia.* Translated by Eden and Cedar Paul. 2nd edition. 2 vols. New York: Macmillan, 1955.

Meijer, J. M. *Knowledge and Revolution: The Russian Colony in Zurich, 1870–1873.* Assen: Van Gorcum, 1955.

Mendel, Arthur P. *Dilemmas of Progress in Tsarist Russia.* Cambridge, Mass.: Harvard University Press, 1961.

Narodnicheskaia ekonomicheskaia literatura. Edited by N. K. Karataev. Moscow: Sotsekgiz, 1958.

Noetzel, H. G. *Petr L. Lavrovs Vorstellungen vom Fortschritt für Russland aus den Jahren vor seiner Emigration.* Cologne, 1968.

Obshchestvennoe dvizhenie v poreformennoi Rossii. Edited by E. S. Vilenskaia, L. I. Ivanov, B. S. Itenberg, et al. Moscow: Nauka, 1965.

P. L. Lavrov: Stat'i, vospominaniia, materialy. St. Petersburg, 1922.

Pazhitnov, K. A. *Razvitie sotsialisticheskikh idei v Rossii.* Vol. 1. Khar'kov, 1913.

Polevoi, Iu. Z. *Zarozhdenie Marksizma v Rossii.* Moscow: Izdatel'stvo akademii nauk SSSR, 1959.

Revoliutsionnaia Rossiia i revoliutsionnaia Pol'sha. Edited by V. A. D'iakov, I. S. Miller, and N. P. Mitina. Moscow: Nauka, 1967.

Revoliutsionnaia situatsiia v Rossii v 1859–1861 godakh. Edited by M. V. Nechkina. Moscow: Nauka, 1965.

Rusanov, N. S. *Biografiia Petra Lavrovicha Lavrova.* St. Petersburg, 1899.

––––––. *Sotsialisty zapada i Rossii.* St. Petersburg, 1908.

––––––. *V imigratsii.* Moscow, 1929.

Russkaia zhurnalistika. Shestidesiatye gody. Edited by V. Polianskii. Moscow, 1930.

Sedov, M. G. *Geroicheskii period revoliutsionnogo narodnichestva.* Moscow: Mysl', 1966.

Snytko, T. G. *Russkoe narodnichestvo i pol'skoe obshchestvennoe dvizhenie, 1865–1881 godov.* Moscow: Nauka, 1969.

Thun, A. *Istoriia revoliutsionnykh dvizhenii v Rossii.* Moscow, 1923.

Venturi, F. *Roots of Revolution.* New York: Grosset and Dunlap, 1966.

Verevkin, B. P. *Russkaia nelegal'naia revoliutsionnaia pechat'.* Moscow: Vysshaia partiinaia shkola, 1960.

Vilenskaia, E. S. *Revoliutsionnoe podpol'e v Rossii 60-e gody XIX veka.* Moscow: Nauka, 1965.

Vitiazev, P. *P. L. Lavrov i N. K. Mikhailovskii.* Petrograd, 1917.

––––––. *Ssylka P. L. Lavrova v vologodskoi gubernii i ego zaniatiia antropologiei,* Vologda, 1915.

Vodolazov, G. G. *Ot Chernyshevskogo k Plekhanovu.* Moscow: Izdatel'stvo moskovskogo universiteta, 1969.

Volk, S. S. *Narodnaia volia 1879–1882.* Moscow: Nauka, 1966.

Yarmolinsky, A. *Road to Revolution.* New York: Collier Books, 1962.

Vosstanie 1863 goda i russko-pol'skie revoliutsionnye sviazi 60-kh godov. Edited by V. D. Koroliuka and I. S. Miller. Moscow: Izdatel'stvo akademii nauk SSSR, 1960.

Vpered! Sbornik statei. Edited by P. Vitiazev. Petrograd, 1920.

Vucinich, A. *Science in Russian Culture 1861–1917.* Stanford: Stanford University Press, 1970.

Walicki, A. *The Controversy over Capitalism.* Oxford: Clarendon Press, 1969.

Wildman, Allan K. *The Making of a Workers' Revolution.* Chicago: University of Chicago Press, 1969.

Wortman, Richard. *The Crisis of Russian Populism.* Cambridge: At the University Press, 1967.

Zaionchkovskii, P. A. *Krizis samoderzhaviia na rubezhe 1870–1880-kh godov.* Moscow: Izdatel'stvo moskovskogo universiteta, 1964.

Selected Articles, Published Documents, and Short Memoirs

Al'tman, V. V. "P. L. Lavrov i parizhskie kommunary: Iz arkhiva P. L. Lavrova." In *Evropa v novoe i noveishee vremia*. Moscow, Nauka, 1966.

Al'tovskii, A. I. "Lavrov kak teoretik sotsializma." *Sotsialist-revoliutsioner*, 1910, no.2.

Antonov, M. "Politicheskaia deiatel'nost' P. L. Lavrova." *Byloe*, 1910, no. 13.

Antonovich, M. A. "Po povodu stat'i N. S. Rusanova 'P. L. Lavrov.'" *Byloe*, 1907, no. 4.

Bachman, J. E. "Recent Soviet Historiography of Russian Revolutionary Populism." *Slavic Review*, vol. 29 (1970).

Bernstein, Eduard. "Karl Marks i russkie revoliutsionnery." *Minuvshie gody*, 1908, nos. 10 and 11.

"Delo o publichnikh lektsiakh v 1860-kh godakh." In *Istoriko-literaturnyi sbornik*. Izdanie otdeleniia russkogo iazyka i slovesnosti rossiiskoi akademii nauk. Leningrad, 1924.

Deutsch, L. G. "O sblizhenii i razryve s narodovoltsami." *Proletarskaia revoliutsiia*, 1923, no. 8.

Dmitriev, S. S. "Stikhotvorenie-pamflet na koronatsiiu Aleksandra II." *Literaturnoe nasledstvo*, vol. 63 (1956).

"Dokumenty dlia istorii Obshchestva Krasnogo Kresta Narodnoi Voli." *Byloe*, 1906, no. 3.

Firsov, N. N. "Vospominaniia o P. L. Lavrove." *Istoricheskii vestnik*, 1907, nos. 1 and 2.

Freidfel'd, L. "Svetloi pamiati Sofii Mikhailovny Ginsburg." *Katorga i ssylka*, 1924, no. 12.

Gintovt-Dzebaltovskii, V. "Parizhskie vstrechi." *Sibirskie ogni*, 1927, no. 2.

Gizetti, A. A. "Istoriko-sotsiologicheskie vozzreniia P. L. Lavrova." *Voprosy obshchestvovedeniia*. 1911, no. 3.

————. "P. L. Lavrov i *Vpered!*." *Byloe*, 1925, no. 2.

Gol'denberg, L. "Vospominaniia." *Katorga i ssylka*, 1924, no. 5.

Iokhel'son, V. I. "Iz perepiski c P. L. Lavrovym." *Byloe*, 1923, no. 21.

"Iz materialov o P. L. Lavrove." *Krasnyi arkhiv*, vol. 3 (1923).

Kamkov, B. "Istoriko-filosofskie vozzreniia P. L. Lavrova." *Zavety*, 1913, nos. 6 and 7.

Kareev, N. I. "Iz vospominanii o P. L. Lavrove." *Byloe*, 1918, no. 3.

Kareev, N. "Nauchnaia rabota P. L. Lavrova." *Severnye zapiski*, 1915, no. 1.

Karpovich, M. M. "P. L. Lavrov and Russian Socialism." *California Slavic Studies*, vol. 2 (1963).

Kimball, A. "The Russian Past and the Socialist Future in the Thought of Peter Lavrov." *Slavic Review*, vol. 30 (1971).

Kirichenko, T. "K voprosu ob obshchestvenno-politicheskikh vzgliadakh P. L. Lavrova v 70-kh-80-kh godakh XIX veka." In *Moskovskii istoriko-arkhivnyi institut: Trudy*. Vol. 18, pp. 443–63. Moscow, 1963.

Knizhnik-Vetrov, I. S. "Lavrov o Chernyshevskom." *Literaturnoe nasledstvo*, vol. 7-8 (1933).

Kovalevskii, M. "Stranichki iz vospominanii." *Vozrozhdenie*, 1951, no. 15 (Paris).

L.———r, N. "P. Lavrov o roli partii v proletarskoi revoliutsii." *Molodaia gvardiia*, 1923, no. 4-5.

Ladokha, G. "Istoricheskie i sotsiologicheskie vozzreniia P. L. Lavrova." In *Russkaia istoricheskaia literatura v klassovom osvechenii*. Vol. 1. Moscow, 1927.

Levin, Sh. M. "Predlozhenie Lavrova literaturnomu fondu khodataistvovat' o Chernyshevskom." *Literaturnoe nasledstvo*, vol. 67 (1959).

Librovich, S. F. "P. L. Lavrov kak redaktor *Zagranichnogo vestnika*." *Vestnik literatury*, 1913, nos. 11 and 12.

Lopatin, G. A. "K rasskazam o P. L. Lavrove." *Golos minuvshego*, 1916, no. 4.

Martov, L. "Obshchestvennye i umstvennye techeniia 70-kh godov." In *Istoriia russkoi literatury XIX veka*. Edited by D. N. Ovsianiko-Kulikovskii, vol. 4. Moscow, 1910.

Meijer, J. M. "Lavrov at the end of 1875." *Bulletin of the International Institute of Social History*, no. 2 (1952).

Nechaev, V. N. "Protsess P. L. Lavrova 1866 goda." In *Istoricheskii arkhiv: Sbornik materialov i statei*. Collection 1. Moscow, 1921.

Nicolaevsky, B. "Iz literaturnogo nasledstva V. I. Zasulicha." *Katorga i ssylka*, 1929, no. 6.

———. "Materialy i dokumenty. Tkachev i Lavrov." *Na chuzhoi storone*, 1925, no. 10.

Ovsianiko-Kulikovskii, D. N. "Peredovaia ideologiia 70-kh godov: Lavrov i Mikhailovskii." In *Istoriia russkoi intelligentsii*. Vol. 8, part 2. Moscow, 1906.

"Pamiati M. M. Kovalevskogo." *Russkie zapiski*, 1916, no. 3.

Parchevskii, K. "Lavrovskie chetvergi." *Poslednie novosti*. 9 December 1937 (Paris).

Pipes, Richard. "Russian Marxism and the Populist Background." *Russian Review*, vol. 19 (1960).

Poglubko, K. A. "O sviazakh zhurnala *'Vpered!'* s serbskimi sotsialistami." In *Balkanskii istoricheskii sbornik*. Vol. 1, pp. 95–127. Kishinev, Akademiia nauk Moldavskoi SSR, Institut istorii. 1968.

Rappaport, S. "M. Kovalevskii i I. Mechnikov v ikh snosheniiakh s P. L. Lavrovym." *Russkie vedomosti*. 15 June 1916 (Moscow).

————. "Pierre Lavroff." *Le mouvement socialiste,* 1900, nos. 28 and 29.

"Rech' N. F. Annenskogo o P. L. Lavrove." *Katorga i ssylka,* 1925, no. 1.

Rusanov, N. S. "Lavrov—chelovek i myslitel'." *Russkoe bogatstvo,* 1910, no. 2.

————. "P. L. Lavrov." *Byloe,* 1907, no. 7.

————. "Petr Lavrovich Lavrov." In *Istoriia russkoi literatury XIX veka.* Edited by D. N. Ovsianiko-Kulikovskii. Vol. 4. Moscow: 1910.

Sapir, B. "Unknown Chapters in the History of *Vpered!.*" *International Review of Social History* 2 (1957).

Shilov, A. "N. G. Chernyshevski v donoseniakh agentov III otdeleniia." *Krasnyi arkhiv* 14, no. 1 (1926).

Shtakenschneider, E. A. "Iz vospominanii E. A. Shtakenschneider o Lavrove." *Golos minuvshego,* 1915, no. 12.

————. "P. L. Lavrov." *Golos minuvshego,* 1915, no. 7-8.

Tcheksis, L. A. "La philosophie sociale de Pierre Lavroff." *Revue de synthèse historique,* vols. 25 and 26 (1913).

Venediktov-Beziuk, L. "Pobeg P. L. Lavrova iz ssylki." *Katorga i ssylka,* 1931, no. 5.

Vinitskaia, A. A. "Iz prikliuchenii v Parizhe." *Istoricheskii vestnik,* 1912, no. 1.

Vitiazev, P. "P. L. Lavrov i ego korrespondenty." *Literaturnoe nasledstvo,* vol. 19-21 (1935).

————. "Chem obiazana russkaia obshchestvennost' P. L. Lavrovu?" *Ezhemesiachnyi zhurnal,* 1915, nos. 2 and 3.

————. "P. L. Lavrov v vospominaniiakh sovremennikov." *Golos minuvshego,* 1915, nos. 9 and 10.

————. "P. L. Lavrov i Saltykov." *Literaturnoe nasledstvo,* vol. 13-14 (1934).

————. "P. L. Lavrov v epokhu 60-kh gg. i ego stat'ia 'Postepenno.' " *Kniga i revoliutsiia,* 1922, no. 6.

————. "P. L. Lavrov v 1870–1873 gg." In *Materialy dlia biografii Lavrova.* Petrograd, 1921.

Vyrubov, G. N. "Revoliutsionnye vospominaniia." *Vestnik evropy,* 1913, no. 2.

Walker, F. A. "The Morality of Revolution in P. L. Lavrov." *Slavonic and Eastern European Review,* vol. 41 (1962).

Zamiatnin, V. "Ekonomicheskie vzgliady P. L. Lavrova." *Ekonomicheskie nauki,* 1961, no. 3.

Lavrov, Peter Lavrovich—(*cont.*)
Petersburg, 26; and Lopatin,
117; marriage of, to Antonina
Khristianovna, 12–13; and
Marx, 67, 123, 126, 155, 158,
182, 227; and Marx and Engels, 126–27; and Marxian
theory of surplus value,
181 n99; and Marxism, 123–
24; as mathematician, 79 n; and
I. I. Mechnikov, 220; as member of *zemstvo,* 71; and M. I.
Mikhailov, 53; and Nicholas
Mikhailovskii, 139 n; military
service of, 15; and John Stuart
Mill, 67; and Narodnaia Volia,
xiv, 28, 206, 208–10, 212–13,
215, 217–219; and Narodnik
movement, 182; neo-Kantianism of, xvii, 31, 33, 80–81, 97,
109, 227; and nihilist subculture, 68; and Paris Commune,
xvi, 119–25, 136, 163, 218;
physical appearance of, 13; and
Pisarev, 48–50; pleas for clemency for, 79; and Plekhanov,
214–16; political verse of, 16–
17, 27; as polymath, xiii, 15;
and positivism, 88; preparationism of, 19–20, 52, 139, 147,
160, 185, 187, 200; prose style
of, 22; and Proudhon, 36–37,
40 n, 66, 109; psychology of,
2–3, 6–11, 31, 81, 109–10,
127–28, 134–35, 139–40, 161–
62, 185, 222–23, 226–28; as
public lecturer, 45–46; radical
commitment of, 127–28, 135;
radical evolution of, xvi–xix; as
rationalist, 91–92; and raznochintsy, 43; and realism, 36, 87,
102, 108; resignation of, as
editor of *Vpered!,* 196; and
revolutionary generations, xv–

xvi, 130, 166, 228; revolutionary strategy of, 180–81, 186–
88, 209, 213; and Riul'man,
76–77; romanticism of, 46; and
Russian colony in Zurich, 154;
and Russian Lavrovists, 153,
172, 198; and Russian liberalism, 61–62, 74–75, 216, 218–
19; and the Russian revolutionary movement, 61–62, 113,
127–28, 142, 153, 178–79,
182–85, 192, 199, 204–5, 212,
219, 224–25, 227–28; and Elena
Shtakenschneider, 26, 28, 38;
socialism of, 38, 108, 114, 116,
126–27, 141, 145–46, 181–82,
212–13, 218; and socialist
émigrés in Paris, 221–22; and
Herbert Spencer, 66; and student movement (1861–62),
54–56; subjective sociology of,
xiii, 66, 88–89, 103; contemplated suicide of, 220; and
terrorism, 204 n, 206–7, 213;
theory of personality of, 35–37,
189; theory of progress of, 38–
39, 47, 61–62, 65–66, 90, 98,
100–101, 108, 181, 218, 228;
and the Third Section, 51, 55,
62; and Tkachev, 157–58, 160;
trial of, 80; and Turgenev, I. S.,
33; and union of Russian revolutionary groups, 172; utilitarianism of, 98; utopian socialism
of, 28, 62, 188, 191–92; and
Vpered! commune, 194–95;
and A. V. Weber, 176–77. *See
also* Lavrovism; Lavrovists,
Russian
Lavrov, Sergei Petrovich (son),
13, 82 n40
Lavrova, Antonina Khristianovna
(wife), 5–6, 12–13; illness of,
60; death of, 72–73

Burtsev, Vladimir, 216
Buturlin, A. S., 137, 151

Censorship, 105, 163; Committee,
    63, 64 n2
Chaadaev, Peter, 96
Chaikovskii circle, The, 113 n8,
    132 n47, 133, 149–50, 169–70
Chaplitskaia, Anna, 82, 83, 86,
    111; death of, 134–35
Cherkezov, Levan, 195
Cherniavsky, Michael, 161 n50
Chernoperedeltsy, 204, 207, 208.
    See also Chernyi Peredel;
    Lavrov, Peter Lavrovich, and
    Chernyi Peredel
Chernov, Victor, 224
Chernyi Peredel, 206, 209, 210
Chernyshevskii, Nicholas, xiii, 37,
    48, 56–57, 59, 68, 70, 72, 84,
    95–96, 112, 200 n134;
    anthropologism of, 39–40; and
    Lavrov, 42; rational egoism of,
    44; and the Russian Enlighten-
    ment, 43; and the student
    movement, 58
Chess Club, The, 53, 59 n68
Chto delat'? (Lenin), 218 n51
"Chto takoe antropologiia?"
    (Lavrov), 29 n9, 39
Civil War in France, The (Marx),
    123
Committee of the Society for
    Struggle with Hunger, 216
Comte, Auguste, 66–67, 87, 90
"Consecrated Guard," The,
    209 n31
Crimean War, 15
Critically thinking minority:
    Lavrov's concept of, 90–92; as
    socialists, 141. *See also*
    Intelligentsia, The

Darwin, Charles, 67, 88, 213

Decembrists, 53, 209
*De la justice dans le révolution et
    l'église* (Proudhon), 36, 101
Delo, 118, 129, 163, 202
Deutsch, Lev, xvii, 204, 206, 211
"Difficult Moment, A" (Lavrov),
    184
Dilke, Charles, 169, 202 n3
Dostoevsky, Fedor, 26, 37, 166
"Dva tipa sovremennykh filosof"
    (Antonovich), 47–48

Education, in Russia, 45, 54, 57
Egaiité, 202
18 Marta 1871 goda (Lavrov),
    122, 202. See also *Parizhskaia
    Kommuna*
"Ekzameny" (Lavrov), 24
Eliseev, G. Z., 58, 68, 86, 133–34,
    118–19, 135, 139 n70; as editor
    of *Vek,* 61
El'pidin, M., 115 n11
El'snits, A. L., 131, 137
Emigré revolutionaries: of the
    1840s, xv; of the 1890s, 217
Encyclopedic Dictionary, 53, 59,
    63, 80

Engel'gardt, Alexander, 26, 55, 59
Engels, Friedrich, 167–68. *See
    also* Marx, Karl, and Friedrich
    Engels
*Essay on the History of the
    Physical-Mathematical Sci-
    ences* (Lavrov), 67, 71–72
Essay on Liberty (Mill), 36. See
    also *On Liberty*
*Essays on Questions of Practical
    Philosophy* (Lavrov), 41, 44,
    65
Ethical sociology, 89. *See also*
    Subjective sociology
Eval'd, A. V., 58

Index

Date Due

APR 18 75			
MY - 9 '00			